BUSINESS
AS A HUMANITY

Business as a Humanity

Edited by

THOMAS J. DONALDSON
R. EDWARD FREEMAN

New York   Oxford
OXFORD UNIVERSITY PRESS
1994

Oxford University Press

Oxford   New York   Toronto
Delhi   Bombay   Calcutta   Madras   Karachi
Kuala Lumpur   Singapore   Hong Kong   Tokyo
Nairobi   Dar es Salaam   Cape Town
Melbourne   Auckland   Madrid

and associated companies in
Berlin   Ibadan

Copyright © 1994 by Oxford University Press, Inc.

Published by Oxford University Press, Inc.
200 Madison Avenue, New York, New York 10016

Library of Congress Cataloging-in-Publication Data
Business as a humanity / edited by Thomas J. Donaldson
and R. Edward Freeman.
p. cm.—(The Ruffin series in business ethics)
Includes bibliographical references and index.
ISBN 0-19-507156-5
1. Business ethics.   2. Management—Moral and ethical aspects.
I. Donaldson, Thomas, 1945–   . II. Freeman, R. Edward, 1951–
III. Series.
HF5387.B864   1994
174'.4—dc20   94-8233

9 8 7 6 5 4 3 2 1

Printed in the United States of America
on acid-free paper

FOREWORD

The purpose of The Ruffin Series in Business Ethics is to publish the best thinking about the role of ethics in business. In a world in which there are daily reports of questionable business practices, from insider trading to environmental pollution, we need to step back from the fray and understand the larger issue of how business and ethics are, and ought to be, connected. We need to integrate the teaching and practice of management more closely with ethics and the humanities. Such an integration will yield both a richer ethical context for managerial decision making and a new set of practical and theoretical problems for scholars of ethics.

During the past twenty years, scholarship in business ethics has blossomed. Today, more than ever before, there is a growing consensus among management scholars, ethicists, and business executives that ethics should be a vital part of the teaching and practice of management.

Responding to this need, in 1987 the Peter B. and Adeline W. Ruffin Foundation established a fund at The Darden School, University of Virginia, to create a distinguished lecture series in business ethics. The Ruffin Series in Business Ethics will publish these lectures, as well as other distinguished books of interest to management scholars, ethicists, and practicing managers. Each of these three audiences is important because it is only through a sustained dialogue among management thinkers, philosophers, and managers that lasting progress can be made in bringing ethics into the daily business of business.

It is a distinct pleasure to present the second volume of the Ruffin Lectures. A distinguished interdisciplinary group of scholars gathered in Charlottesville in the fall of 1989 to discuss the papers of Ruffin lecturers Richard De George, Joanne Cuilla, Robert Solomon, and Clarence Walton. Over the next few years a number of scholars undertook the project of developing the themes these lectures called to mind. The resulting volume can be viewed as a series of sketches, an interweaving of various strands of thought, that hangs together by virtue of the richness of the questions raised.

The essays in this volume call for a rethinking of the very foundations of business and business schools. The authors ask us to entertain the idea of seeing business in the same light that we see art, literature, and philosophy: business as a humanity. Such a rethinking process cannot be completed within the confines of this volume, but it is our hope that the essays included here can serve as the basis for an ongoing dialogue. Such a conversation must seek to revitalize our schools of management and meet the challenges that executives face in the business world of the twenty-first century.

R. Edward Freeman

PREFACE

Business and business education are at a crossroads. On the one hand, corporations are beginning to understand that their only source of competitive advantage lies in the hearts and minds of the people who are employees. On the other hand, the forces of global competition have made many businesses try to "get the cost out of the business" through layoffs, restructuring, and reengineering. Our current ways of thinking about business do not help us to think very deeply about how to increase the skills and abilities of employees in order to become more competitive while at the same time managing a continuous process of restructuring and downsizing.

Focusing on the normal business disciplines of economics, accounting, finance, production, and marketing will not allow executives to understand the systematic and profound changes affecting business today. The business thinkers in this volume all insist that we must add the humanities to the repertoire of business education if managers and employees are to understand the world they currently face.

The humanities are relevant to business precisely because they inform us about our culture and the cultures of other societies. They force us to consider the depth and complexity of the people who are responsible for the success of businesses. They ask us not to see people as motivated solely by economic goals but to view the problem of motivation as a complex process of how human beings achieve joint ends by working together.

Finally, business schools themselves are in desperate need of revitalization. The criticisms leveled at them and their main product, the M.B.A, range from "M.B.A.s know tools and not people" to "M.B.A.s are American, not global." The standard business disciplines cannot revitalize the M.B.A. programs by simply being more efficient or by adding more business techniques and buzzwords. Business ethics can have a large role to play in this revitalization, but it is frequently conceptualized too narrowly along purely philosophical lines.

What business and business schools need is some new thinking about how to reconnect the very best thinking about human society and institutions with the world of business. The essays in this volume begin this process by asking us to conceptualize how business can benefit from the humanities. The essays themselves cover a wide territory, as do the humanities.

We hope that thoughtful executives will profit from these essays by being exposed to new modes of thought. Ethicists and other business thinkers will be challenged to look beyond the traditional boundaries of their disciplines—to reconceptualize problems that speak from humanist and cultural traditions to the very pressing problems of business today. Finally, in the epilogue we suggest an agenda for further thinking about business and the humanities and make some rather concrete proposals for the revitalization of business schools.

As with all the volumes in this series, we hope to stimulate the very best thinking about the role of ethics and business, thereby setting the stage for more and better work in the future.

Washington, D.C.   T.J.D.
Charlottesville, Va.   R.E.F.
March 1994

ACKNOWLEDGMENTS

For their contributions to the development of this volume we wish to thank The Darden School Foundation and the Olsson Center for Applied Ethics at the University of Virginia and the John Connelly Program in Business Ethics at Georgetown University. We especially appreciate the support of John Rosenblum, Robert Harris, James Freeland, and Leo Higdon of the Darden School administration, and Robert Parker, dean of the School of Business Administration at Georgetown. This book would not have been possible without the efforts of Julie Eddinger of Georgetown and Karen Musselman, Patricia Bennett, Henry Tulloch, and Tara Radin of the Olsson Center. Our faculty colleagues at Georgetown and Virginia have also provided an important source of encouragement to us. Herb Addison and the Oxford University Press team have provided their usual outstanding support.

The John Connelly Program in Business Ethics at Georgetown University would not exist without the generosity of the Connelly family. The Olsson Center for Applied Ethics at the University of Virginia, owes a great debt to the Olsson family and Sture Olsson in particular. Edward and Brian McAnaney and the Ruffin Foundation have made the Ruffin lectures possible by generously supporting the Olsson Center. This book is therefore appropriately dedicated to the Connelly, Olsson, and Ruffin families for making it all possible.

CONTENTS

III

IV

CONTRIBUTORS

Kenneth R. Andrews
Harvard Business School

George Brenkert
University of Tennessee

Joanne B. Ciulla
University of Richmond

Richard T. De George
University of Kansas

Thomas J. Donaldson
Georgetown University

Thomas W. Dunfee
University of Pennsylvania

David A. Fedo
Curry College

Peter A. French
Trinity University

R. Edward Freeman
University of Virginia

Ronald M. Green
Dartmouth College

Edwin Hartman
Rutgers University

W. Michael Hoffman
Bentley College

Robert C. Solomon
University of Texas

Manuel G. Velasquez
Santa Clara University

Clarence C. Walton
The American College

Patricia H. Werhane
University of Virginia

BUSINESS
AS A HUMANITY

Introduction

Thomas J. Donaldson

In many ways this volume reflects the evolution of existing trends in business education. For the purpose of confronting pressing problems of managerial responsibility, employee rights, and organizational justice, business academics have turned to political philosophers and ethicists. In order to understand the complex historical roots of modern democratic capitalism, they have turned to historians. In order to understand poignant problems of leadership, they have turned to literature and drama. This volume analyzes the panoramic implications of these evolutionary trends and proposes specific directions for future business education, including directions for curriculum design. The contributors conspicuously disagree about means more than they do about ends. Indeed, the variety of selections included here leaves the clear impression that the humanities must contribute to contemporary business education through the breadth of values they encompass. On this point the authors agree, but they disagree over the ways these values are to be realized.

The notion of "the humanities" originated in the Renaissance, when the term referred to an emerging revolution in the means and modes of education. The astounding evolution of intellect and the rediscovery of ancient Latin and Greek classics, including rhetoric and poetry, led to a break with pedagogical dogma at the same time that it legitimated human studies as equal in importance to the study of God and the natural world. It was a liberating revolution. For those contemporary educators steeped in twentieth-century techniques of business education, for those accustomed to understanding business solely through methods familiar to the natural and social sciences, the transition to understanding business as a humanity can be equally shocking—and liberating.

3

Since the title of this volume, *Business as a Humanity,* implies a new direction for business education and research, it is fitting that the contributors themselves embody the eclectic creativity this direction requires. Drawn from departments of humanities as well as from schools of business—with a few individuals holding joint appointments—the fourteen contributors endorse the metamorphosis of business education from its existing state, that is, from a technical, scientifically-inspired regimen, to something broader, more inclusive, and more humanity-driven. While often divided about the best means for achieving this metamorphosis, the contributors all agree that it is necessary. They articulate, in short, a conception of "business as a humanity."

The spectrum of issues surrounding the concept of business as a humanity may be divided into a few subareas. Foremost among these is the role of the humanities in the education of business managers, an issue relevant to each of the selections in this volume. The thread that unites the varying approaches within this subarea is the claim that philosophical essays, historical treatises, and literary works such as plays, short stories, and novels, as well as the methods of understanding implicit in such works, should be assigned in the business classroom. In the matter of pedagogical materials, then, the connection between business and the humanities is seen by the authors to be real and practical.

Closely connected is the subarea of classroom topics. Business education, like all education, is a function of both topics and style: the former sets the agenda, while the latter delivers it. But the choice of topics takes on special significance in a business setting. If the subject matter of business education is limited to functional questions—How can market share be enhanced? How can efficiency be maximized? How can accounting be simplified?—human issues are intentionally excluded. Their omission simply creates a vacuum that is conveniently filled by additional functional issues. Instead, as Patricia H. Werhane points out in her essay, other types of questions—Who is affected by my decision? Is this the kind of decision that a disinterested, reasonable person would make? Does my decision violate any basic human rights?—are critical for business education because they transcend the simplistic logic of means and ends so common in business education.

In this vein, it is worth noting that the one humanities topic that, more than any other, has galvanized modern business is "business ethics." The essays in this volume investigate business ethics in considerable detail, especially in relation to pedagogy. For example, Richard T. De George discusses ways in which the debate over teaching ethics frequently founders on a single problem, namely, whether professors should be in the business of teaching knowledge or virtue. Do we seek students who have a grasp of moral theory or those possessing high moral character? Furthermore, are these two distinct goals individually attainable and, if so, are they jointly compatible? Op-ed pieces appear with disturbing regularity arguing that business ethics courses are useless because people past the age of sixteen cannot be made virtuous through classroom instruction. While most ethicists agree that at least the elements of moral reasoning and theory can be taught, the question remains as to whether the fundamental character traits of virtue or fairness can be taught. Furthermore, while empirical research tells us that people do not stop developing morally in their twenties or thirties, is their moral development enhanced by taking a course in ethics?

The contributors to this volume are optimistic about the answers to such questions. Ethics may not be teachable in the same way as astronomy or psychology, but it *can* be taught. Part of a successful teaching strategy involves drawing lessons from the humanities, which resuscitate habits of the mind and of the heart, both too often suffocated by mere technical training.

To say this is not to deny skeptics their due, and in his essay Robert C. Solomon is quick to vindicate a brand of humanities cynicism. He agrees with the skeptics who say, for example, that a suspicious gap exists between the character-building aims promoted by some business ethics advocates and the often abstract and dialectical contents of the courses business ethics professors often teach. "Born-again" ethics is not the result of another technical interpretation of the categorical imperative. But the moral of the story is not that one should ignore all theoretical acumen in the interest of developing virtue; as Richard De George reminds us, unless virtuous people are morally articulate, their voices will not be adequately heard in the marketplace.

Pedagogical style and substance are inseparable. The best subject matter, or the correct topical agenda, requires a compatible pedagogical style—and the relationship between style and content constitutes the next subarea. "Seeing the round earth squarely," to repeat the memorable phrase used by Clarence C. Walton in his essay, implies that certain items of pedagogical substance, that is, certain themes, must unify a student's conception of humanity in business. For example, the theme of truth certainly is relevant for an economic system in which disclosure, misleading advertising, honesty in packaging, and intelligence gathering are all constant issues. And surely the theme of justice is critical for a society in which women, blacks, Chicanos, and Native Americans repeatedly find themselves in positions subordinate to white males. But if such themes are relevant, then it also follows that the writings traditionally hailed for discussing those themes—including the works of Plato, Aristotle, Kafka, Twain, and Rawls—may have a role in business classrooms. Indeed, the use of such vehicles may mitigate the problem underscored by Robert Solomon and Peter A. French in their essays, namely, that the academic discipline of ethical theory, associated with departments of philosophy, has deteriorated into a miserable state that results in bored students and that strikes practical decision makers as irrelevant. The antidote may be inspiration from another branch of the humanities. "The great books," Solomon asserts, "allow us to get involved in and to live vicariously through the difficulties and dilemmas of life, and those difficulties and dilemmas are, to a large extent, ethical quandaries, predicaments of loyalty and honor, or occasions for shame."[1]

Closely related to the question of pedagogical style and substance is a subarea that affects business education at its core—the nature of ethics itself. Is ethics to be conceived of as an abstract inquiry into the "big questions" or as something more practical? In other words, is it to be conceived of in the way that present-day philosophy departments in universities are inclined to conceive of it, or is it to be understood as a unique, reconstructed enterprise? Solomon notes that those who have managed, from time to time, to bring philosophy into the board room "now know from experience that . . . favorite academic disputes have a way of sinking faster than a heavy metal zeppelin. . . ."[2] For Solomon, what is needed is not only exposure to literature and history but a new conception of the enterprise of business ethics that draws on the rich and distinctive approach adopted by Aristotle in his *Nicomachean Ethics*. Both Edwin Hartman and Peter French are frequently critical of Solomon's views, but they share his fundamental displeasure with the current state of academic moral philosophy and with approaches to business ethics that simply overlay business contexts with a veneer of moral theory. Solomon, as Hartman notes, reflects Aristotelian tendencies by preferring "virtue talk" to anything that admits of calculation. But while Hartman is willing to grant that a "virtue ethics" is more easily compatible with the personal struggles of individual managers in business than, say, the more theoretical concepts of utilitarianism and justice, he notes that managers drawing high salaries need guidance as to how to deal with the company stakeholders who "speak in many voices." Dealing with them, he argues, means more than employing the somewhat inexact language of "virtue" and "practical wisdom." It means occasionally employing rules and calculative reasoning in order to make sense of specific dilemmas. This kind of reasoning, moreover, is reasoning that Aristotle himself endorses from time to time in his *Nicomachean Ethics*.

Peter French accepts Solomon's concern about sterilizing ethics by reducing it to impersonal rational calculation, but he wants to push Solomon's thesis one step further. If we relinquish the view of moral actors derived from the tradition of Kantianism and utilitarianism, that is, the view that sees moral persons as identical, faceless, atomistic individuals, then how are we to view the organizations they inhabit? For example, how are we to view the business corporation if not simply as a collection of atomistic moral egos? While rejecting the view that corporations are reducible to the *persona fictas* of corporate law, French grants that these suprahuman entities have moral personalities. Simply put, he argues that "there is a point to blaming corporations" and to "keeping a kind of moral ledger on them."[3] Note the way most people responded to the Exxon Valdez oil spill in Alaskan waters. They assigned moral culpability to Exxon and not merely legal liability. Finally, French argues that even punishment— a concept many ethicists wish to reserve entirely for human agents— is appropriate and can be exacted of corporate entities under certain circumstances.

When a person looks at the history of ethical thought, he or she is struck by the fact that, beginning at least with the Platonic dialogues, Western intellectual history has refused to restrict the pedagogy of ethical instruction to the proclamation of rules and theories. The classics of the ethical literature reveal a richness and variety of method, and this, in turn, sheds light on the contemporary case study method. For example, it is easy to lose sight of the fact that the Socratic method, derived from Socrates' dialectical style, was utilized by Plato when discussing ethical topics such as justice or courage; this method was also consciously used as a model by many founders of the case study method. As Joanne B. Ciulla argues in her essay, even the tradition of casuistry, with its discussion of moral dilemmas and quandaries, exhibits a striking similarity to current case study methodology. Business professors who discuss business ethics through cases should see themselves not as intellectual orphans but as "part of a family of scholars who systematically discussed cases about the moral problems of doing business."[4]

This is not the same as validating the case study method as a sufficient pedagogy for teaching ethics. George Brenkert notes that although many views are possible about the relationship between abstract understanding and good judgment in specific cases, any view that fails to give significant meaning to both moral principles and the particular details should be rejected. The case study method, with its use of casuistical techniques, must build not only instinct but understanding.

Recent history can also inform efforts in integrating the humanities with business. Thomas W. Dunfee highlights the historical evolution of the humanities component of a business school education, observing both that the role of the humanities is not entirely new and that business schools have not been so immune to new ideas as many observers (including, in his opinion, Richard De George) imply. In a similar vein, Ronald M. Green notes that the recent yet surprisingly rich history of the development of medical ethics issues can suggest lessons for business teaching. He notes that in the late 1960s medical education confronted a new brand of criticism which asserted that the traditional medical school curriculum was too narrowly based on the sciences alone. This period, Green notes, "saw the emergence of criticism of the profession for its broad failures of social responsibility—including its neglect of preventive medicine and its fostering of an overconcentration of doctors in highly paid but socially questionable medical specializations."[5] The result was a growing attempt to integrate the humanities with medical education, an attempt that garnered only mixed reviews. Many students shied away from the new humanistically motivated courses because their training had led them to conceive of the humanities as "soft" and the sciences as "hard." The solution to this problem that appears to be evolving in medical education, says Green, is for the humanities and the social sciences to make a contribution at a level that both researchers and students can respect. Green's point seems to be that teaching in business ethics, like teaching in medical ethics, can be successful only if it occurs in a context in which ethics research makes a substantial contribution to the ongoing evolution of knowledge in business.

In conclusion, this volume connects issues of teaching, theoretical ethics, and business education to a guiding concept of business as a humanity. The contributors have not attempted to reduce business to a humanity; they merely insist that both research and pedagogy in business must confront the humanity already implicit in business life. In the end, their views about teaching ethics to business professionals is remarkably similar to that of the philosopher John Stuart Mill. Almost two centuries ago Mill remarked that "people are people before they are lawyers, or physicians, or merchants, or manufacturers; and if you make them capable and sensible people, they will make themselves capable and sensible lawyers, physicians, or merchants."

NOTES

1. Robert C. Solomon, "Business and the Humanities: An Aristotelian Approach to Business Ethics," in Thomas J. Donaldson and R. Edward Freeman, eds., *Business as a Humanity* (New York: Oxford University Press, 1994), p. 73.

2. Ibid., p. 47.

3. Peter A. French, "Responsibility and the Moral Role of Corporate Entities," in Donaldson and Freeman, eds., *Business as a Humanity*, p. 93.

4. Joanne B. Ciulla, "Casuistry and the Case for Business Ethics," in Donaldson and Freeman, eds., *Business as a Humanity*, p. 167.

5. Ronald M. Green, "A Response to Richard T. De George's 'Business as a Humanity: A Contradiction in Terms?' " in Donaldson and Freeman, eds., *Business as a Humanity*, p. 30.

I

Business as a Humanity:
A Contradiction in Terms?

Richard T. De George

The battles over whether and how to include business ethics in the M.B.A. curriculum were symptomatic of deeper issues that are now emerging. The inconclusiveness of those battles can be taken as evidence that the issues being fought were not simply a matter of ethics; after all, most participants agreed that people going into management positions and being trained for the senior posts in management should be ethical. People who opposed attempts to introduce business ethics courses on the M.B.A. level perhaps instinctively felt that there was more at stake than just one course or one module. Those who reluctantly acceded to the demands from the business community, students, and teachers of business ethics that a course or module on ethics be introduced into the curriculum often and mistakenly assumed that that one course or module would suffice. They also assumed that the new course would not greatly affect the curriculum as a whole and that it would leave the rest of the faculty free to continue to carry on their business as usual. They were mistaken. The people who pushed for business ethics courses were unconsciously part of a bigger and still largely unarticulated movement, the unwitting spearhead of a challenge to the business education curriculum as constituted. They wrought more than they knew or intended.

An indication of the larger war that is beginning to emerge can be gleaned from an article on the first page of the *Wall Street Journal* for February 27, 1989, entitled GOING GLOBAL: THE CHIEF EXECUTIVES IN THE YEAR 2000 WILL BE EXPERIENCED ABROAD and bearing the subtitle A COMEBACK FOR LIBERAL ARTS.[1] The issue in the incipi-

11

ent war is whether the increasingly narrow, specialized, analytical training that constitutes the M.B.A. curriculum in the major business schools is the proper training for top managers who will be operating in the twenty-first century.

Business education at one point at least nominally covered three main areas. A successful manager had to have analytical skills, organizational skills, and people skills. Business schools did best at producing people with analytical skills, partly because those skills are the most clearly defined and the easiest to teach and learn, even though the courses themselves are often difficult. Research in those areas is quantifiable and "hard," rather than mushy and "soft." As a result, analytically inclined faculty became more and more influential in schools of business; the better the school, the more analytical its professors, their research, and their teaching. This emphasis on analysis partly explains why the demand for M.B.A.s has remained especially strong in finance, while it has softened in other areas of management.

At the heart of the impending war is the very nature of business education. What is business education for? Should it consist of what business schools can teach best, that is, analytical topics such as accounting, finance, microeconomic analysis, and computer modeling? This is the competence model. Should business schools teach what business firms want or think they want, that is, should they be reactive and consumer-driven? This is the consumer model. Or should business schools be proactive, ahead of their time, teaching what businesses in the future will need, attempting to form a vision of business larger than that even of most of today's top managers and leading the way by producing potential leaders with such vision? This is the leadership model. The internal dynamics of the better business schools lean toward the first option; the demands of the current market drive the lesser business schools toward the second option; and the realities of the changing nature of business as it will be practiced in the twentieth-first century call for implementing the third option.

Wars are always waged under ideological banners. The banner for the coming war is labeled "leadership," a label acceptable to business and business schools. There are more and more conferences on leadership, more and more books and articles devoted to it, and much hand-wringing about it. The cry for leadership from the business schools hides part of the true nature of the debate, which is not unrelated to the cries for ethics. Both stem from a vaguely perceived failure of M.B.A.s to provide the leadership and the moral fiber that business needs. Lurking below the surface is the suspicion that analytical skills do not a successful business make, that they are a necessary but insufficient condition for business success. Moreover, those with the necessary analytical skills can be hired to perform the technical tasks. The overriding questions are where the business leaders are to come from, how they are to be trained, and whether the business schools are unwittingly training leadership out of their products. The hidden agenda is the training of human beings for the human endeavor called business. What is sought is what was once identified with the humanities, not as technical disciplines but as subjects that broadened one's understanding of what it means to be human, that offered ideals of human achievement towards which to strive, and that helped give meaning to human activity.

The *Wall Street Journal* article I mentioned referred to the liberal arts.[2] Those in business ethics have pushed for philosophical ethics. A serious consideration of the third model of business education leads to the question of the relationship between business education and the humanities. What I shall argue for is not a union of business education and the humanities in the usual way of adding philosophy, literature, and history courses to the curriculum. For I believe that any such attempt will lead us back to the same battles that were fought and continue to be fought with respect to business ethics, battles over whether the humanities are simply to be added as two, three, or more courses to an already crowded curriculum; whether they will simply be an appendage to the core business courses, seen as such by students; whether they will be taught by humanities or by business faculty; and whether they should be integrated across the curriculum by existing faculty. Those battles cannot be won.

I have used the metaphor of war consciously, for the third model involves a revolution in the business school and its curriculum, and the revolution may be as bloody as any academic war has been.

I begin with a retrospective look at both the humanities and the business school curricula. I then ask what purpose business education is intended to serve. Finally, I suggest that, given the goal of business education, at least some—and some of the best—graduate schools of business should be producing leaders for the twenty-first century. These leaders will require the broad vision that has characterized the humanities at their best. The revolution I shall advocate, however, does not require teachers of the humanities to breach the barricades at the business school with their graduate humanities courses. For the humanities in their way have become as narrow and specialized as the business schools. What is required is a humanization of business education to fit the required humanization of the business world. A mistake of those promoting business ethics has been to think that ethics requires simply virtuous people instead of a dramatic change in the very nature of business and the way it is structured and carried on. The same mistake should not be made as we discuss the humanities and business education. What is required

is more than graduate humanities courses, which can often be
counted among the least broadening in the university curriculum.

BUSINESS EDUCATION AND THE HUMANITIES:
A HISTORICAL GLANCE

Although business schools are considered professional schools on
most campuses, business, unlike medicine and law and like journalism and education, is not a profession. There is no body of knowledge that we can identify as business. In law school there is a body
both of law and of jurisprudence, a body of knowledge with a long
tradition and history. The same is true of medicine, even though
medicine is still often more of an art than a science. There is a body
of knowledge that those who practice medicine are required to have
mastered. There is no comparable body of knowledge that we can
identify as business.

It is true that C.P.A.s must be certified, just as doctors and lawyers
are, through an examination. There is some basis for saying that
C.P.A.s form a profession and that there is a body of accounting
knowledge. But even if one were to grant that, it does not make
business as a whole a profession with a coherent body of knowledge.
In fact, the justification for a school of business or of management
or of administration is not the existence of a coherent body of
knowledge but the claim that success in business requires a variety of
kinds of knowledge—accounting, economics, finance, management,
organizational behavior—that no single discipline provides. The
needed knowledge cannot adequately be obtained in any single department within the university (e.g., economics, math, accounting,
psychology, political science) and still achieve the depth and diversity
required. Why couldn't accounting be taught in the math department, organizational behavior in the sociology department, organizational psychology in the psychology department, and so on? They
could and they are. But those departments do not specialize in business applications for their fields. Why couldn't business hire mathe-
maticians, psychologists, and sociologists instead of people from
business schools? Again, they can and they do. But they must then
train them in business. Businesses often prefer to have that training
done on a campus in the business school.

The claim that there is no body of business knowledge explains
why there was no graduate school of business until 1906. Nor in
1906 did such a body of business knowledge suddenly appear. The
absence of any such body of knowledge was at the heart of the debate over establishing the Graduate School of Business at Harvard
University. One of those championing the school was the eminent

Harvard philosopher Alfred North Whitehead, who in a 1927 address to the American Assembly of Collegiate Schools of Business chose as his topic "Universities and Their Function," a theme to which I shall return. Whitehead noted that "[t]he universities have trained the intellectual pioneers of our civilization—the priests, the lawyers, the statesmen, the doctors, the men of science, and the men of letters. They have been the home of those ideals which lead men to confront the confusion of their present times. . . . The conduct of business now requires intellectual imagination of the same type as that which in former times has mainly passed into those other occupations."[3] In referring to the university, an institution that began in the Middle Ages, he notes that its "existence is the reason for the sustained, rapid progressiveness of European life in so many fields of activity."[4]

Universities played a significant role in the development and transmission of what we call Western civilization. The notion of the humanities first emerged during the Renaissance. Its early application in the fifteenth and sixteenth centuries was related in particular to the study of the ancient Latin and Greek classics—which included grammar, rhetoric, and poetry—in opposition to the study of divinity or theology. Francis Bacon distinguished among Divine Philosophy, Natural Philosophy, and Human Philosophy, or Humanite, in his *Advancement of Learning* (1605).[5] The humanities only slowly came to be equated with the classics, philosophy, literature, and history—or with those studies that deal with man or humanity, as opposed to the natural world (science) or God (theology). Moreover, the humanities dealt not only with humanity but with human values. The division of the curriculum into science, the humanities, and the social sciences is of even later origin, since the social sciences did not start to develop as separate disciplines until the nineteenth century.

The humanities are sometimes equated with the liberal arts, which in the medieval university included the *trivium* (grammar, logic, and rhetoric) and the *quadrivium* (arithmetic, geometry, music, and astronomy). By the eighteenth century the arts included logic, physics, and morals and were distinguished from theology and law.

In the present-day American university the humanities continue to include philosophy, literature, the classics, and sometimes history. They also include what we call foreign language departments, which include foreign literature departments. The learning of a foreign language is not humanistic in itself, but it is liberal in the sense that it opens up to the student the culture and literature of which that language is a part and, in doing so, enlarges a student's perspective on and insight into what it means to be human.

History is currently sometimes considered a humanity, sometimes a social science, and history departments are frequently split in their self-identification. Those who are trained in the techniques of investigating data, which are similar to the techniques used in the social sciences, tend to identify with the latter. Those who identify more with literature, values, and the meaning to be gained from the study of history tend to identify with the humanities.

As a humanity, history can offer insight into the development of human society. It can enlarge one's perspective so as to preclude equating one's own experience or current conditions with what humanity is or must be. We can learn from the past. This is just as true of the history of business as it is of political history. A graduate student of business with no appreciation of the historical development of business and of the relationship of business to society in its broader context starts out with blinders and probably with the misconception that business is and must be as described in the latest courses offered in the business school. Where else, if not in business school, will the student get a historical perspective on business?

Business schools have tended to teach organizational behavior, group dynamics, and the psychology of marketing from texts and theories developed in the social sciences. By ignoring the storehouse of material available in literature they miss the opportunity to present the student with subtlety of insight, beauty of language, imagination, and vivid description that puts most texts to shame. Students do not need psychosociological jargon in their business interactions. They do need to understand people and their motives, to know how to read and judge character, and to have the ability to imagine themselves in another's shoes, be they those of a competitor, a boss, or a subordinate. For those dedicated to the case method, novels, short stories, and plays offer an inexhaustible storehouse of riches, more detailed, subtle, and complete than most cases written up for courses.

Students need not know the latest technique of literary criticism. Nonetheless, training in how to read a text critically is a skill most business people can use. And the ability to read business activity as a text (to use the language of contemporary literary criticism) would throw fresh light on business. Business executives should know how to write not only fluently but imaginatively and to communicate effectively. How better to learn this than from the great masters of the English language? Teaching all of this is possible while at the same time covering the nuts and bolts of organizations and management. The medium, however, makes the message very different.

If literature provides concrete images, philosophy provides abstractions and the practice of dealing with them. Philosophy by its nature is a questioning enterprise in which everything is up for review and challenge and in which presuppositions, arguments, and the meaning of terms are all subject to analysis. The great philosophical systems of the past also offer examples of imagination and of attempts at broad synthesis. One of the benefits of philosophy is that it helps students put themselves and their endeavors in perspective and encourages them to think of issues, values, and concepts other than those encountered in everyday life.

A course in the philosophy of business would enable students to think about the foundations of business—its values, ends, purpose, and justification. Once again, students need not know about the latest debates about modernism and postmodernism or the latest theory of mind. But such knowledge could well be helpful. Critical theorists and postmodernists attack the instrumental view of reason that pervades business and modern society. They attack as well the concept of the individual that emerged in the sixteenth and seventeenth centuries and that forms the basis for the view of the rugged individual that is so central to the American business image. Knowledge of such attacks might lead students as well as faculty to question the ideas, the theories, and the models built on such foundations. This suggests that philosophy could add a critical element to business education, an element that would keep business education always alive and prevent it from becoming an accepted, orthodox ideology.

The word "business" is derived from the term "busy" and refers to what one is busy about—one's function, duty, or occupation. Only in the seventeenth century, with the rise of the modern period and of capitalism, did it come to be attached to trade or commerce, taking on the meaning imputed by business schools. Interestingly enough, Webster's also translates "business" as meaning "calling" and "vocation."

Business education grew out of vocational training and was and is based on certain assumptions about the nature of business. Who decides what business is is a question rarely asked or answered. Schools of business are variously called schools of management or schools of business administration or schools of commerce. Education in general is geared to prepare one for one's future expectations and business is what those who go to business school expect to spend their lives engaged in. Business is an activity by which human beings associate with one another in the production and exchange of goods and services for their mutual advantage. It is not an end in itself. Too often it is seen in terms of dollars and cents, rather than in terms of people. Business is a human activity, the way that those engaged in it express and develop themselves. Engaging in business should and could be a human and humanizing experience. That it is not for so many people is an indictment of business as it is practiced and is both a call and an opportunity for humanizing it. Business schools can and should take the lead in that project.

It is a historical accident that business schools, growing out of practical training schools, chose to emphasize the social sciences, rather than the humanities. For both fields approach human life, although in different ways. That the social sciences model is dominant in business schools has helped create some of the difficulties perceived today by so many critics.

The impending war that I referred to earlier is a war between those who wish to continue along a more and more technical line, with economics and analytical skills growing in importance and dominating the curriculum, and those who wish to change the current approach to a people-centered one. Not only do some question the validity of the theory behind some social science disciplines—think of the scathing attacks by critical theorists within those disciplines—but there is also the conflict over the fact that the social sciences have sought to be value-neutral and have mistakenly often claimed to be so. This supposed value-neutral approach has in turn infected business education. Yet business is not value-neutral or value-free but value-laden. The recent appeals for ethics and leadership in business are appeals for proper values in business and for unmaking what I have called the myth of amoral business. It is the humanities that have traditionally and openly embodied values, that have developed techniques for dealing with them, and that are needed to supplement, if not replace, social scientific approaches to business.

The debate over business ethics foundered in part on the issue of whether what was needed was knowledge or virtue. Did we want moral and virtuous people, or did we want people with knowledge of ethical theory and moral reasoning? The latter skills could be taught in courses; morality and virtue themselves must be taught in life, usually as one grows up. The relation of the two sets of qualities is tenuous and not analytical. Teaching theory and method to those not inclined toward virtue can turn them into sophists skilled at defending their immorality and at covering it with seemingly moral language and arguments. It will not make the vicious virtuous. But teaching moral theory and method to those who seek virtue can help make them morally articulate. And that is its justification. After each business scandal we hear cries for ethics to be taught in the business schools. What the cries seem to be really calling for is virtuous people, not necessarily people skilled in ethical theory. What the business schools can produce is the latter, and the two should not be confused. Nonetheless, unless virtuous people are morally articulate, their voices will not be adequately heard in the marketplace.

The same sort of problem arises with respect to the humanities. What business may want and need is people with broad vision and background, not necessarily people with certain knowledge about theories within the disciplines of the humanities. What the universities are prepared to teach may not be what is expected or demanded. Breadth and vision are comparable to virtue. Can they be taught, or can we at best cultivate potentialities in individual students in whom the sensitivity to such issues already exists and who require only that we nurture what is already there? These people are probably the real leaders, and business schools should nourish, not snuff out, their potential.

THE UNIVERSITY AND THE BUSINESS SCHOOL

Why have a business school or an M.B.A. program in a university? Business does a great deal of on-the-job training. Technical business courses are and can be made available in specialized institutes or schools. Business can set up its own programs. These are all possible alternatives to traditional business school education. If schools of business are located at universities, it should be for some reason attached to the nature of a university. That nature should infuse the business school, as well as every other part of the university. The business school should also contribute to the life of the university. It is extremely narrow-minded and shortsighted to consider business education apart from the university and apart from the nature of university education. To do so is to envisage the business school and what takes place within it as somehow different and separate from the rest of the university. Although this may well be the status of some business schools on some campuses, their rationale for being part of the university consists in their sharing its goals.

A university is a place where knowledge is king. The university has as its function the development, transmission, and preservation of knowledge, which is pursued by both faculty and students. The knowledge that is developed and transmitted is not simply the knowledge that is already preserved in books in the library or on computer tapes; it is living knowledge, reworked and vitalized as it is transmitted to students. If it is not, then students would do as well without teachers, using instead only books or computers, as they do with teachers.

A university is a place where objective, systematic, unified knowledge can and should be sought. To call knowledge objective is to emphasize that it is communal and shareable, rather than completely subjective and private. Such knowledge is not simply belief but is based on evidence and argument. It is critical in the sense that it is continually being rethought. Such knowledge is not a mass of details or facts, but it is ordered—frequently with high-level general principles serving to organize, make coherent, and unify the facts or data.

The reason all the various disciplines are gathered together at the university is that bounds to knowledge are arbitrary. One portion spills into or requires another.

The university serves as a place where such knowledge can be pursued. By bringing scholars and teachers together in one place, the university makes possible interactions among them and allows students access to a great store of knowledge. The period of university education is a time when students are allowed to pursue the life of the mind, to learn, to make mistakes, and to develop their skills without the pressures of the workaday world. The point is not for them to do but to learn and to take the time to consider their goals and the larger questions of human life and society.

Knowledge, as rethought, is always critical. This critical aspect of reason, like the university itself, serves a social function. The university provides a place from which the ideas, ideals, structures, and institutions of a society can be evaluated, rethought, criticized—and in this way improved, either by being bolstered or by being reformed. Critical thought is neither necessarily radical nor necessarily conservative. It depends on the society and the conditions in which it finds itself.

Education aims not only to teach students what is known but to teach them how to learn, how to think critically about whatever knowledge they encounter. It also and importantly aspires to teach them the best that humankind has achieved so that they may have touchstones for what they find around them and how they live their lives.

If this characterization of the university is accepted, it shapes the role of all of its parts, including that of the business school. The goal of the business school is to develop knowledge appropriate to business, evaluate it critically, and pass it on to its students. What may well differentiate business training as found in a company classroom from that found in a university is that the former may be appropriately narrow and infused with the values, ideology, or culture of the company, whereas the latter should be neither. University business education should be broad in the sense that what is most important are concepts, theories, and approaches that can grow and be applied in a variety of different businesses and be used in solving a variety of tasks. In truly learning, the students should learn how to continue learning; in mastering any theory, students should learn how to think through a theory, appreciate its strengths and weaknesses, evaluate new theories, and evaluate them and know when to revise or change their own theories.

The essence of the critical task, university training, is in contrast to corporate inculcation of values. The purpose of university education is not indoctrination but expansion. It should open one up to more than one's self and one's parochial interests. It should help one learn how to deal with values.

In all of this various qualities of mind are essential, and it is the task of education to develop and hone these qualities. The ability to evaluate critically is one component. Imagination is another vital one. The difference between routinely assimilating and creatively thinking is not only the ability to criticize and evaluate but the ability to imagine what might be, as well as to see what is.

A goal of the university in the contemporary world is to help humanize society, to help make it more human by training large numbers of people to think clearly, critically, and imaginatively about themselves, their lives, and their society. As societies become more and more closely intertwined, the need for internationalizing the curriculum has become increasingly apparent as educators strive to enlarge students' horizons and views of themselves and to prepare them to understand humanity, not only in their own person but in that of others in other lands. The spread of the university is linked with the spread of civilization and the enrichment and appreciation of culture as well as of cultures.

Business is an interaction among people. It is an extremely pervasive and important component of our society. The purpose of a business school that is consonant with that of a university is to humanize business, just as the university attempts to humanize society. This involves criticism and imagination as central ingredients. Critical and imaginative approaches to business education involve more than simply turning out people with the skills that business wants. If business wants people with special skills, it can train them itself. What business should expect from a business school and what a business school should provide is something that business cannot itself produce. It may appear arrogant for a business school to claim to know better than business itself what is good for business and what business needs. But if businesses knew better what they need, they would provide it for themselves.

The task is to determine how to build a critical and imaginative humanistic approach into a business curriculum. The key lies in the purpose of a business school and of graduate training in business. If its purpose is truly to humanize business, then its courses must be developed accordingly. Business education cannot humanize business unless its products are able to conduct business successfully. The humanistic revision does not imply any lack of attention to accounting or finance, for instance, even if it calls for questioning some of their assumptions and approaches. Nor does it deny the need for developing students' organizational and people skills, even if it calls for some different approaches to teaching these, as well.

HUMANIZING THE BUSINESS SCHOOL CURRICULUM

What does this mean for business schools and business education? Let me start by indicating what it does not mean. The aims of the university, as I have portrayed them, are sometimes linked with the aims of liberal education and with the humanities. Although any such equation is much too narrow, there is some basis for the equation. It is much too narrow, for all aspects and parts of the university should be informed by them. A liberal education should not be equated with the liberal arts, which are frequently equated with the humanities. The sciences can be as liberating as the humanities. They can serve as a valid means for training the mind to be critical (as does philosophy) and to be imaginative (as does literature)—even if they do so in different ways. The same can be true of the so-called professional and business schools.

Many of those inside as well as outside universities claim that undergraduate education should be humanistic or broadly based, as the traditional liberal arts education has been. The point is well taken, but it does not follow that graduate professional education, presupposing humanistic undergraduate training, can then be anti-humanistic or strictly technical. The technical approach to medical school education has produced doctors who are more interested in medicine than in patients. The law schools have produced lawyers more interested in success than in justice. The business schools have produced managers more interested in profits than in people, goods, and services.

What is not required to humanize the business school curriculum is the introduction of graduate courses in the humanities. The disease of professionalism in the professional schools is present also in the humanities graduate programs. A graduate-level course in the humanities may be no more humanistic, no more liberal, no more broadening than a graduate course in accounting or management. If this is the case, then those who advocate making the business curriculum more humanistic will not achieve their goal simply by requiring one or more courses in the humanities. Any attempt in this direction is misplaced for a number of other reasons. Graduate courses in the humanities are usually narrow and specialized and require a large number of previous courses in the discipline. One cannot teach a graduate level course in history or English literature or philosophy to those without a certain amount of training in those areas. One cannot make a course a graduate-level course simply by offering it to people in graduate programs of engineering, law, medicine, or business. If my observation that these courses are not especially humanistic in their own right is correct, then adding them to a business school's curriculum will not achieve the purpose of making that curriculum more humanistic.

An alternative suggestion might be to teach the broad humanistic courses, usually taught on the undergraduate level, in the M.B.A. programs. But if the courses are undergraduate courses, why should they be taught to those in graduate programs? They are courses the student should have had as an undergraduate and would be at best remedial courses that should not carry graduate credit.

It is not only the content of a particular course that makes that course humanistic. Philosophy may be as technical as accounting and may be taught as a technical as opposed to a liberal arts course. In each of the subjects traditionally included in the humanities, we can distinguish content and method. Neither, by itself, makes the humanities humanistic; there is no one humanistic method. I have emphasized values, criticism, imagination, insight into the human condition, and focus on basic human concerns as important in the humanities for purposes of business education. In literature and the humanities there are classics—great works—that cross time and national boundaries. They continue to touch something fundamental in people. These works can be used effectively in business education because they provide useful paradigms. They are used in many executive seminars, many of which emulate the Aspen seminars developed by Mortimer Adler. It is noteworthy that the classics of literature and philosophy are taught to CEOs and corporate presidents and vice presidents but rarely to M.B.A.s.

Humanizing business means bringing to the business activity an awareness of the place of business in society and of its impact on people and keeping in mind that society allows business activities because of the good business can do for society and its people. In a democratic society, the values of democracy should not be infringed upon when entering corporate walls. At their best, business schools should develop and articulate a vision of what business at its best can and should be and then attempt to inculcate that vision through their training. This means a value-filled, rather than a value-neutral or value-empty, curriculum.

One problem with graduate schools of business is that they lack vision. Like most graduate teachers, professors of business too often teach what they do research in. To the extent that their research is narrowly analytic, that is what they teach. This is appropriate for a Ph.D. program in which the aim of teaching is to produce the scholars to replace oneself. It is not appropriate at the M.B.A. level. To the extent that analytic research skews the curriculum, it distorts the aim of humanizing business. To humanize business, business schools must first humanize their curriculum.

I mentioned that graduate courses in philosophy or literature may be technical and nonhumanistic. Undergraduate courses in these areas may also be of this type. To the extent that teachers treat their undergraduate courses as extensions of their research, these courses too often are nonhumanistic; however, they can be broadening and throw critical and imaginative light on what it means to be human and to be a human being in a society where one can have not only a place but a voice. It is possible to infuse education with a vision of a good society or a good life, rationally, critically, and imaginatively drawn.

Business schools are utilitarian as well as educational. Ideally the two go hand in hand. The aim is to produce persons who can work effectively in business. If the end of business is to provide goods, services, and employment for society, it is expected that those who do so will be rewarded. Clearly, monetary as well as moral incentives are operative. Difficulties arise when the monetary incentives drive out the moral ones and when the aim of business is not to serve society but to enrich itself. One can aim to enrich oneself by serving society in business. That is different from having as one's primary aim enriching oneself. The latter leaves society out of the picture and justifies enriching oneself at the expense of society. To do so is to invite society's wrath. That should not be the aim of business schools.

It is noteworthy that the article in the *Wall Street Journal* to which I referred earlier emphasized the internationalization of business.[6] The skills needed to operate abroad include knowledge of the language of the nation in which one will work, as well as knowledge of the culture. What is significant is that the foreign culture is something the manager must know. If that is true abroad, is it not just as true that managers must know and appreciate their own culture? Yet the typical business school curriculum does not include much if anything about American culture in its broad aspects.

It does not seem appropriate that history, philosophy, or literature as disciplines be taught or studied as such in business schools. As vehicles, however, these subjects can be well used to teach management or administration as activities that involve people and as fields of study that need not only social scientific approaches but humanistic approaches as well—or instead.

If we look at how the business faculty develops, we find that it often includes people trained in the social sciences, who then develop courses that apply their knowledge of sociology or psychology or anthropology. One step in the change toward a humanistic business curriculum is to hire those trained in humanities disciplines. They would not be expected to teach graduate philosophy or history or literature, but neither should they be expected to teach social science courses developed by others. The challenge given them would be to develop courses in administration or management or organizational behavior as perceived by someone trained in the humanities. This is the answer to the question as to whether business courses can be taught as humanities.

The battle over whether and how to teach ethics can be taken as a model. The difficulty is whether to teach ethics as a separate course and whether it is to be taught by those in business or by those trained in philosophy and ethics. A straw in the wind is that several people trained in philosophy have full-time appointments in schools of business, rendering moot the question of whether business ethics should be taught by the faculty in philosophy or the faculty in business, for these faculty members are both. We can expect the courses taught by such people to be different both from those they would teach if they were located in philosophy departments and from ethics courses taught by those in business who have no training in ethics.

The key to humanizing the business school curriculum is not to impose humanities courses taught by humanities faculty on the curriculum and not to expect that many of the business school faculty teaching today will be interested in humanizing their teaching in any of the ways I have suggested. Instead, the key is twofold. First, business schools need to seek out applicants with strong humanities or liberal arts educations that have helped to shape their critical and imaginative skills, skills that can be developed further on the graduate level in business school. An undergraduate business education should be a liberal arts education. Unless students have a broad humanities or liberal arts background, they should be considered to have deficiencies and should either be rejected or be required to make up those deficiencies before entering an M.B.A. program.

The second step is to hire faculty trained in the humanities to teach the existing standard courses in business and to help develop new ones. This faculty should not be expected to teach from the same texts currently used, for that would defeat the purpose of hiring them. They hopefully would develop new material, perhaps slowly in the beginning, and work it in with traditional material, experimenting, and leavening the offerings in a new way. Enough humanities-trained faculty members should be added to the business faculty over a small number of years to allow them to support one another's endeavors and to cooperate with one another, as well as with the rest of the faculty, and to keep them from feeling like outsiders. Some new cooperative programs in business and the humanities might be formed to train new Ph.D.s in the humanities with an interest in teaching in business schools, similar to programs that have developed in law and business and law and philosophy.

I have no ideal curriculum to lay out or propose, even though I have suggested the inclusion of literature, philosophy, and history in a variety of ways. Nor do I believe there is any ideal curriculum. But there are poor curricula, and any curriculum that does not fulfill in substantial part the goal of university education is seriously deficient. Given the realities of business schools, such changes as I have proposed must be made by the faculties of the schools, probably with much discussion, debate, soul-searching, and internecine warfare. I do not know whether graduate accounting can—or even should—be made humanistic. I do think it can be taught imaginatively. I know it can also have a critical component.

The notions of business as a vocation and of humanizing business are key notions that, if taken seriously, will lead to important changes in the nature of business school education and in the role that those trained in business will fill. The change will prepare business school graduates to become leaders in humanizing business. The time is ripe, and the goal is worth the effort. Some revolutions have been peaceful. We should all hope that this revolution, which is already smoldering, will on the whole be at least as peaceful as major educational revisions can be.

NOTES

1. Amanda Bennett, "Going Global: The Chief Executives in the Year 2000 Will Be Experienced Abroad," *Wall Street Journal,* February 27, 1989, p. 1.

2. Ibid.

3. Alfred North Whitehead, *The Aims of Education* (New York: Mentor Books, 1961), p. 99.

4. Ibid., p. 100.

5. Francis Bacon, *Advancement of Learning,* ed. William Aldis Wright, 4th ed. (Oxford: Clarendon Press, 1891).

6. Bennett, "Going Global," p. 1.

A Response to Richard T. De George's "Business as a Humanity: A Contradiction in Terms?"

Ronald M. Green

As we have come to expect, Richard De George has given us a rich and thoughtful discusson of the role the humanities might play in business education. My aim in this comment is not to take issue with De George. Rather, because I substantially agree with almost everything he says, I want to identify one ambiguity in his argument and sharpen the separate points within it. To assist in this, I propose to draw on the related area of medical education. Medical educators have had longer experience than business educators in trying to integrate the humanities into their curricula. By looking at their efforts we can better understand the challenges facing the humanities in business education.

De George's discussion is an appeal for the "humanization of business education" as part of the "humanization of the business world."[1] This appeal is partly grounded in an understanding of the nature of business education in the university setting. At one of the most important junctures of his argument, De George raises a central but infrequently asked question: "Why have a business school or an M.B.A. program in a university."[2] Why not consign business education to a freestanding technical or vocational school or to programs located within business enterprises themselves? De George's answer is that business education belongs in the university because, in its most valuable forms, it shares the university's goals. These include participation in the critical exercise of reason and the advancement of knowledge. Although De George does not say so, he might add that this need to participate in the process of critical inquiry is not merely an expression of idealism on the part of business educators. Business school faculty members and students have chosen to be part of the university in order to tap the stream of knowledge so essential to technical mastery in their fields. As De George makes clear, however, business educators' utilization of the opportunities afforded by the university setting entails corresponding responsibilities. If business education profits by its location in this setting of critical inquiry, it must also be prepared to expose itself—its assumptions, goals, and values—to this same process of critical inquiry. It follows from this that the special task of the business school, according to De George, is "to develop knowledge appropriate to business, evaluate it critically, and to pass it on to its students."[3]

As much as I agree with De George's position here, I would point out that the precise nature of the tasks he sets for business education—and specifically for the humanities' contribution to it—is not clear. If university-based business education is to be a critical enterprise, where and how is that criticism to transpire? What is the locus of critical inquiry, and what is its object? If business education is to employ the humanities in order to humanize the business world, precisely how is that humanization to be effected? To see the ambiguity inherent in these proposals, consider two very different approaches to using the humanities as a critical element in business education. One approach focuses on students. It seeks to impart to them the skills of analysis and the breadth of experience needed to make them more creative and responsible business citizens. A second approach focuses directly on business itself and on the process of business education that leads to it. In this approach humanistic scholarship in philosophy, literature, or history aims at affecting business practice not so much by changing its practitioners as by pursuing research and critical inquiry in order to challenge the assumptions, goals, and values that underlie business and business education.

I believe De George has both these approaches in mind when he sketches the role he envisions for the humanities, but he does not always distinguish these two approaches as clearly as he might. For example, early in his essay, in connection with the task of business ethics, he speaks of the importance of recognizing that improving business ethics requires not only "virtuous people" but also a potentially "dramatic change in the very nature of business and the way it is structured and carried on."[4] This suggests the dual focus of the humanizing task of business ethics. Yet later in the essay, while illustrating his point that the goal of business education is "to develop knowledge appropriate to business," he focuses almost exclusively on ways to mold students into critical thinkers. They must be given the qualities of mind that will enable them to transcend particular or parochial contexts and to continue to question and learn throughout their careers. Here De George gives very little attention to the direct critical and ethical examination of business and business education within the context of a university-based business curriculum. Although he again tells us that, at their best, "business schools should develop and articulate a vision of what business at its best can and should be,"[5] he says very little about the research and scholarly activity that necessarily underlie this process.

I can further illustrate the nature and importance of the distinction I am drawing by tracing the evolution in thinking undergone in connection with the role of the humanities in medical education. Medical education did not always take place in the university setting. As was true of business until more recently, medical training was frequently acquired in the practitioner context. This changed in the nineteenth century for a variety of reasons, not the least of which was that physicians sought to upgrade the social standing of their profession by tapping into the prestige associated with university education. For example, in 1847 a member of the Royal College of Physicians wrote a treatise in which he remarked upon

> the great advantages which result to society from there being an order of men within the profession who have had an education with the members of other learned professions; from a certain class of the medical profession having been educated with the gentry of the country and having thereby acquired a tone of feeling which is very beneficial to the profession as a whole.[6]

Considerations of social status may have prompted this writer to want to move doctors into the university and have them humanistically educated to become the model of the Complete Physician, but by the early twentieth century a university setting for medical education had become technically unavoidable. In the United States this development was spurred by the Flexner Report of 1910, which argued for the incorporation of basic science in the medical curriculum. This report led to the closing of scores of independent proprietary medical schools and to the establishment of the modern pattern of postgraduate, university-based medical education. Medical educators needed the university, as well as the creative and critical context of scientific inquiry it presupposed, to move their profession forward and ward off the challenges posed by less well educated practitioners of alternate forms of medicine.

In the late 1960s medical education entered a new phase when many critics inside and outside the profession came to believe that the medical school curriculum was too narrowly based on the sciences alone. This period saw the emergence of criticism of the profession for its broad failures of social responsibility—including its neglect of preventive medicine and its fostering of an overconcentration of doctors in highly paid but socially questionable medical specializations. This period also witnessed growing concern about the creation of a generation of doctors more skilled at treating the disease than the patient. Predictably, many critics of medicine saw the integration of the humanities into medical education as a solution to these problems of value neglect and technical myopia. This was the period when courses on medical ethics and programs and even departments of humanities began to spring up in medical schools across the United States. By exposing students to philosophy, literature, and history, it was argued, humanization of the profession might occur and a genuine conversation could be established between the medical profession, medical educators, and the other departments of the university charged with understanding and responding to society's broad needs.

During the first phases of these initiatives, the principal focus of this process of humanistic education was on the individual student. Courses (usually electives) were elaborated upon and offered to students as an enrichment to their education. These efforts were predictably not always as successful as humanists or others had hoped. Profoundly shaped by their own previous training, as well as by the existing context of the medical school and the structure of the profession that it served, many of the best students avoided these courses and eschewed the "soft" and "unreal" domain of the humanities for the "hard" and "real" world of the laboratory or clinic. In this setting humanities instructors frequently felt themselves to be both marginal and marginalized: at best, modest change agents; at worst, a glossy but misleading embellishment on a deeply inhumane curriculum.

More recently, this picture of limited success for the humanities has undergone change with what I discern to be the beginning of a different approach to the inclusion of a self-critical and humanistic component in the medical curriculum. This approach places emphasis on the direct contribution medical humanists and medical social scientists can make as scholars and researchers whose critical gaze is turned on the profession itself and its associated pattern of education and organization. Some of this research is transpiring within programs or departments of the humanities, some in traditionally "friendly" territory such as departments of community and family medicine. Some research is primarily social scientific; the studies of my Dartmouth colleague Jack Wennberg, drawing national attention to the appalling discrepancies in procedural utilization and success rates across medical centers, are an example. But some research, particularly that by medical ethicists who have chosen to examine moral issues of health care availability or therapeutic priorities, is deeply humanistic.

I don't wish to overstate the successes or even the degree of activity of this sort. Its importance lies less in any finished record of achievement than in its role as a reminder that critical inquiry and humanization in a graduate professional context can take two very different (albeit related) forms. One approach aims at making the humanities available to the student for his or her personal edification. A second approach stresses the role of the humanities in enabling observers to understand critically and evaluate the educational and professional context in which students and practitioners operate. What the efforts of medical humanists to incorporate humanities in the medical curriculum show, I believe, is that the first approach without the second is severely limited. In this setting, humanists find that even their rudimentary efforts at humanization are held hostage to unexamined and unexplained practical imperatives dominating the educational and professional environment in which they are trying to operate.

What are the lessons of this excursion into the history of the medical humanities for those considering the role of humanists in the business setting? There are two, I think. First, it is important to be clear about just how the processes of critical inquiry are imagined to transpire. Without direct attention to the context, all the energy focused exclusively on students may have little import on business education and on the business world as a whole. This is why I have been compelled to tease out and develop the different implications of De George's somewhat ambiguous call for "humanization." Second, this brief review of history suggests some considerations worth keeping in mind as humanists enter this environment. They must not, for example, be afraid, even if they feel a bit like invited guests, to ask sharp questions about their context and their colleagues, and they must incorporate these questions into their teaching and research. In addition, both humanists and other members of business schools faculties must recognize that this kind of teaching and research requires a context of support. Although single individuals may bravely raise such questions, their ability do so is greatly facilitated by the existence of departments or programs where critical inquiry is institutionalized. De George makes this point emphatically when he calls for the addition of enough humanities-trained faculty in the business school to allow them to support one another. In medicine, we saw that the most creative interrogations of the professions have emerged from programs or departments where a critical density of researchers has been achieved and where these researchers have been able to reinforce and stimulate one another's work and carry it to the faculty as a whole. I am not here calling for the creations of departments of the humanities in business schools, although that may come. What is important is the lesson that in whatever sub-groups they gather, whether with other humanists or with business educators in congenial functional areas, humanists should not allow themselves to become separated and isolated, and they should not permit their contribution to be oriented solely to students, rather than to the business school community and business as a whole.

NOTES

1. Richard T. De George, "Business as a Humanity: A Contradiction in Terms?" in Thomas J. Donaldson and R. Edward Freeman, eds., *Business as a Humanity* (New York: Oxford University Press, 1994), p. 13.

2. Ibid., p. 19.

3. Ibid., p. 20.

4. Ibid., p. 13.

5. Ibid., p. 23.

6. Magali Sarfatti Larson, *The Rise of Professionalism: A Sociological Analysis* (Berkeley: University of California Press, 1977); quoted in Eric J. Cassell, *The Place of the Humanities in Medicine* (Hastings-on-Hudson, N.Y.: Institute of Society, Ethics and the Life Sciences, 1984), p. 9.

A Response to Richard T. De George's "Business as a Humanity: A Contradiction in Terms?"

Thomas W. Dunfee

Richard De George's eloquent call for a true humanizing of the business school curriculum encompasses many valid points. I agree in general with De George's position but find that I have a quite different perspective concerning several of his claims. My perspective is that of someone who has been a business school faculty member for the last two decades and my view represents a qualified and limited defense of business school curricula and research. My basic position differs from De George's in five key respects.

First, it is important to understand that the debate over the role of the humanities in business school education is not new; rather, it has been actively joined for more than three decades. Consistent with De George's admonition that historical perspectives enhance insight, I will briefly summarize the historical evolution of the humanities component of business school education later in this response.

Second, business school faculty are not as closed to new ideas and methodologies as De George implies. I would claim, to the contrary, that business school faculty have recently been more open to new perspectives than have most of their academic brethren have been. This openness is reflected in particular in the extensive assimilation of social science research methodologies into business school research, a phenomenon driven by the demonstrated power of the absorbed techniques, not just by historical accident, as De George suggests.

Third, it is true that some—perhaps most—faculty at the major business schools would question whether the humanities should have more than a strictly limited, peripheral role within the business school. The concerns of such skeptics cannot be summarily dismissed. Advocates must ultimately demonstrate how the humanities relate to valid business school objectives. Frankly, I don't think that a conclusive case has yet been made.

Fourth, De George needs to make a careful distinction between the needs of the undergraduate and the graduate curricula. Graduate business programs have special pedagogical goals and take place in an environment very different from their undergraduate counterparts. Humanization is compatible with the objectives and context of undergraduate business programs, and it should not be surprising that greater integration has occurred at that level. At the graduate level, advocates of humanization must demonstrate convincingly that a master's program in a professional school is an appropriate place to achieve broader educational goals. After all, M.B.A. programs can easily require prerequisites in the humanities or consider an applicant's breadth of undergraduate study in the admissions process. I don't think that De George sufficiently directs his arguments to the special needs and objectives of M.B.A. programs.

Fifth, De George's two primary solutions are (1) to suggest that business schools emphasize the undergraduate background of M.B.A. students in the admissions process and (2) to advocate the use of humanities-trained faculty to teach functional business courses. I agree wholeheartedly that *requiring* M.B.A.s to take graduate humanities courses is neither feasible nor desirable. Hiring humanities-trained faculty, particularly those also trained in a functional business subject, is a good idea but realistically can involve only a small number of people. Although De George is not enthusiastic about their potential impact, efforts to modify the curriculum and encourage the melding of research in the humanities and research in the business disciplines are likely to pay higher dividends.

A BRIEF HISTORY OF EFFORTS TO BROADEN THE BUSINESS SCHOOL CURRICULUM

Excerpts from two important studies of business school education, separately sponsored by the Carnegie and Ford foundations in 1959, demonstrate that De George's concerns and proposed solutions are built on a long-standing tradition. To cite from the Carnegie Foundation study, "Undergraduate preparation for business necessarily rests on a number of subjects in the liberal arts area. The work in these subjects should be pursued beyond the first-year introductory level. The student should be given every opportunity to transfer general knowledge to applications in the business area."[1] According to the Ford Foundation study, "Undergraduate schools of business clearly have a responsibility for general (or 'liberal') as well as for professional education. The school of business cannot avoid this responsibility by confining its jurisdiction to the last two years, leaving the first two years for whatever the student wishes to study or for whatever the liberal arts college chooses to require."[2]

As suggested by these excerpts dating back thirty-five years, the "impending" war that De George describes has been going on for a long time. To those who favor the inclusion of more humanities in the business school curriculum, significant progress has been made. What is different now is that some new troops, philosophers and similarly inclined colleagues interested in applied ethics, are entering the fray. These new soldiers are primarily outsiders and will not have an impact on the battle unless they are supported by key faculty allies within the business school. I fear, however, that joinder with likely allies may not occur for a variety of reasons or that, worse, natural allies may end up fighting among themselves over what is perceived as very limited available space in the business curriculum.

Those seeking to influence change in the business school curriculum must understand the process by which the curriculum reached its current state. The Pierson and the Gordon and Howell studies were done in response to a trend in business schools during the 1950s toward extreme vocationalism and specialization, particularly in industry studies such as insurance, real estate, and banking. A simultaneously amusing and shocking example was provided by Pierson, who listed courses in a baking science major at a large university: Principles of Baking: Bread and Rolls; Principles of Baking: Cakes and Variety Products; Bread and Roll Production–Practical Shop Operation; Cake and Sweet Baked Products–Practical Shop Operation.[3]

Stimulated by the Pierson and the Gordon and Howell studies, significant changes in business school education have taken place during the past thirty-five years. Much of that change has involved movement toward rather than away from De George's position. According to the accreditation standards of the American Assembly of Collegiate Schools of Business (AACSB), general education courses must make up a minimum of 40 percent of the coursework of undergraduate business students, and students can take up to 60 percent of their work outside the formal business curriculum. Humanities courses are specified as part of the common body of knowledge segment of the curriculum. These AACSB standards have changed the type of educational experience encountered by business students.

Another major study of business school education was published several years ago. Written by Lyman Porter and Lawrence McKibbin, the report's title—*Management Education and Development: Drift or Thrust Into the 21st Century?*—is revealing, as is the fact that the study was sponsored by the AACSB.[4] I will address the question of whether the Porter-McKibbin report is likely to have an impact comparable to the two 1959 studies in a later section.

Since the Pierson and the Gordon and Howell reports appeared, the overall quality of business school faculty research has improved, in large part because of the incorporation of research methodologies from the social sciences. In a survey conducted for the Porter-McKibbin report, provosts rated the quality of research done by business school faculty as average or above average when compared to the quality of research undertaken by the faculty of the rest of the university.[5]

Much of the change that has occurred in business education is the result of pressures from both within and without the business schools themselves. The Porter-McKibbin report considers and evaluates the following current criticisms of business school education:

1. insufficient emphasis on generating vision in students
2. insufficient emphasis on integration across functional lines
3. overemphasis on quantitative analytical techniques
4. insufficient attention to managing people
5. insufficient attention to communication skills
6. insufficient attention to the external (i.e., legal, social, political) environment of business
7. insufficient attention to the international dimension of business
8. insufficient attention to ethics

In evaluating these criticisms, Porter and McKibbin found that, in general, business school deans and faculty are satisfied with the status quo.[6] For example, a majority of deans and faculty think that the liberal arts component of the undergraduate curriculum should be left as it is. Twenty-nine percent of deans and 32 percent of faculty think that it should be increased, whereas 6 percent of deans and 13 percent of faculty think that it should be decreased. These percentages are based upon responses from deans and faculty at all levels of business schools. Significantly, a majority of the deans and the faculty at Category I AACSB-accredited schools think that the liberal arts components of the undergraduate curriculum should be increased, with support slipping as the category of school drops. Porter and McKibbin also determined that corporate executives think in general that there is too much emphasis on quantitative topics and too little emphasis on behavioral topics in the modern curriculum.[7]

An optimist could view these findings and conclude that further liberalization of the business school curriculum is likely. Unfortunately, I don't think that an optimistic conclusion is justified. In 1959 the status of the business schools within the academic community was quite low. Today, business schools have the respect of their university colleagues and, as a consequence, there is much less stimulus for change.

Some recent events seem ominous for the liberalization of the curriculum. Yale is apparently moving away from its experimental approach toward a more traditional, functionally dominated curriculum. The student editors of *The Wharton Journal,* the newspaper of the M.B.A. program at Wharton, speculated that one professor was denied tenure "because his specialty is business history." They went on to argue:

> If so many of us have decided that what ——— teaches is an important component of a business education, why is that not enough? Is it because administrators feel that students do not know what is good for them, and that we should be shielded from harming ourselves?

> Take a close look at what ———'s BA905 covers. The course places in historical context how business has evolved, particularly during the last 100 years. If Wharton is trying to teach us to change the status quo . . . don't we need a sense of how the status quo has developed? The course also explores how government regulation shapes business interaction and what the proper role of government in business should be. If we are to be good citizens as well as good businesspeople, isn't that important to know?[8]

As Ken Andrews states elsewhere in the present volume, there appears to be a revival of vocationalism in some quarters, particularly in curriculum relating to real estate. Law courses in business schools have over time moved away from a rule emphasis by incorporating legal and social policy and jurisprudential concepts. The positive implications of this trend are countered by the fact that the importance of law courses in the business school curriculum has steadily declined during the same time period. Although some progress toward humanization has occurred, the situation is static and there are even negative signs concerning what the future may hold.

POSITIONING THE HUMANITIES WITHIN THE BUSINESS SCHOOL CURRICULUM

The business school curriculum is not a monolith and the business school faculty are not uniformly hostile to the arguments advanced by De George. There is diversity and even dissonance within the business school today, characteristics that may be masked to some degree by the current prosperity of the institutions.

Tensions exist among the various subjects taught within the business curriculum and provide an opportunity for the introduction of the humanities, an opportunity that extends well beyond the topic of "leadership" emphasized by De George. Although the concept of leadership is inviting and prophylactic, the term currently carries with it a lot of baggage as an existing research area within the management discipline, and it may actually turn out to be a false beacon.

A broader potential for relevance exists within the tensions provoked by the contrasting views of managers (as well as agents, investors, and economic actors) taught at different places in the curriculum. Business schools somehow meld two very different views of the way people behave. Much of business school education is based upon an image of a monotonic, egoistic manager who responds solely to financial incentives and sanctions. This narrowly focused, selfish creature is the basis for the assumptions that dominate much of the research and, therefore, much of the teaching in economics and finance. In contrast, the polytonic manager responds to values representing interests beyond the purely financial. Not dismissable as merely "tastes" or "mushy preferences," these alternative values often affect actual behaviors. The polytonic manager is the basis for the management discipline courses and the various liberal arts or humanities-oriented courses that have crept into the business curricula.

The question as to which of these views should dominate is critically important to education in business. If the monotonic view is correct, then narrowly defined rational actor assumptions can be considered valid and public policy should be solely structured around economic carrots and sticks such as tax breaks, subsidies, fines, and damages liability. If the polytonic model is more plausible, then there are additional ways to motivate and influence behaviors, including aspirational rule-of-thumb principles of business ethics.

There is a growing empirical literature that supports the polytonic model.[9] People tip when traveling, give blood, vote, consider certain downward adjustment of wages unfair, and otherwise act and think in ways inconsistent with the predictions of the rational actor models.

The polytonic manager is very consistent with the views implicit in De George's essay. This schism in views within the research paradigms of the business disciplines represents a great opportunity for intervention by humanists, who may contribute significantly to our understanding of the additional values that influence behaviors.

HOW BEST TO HUMANIZE THE BUSINESS SCHOOL CURRICULUM

Humanizing the undergraduate business school curriculum can be approached by requiring a set of humanities courses. An obvious issue is whether it is better for the business school to develop a special set of courses offered by its own humanities faculty or instead to ask the humanities faculty of the university to develop courses responsive to the special needs of the business students. It may well be that business schools are not interested in developing their own courses and that humanities faculty are not interested in modifying their courses for business students. If so, the only alternative may be to select as carefully as possible among the humanities courses available to business students as general education courses.

As mentioned earlier in this essay, the situation at the M.B.A. level is more complex. I personally believe that if it could be shown empirically that managers would be more effective as a consequence of more humanities-oriented training, there would be very quick acceptance of such a curriculum. Some acceptance would be likely if it could even be plausibly asserted that management skills would be enhanced by such training.

Unfortunately, some business school faculty would agree with the typo in De George's draft (since corrected to delete the "in" prefix) that "teaching moral theory and method to those who seek virtue can help make them morally inarticulate." More typical, faculty may question whether there is any systematic relationship between education in the humanities and better managerial decision making. Such faculty would find De George's arguments too generalized, perhaps even utopian.

What, then, should be done at the M.B.A. level? I strongly agree with De George that requiring existing humanities courses, graduate or undergraduate, is not the solution. The opportunity exists for increased and direct integration of the humanities if a strong case can be made for the value of such a move. That case would have to be made in the same way that the "case" was made for the incorporation of social science-based material—through demonstrated superiority in dealing with categories of business problems. This has occurred in the marketing discipline, where concepts and methodology from psychology have displaced older, more vocationally oriented approaches. Various quantitative techniques have become an essential part of research in most business school disciplines, influencing both empirical and theoretical research. Humanities research has the potential for having a similar influence on the business schools.

There has been some integration with the humanities already, in particular in management courses emphasizing literature and philosophy and in law courses emphasizing jurisprudence. There has been an American Bar Association-sponsored project on humanities in the business school law curriculum for several years. And some schools have introduced new law courses with a heavy emphasis on the humanities (for example, Wharton has adopted a new undergraduate course on non-Western legal systems).

I certainly agree with De George that the direct employment of humanities-trained faculty is a good idea. My department at Wharton has taken the lead at our institution in this regard and now has on its staff three people with training in philosophy. For this to occur more widely, the research of such faculty must be accepted on its own terms. If humanities faculty are hired and then expected to conduct standard social sciences research, their inclusion on the business school faculty will not have the desired effect. Similarly, if they are treated as second-class citizens, they will not have an impact.

On the basis of my experience and observation, I believe that the most likely areas for the use of humanities faculty in the business school lie in management and law. The least likely areas are finance, accounting, and economics. The potential for substantial integration of business and humanities faculty is quite limited, and there must be some emphasis on the potential for curricular change and for influencing the nature of business discipline research.

CONCLUSION

The war over liberalizing and humanizing the business school curriculum is an old one. Some progress has been made, but much more is needed. Realistically, only small changes are likely in the short term. The greatest potential for long-term change is in research. If research methodologies and publications from the humanities become part of the overall research paradigm of the business disciplines, which after all is essentially a borrowed paradigm, then the entire curriculum and institutional environment will be affected.

Any important changes will have to originate from within the business school. There are natural supporters for change, including management and law faculties, and many executives serve on advisory boards or have other roles through which they may influence the business school. I don't wish to close on a pessimistic note, but I must again mention the potential danger that seemingly natural allies may end up fighting among themselves for what is perceived as a very limited space for nonfunctional subject matter in the business school curriculum. If law faculty and humanities faculty fight over having whose course shall be designated a required course in the M.B.A. core, they can only both lose, and their students with them.

NOTES

1. Frank Cook Pierson, *The Education of American Businessmen* (New York: McGraw-Hill, 1959), p. 163.

2. Robert Aaron Gordon and James Edwin Howell, *Higher Education for Business* (New York: Columbia University Press, 1959), p. 148.

3. Pierson, *The Education of American Businessmen*, pp. 219–20.

4. Lyman Porter and Lawrence McKibbin, *Management Education and Development: Drift or Thrust into the 21st Century?* (New York: McGraw-Hill, 1988).

5. Ibid., pp. 140–41.

6. Ibid., p. 67.

7. Ibid., p. 69.

8. *The Wharton Journal,* April 17, 1989, p. 2, cols. 3–4.

9. See, e.g., Daniel Kahneman, Jack L. Knetsch, and Richard Thaler, "Fairness as a Constraint on Profit Seeking: Entitlements in the Market," *American Economic Review* 76, no. 4 (September 1986): 728–41; Howard Margolis, *Selfishness, Altruism and Rationality: A Theory of Social Choice* (Chicago: University of Chicago Press, 1982); Amitai Etzioni, *The Moral Dimension: Toward a New Economics* (New York: The Free Press, 1988), particularly chapter 4.

II

Business and the Humanities: An Aristotelian Approach to Business Ethics

Robert C. Solomon

> Where there is no shame, there is no honor.
> —*Ethiopian proverb*

Business ethics has finally become an established subject and concern. Ethics courses are now given in virtually every business school in the country and often are required. Elementary textbooks and a few classic case studies have given way to sophisticated theories and hands-on problem solving. The once separate concerns of the humanities and business have started to meet, cooperate, and consolidate their interests and their efforts. "Business ethics" is no longer jeered as an oxymoron. Indeed, it is treated in some business circles with solemnity, even reverence, as a kind of magic that distinguishes the best and most successful corporations. Undergraduate business majors and M.B.A. students crowd into our classrooms, curious about all the fuss and confident, at least, that the very title of the course on their transcript can only do them some good.

Despite this change, almost every month we still read essays in business publications and on op-ed pages in which pundits wonder, twenty-five hundred years after Plato (and often oblivious to his own musings on the subject), whether ethics can be taught at all. One such opinion piece by neoconservative gadfly Michael Levin proclaims that ethics courses are "useless," "pointless exercises" that don't deal with real-life issues. Levin (rightly) insists that "moral behavior is the product of training, not reflection," that it is a good upbringing, not a college or corporate course taken late in life, that teaches the difference between right and wrong. "Bicyclists don't have to think about which way to lean and honest men don't have to think about how to answer under oath," he argues.[1] And, of course, it is true, as Aristotle told us twenty-five hundred years ago, that ethics begins with a good upbringing. But it continues, Aristotle also told us, with practical experience, including the vicarious experiences provided by literature and what we now call "case studies," and it culminates in reflection and a deeper understanding of the practices in which one is and has been engaged. This reflection and deeper understanding of business practices is what business ethics courses, typically offered under the aegis of humanities departments (and in conjunction with business experience), seek to provide.

The skeptics, however, have a point. There is a suspicious gap between the practical aims and personal virtues promoted by business ethics advocates and the often abstract and dialectical contents of the courses we teach. Now that business ethics is an established discipline and no longer on the defensive, it is time to go back to its roots and ask, How do we teach this subject, and what is it that we are trying to teach? Are we trying to "stem the flow of immorality" (as Levin sarcastically puts it), or is our mission more modest? Can one teach virtue? Does a course in ethical theory have any impact on ethical behavior or, for that matter, on ethical understanding? Are case studies—even those drawn from "real life"—sufficient to cultivate real-life habits and ways of thinking? Given that a sizable proportion of the courses in business ethics are taught either in humanities departments (e.g., philosophy) or by humanities-trained professors, we have to ask what the disciplines of the humanities add to the business curriculum and business education. What do our efforts contribute to the presumably honest character of (most of) the students and managers who come to us? Sending them back to Plato's *Meno* isn't going to make them better managers or better human beings, and taking a course in business ethics certainly will not make up for a deficient or vicious upbringing. (Indeed, there is nothing so sinister as the language of ethics skillfully employed by a Machiavellian executive who sees the value of a noble demeanor. The most dangerous crooks are not those who openly extol "the bottom line.") But, then, what can an "applied philosophy" course do in the cultivation and understanding of proper conduct in business?

In this essay (and this volume) it is the connection between business and the humanities that is in question. My conclusion, one can readily anticipate, is that there is a very real and quite practical connection between business and the humanities and that the teaching of business ethics through the humanities does indeed make a difference. The aim of an ethics course, whether for students or seasoned executives, is not to "teach the difference between right and wrong" but to make participants comfortable with what Mark Pastin has rightly called the really "hard choices" of management and to open up the larger framework in which these choices give rise to ethical and not merely practical dilemmas.[2] But those hard choices are not unique to business life, and the habits and ways of thinking that make many of them hard have much to do with the artificial isolation of business language and business thinking. "The humanities" is nothing other than the larger context—of "being a good human being"—in which business decisions must be adequately understood. What business ethics courses provide, accordingly, is not new knowledge but room for reflection and a larger understanding, the luxury of practical reason not constrained by urgency, and, not least, a healthy dose of ethical edification to compensate for an excess of narrow cost/benefit thinking elsewhere. Business ethics courses are intended not to "stem the flow of immorality" but to reinforce morality and to keep our eyes open to the larger context in which all business decisions are made.

It is in this larger context, too, that we have to ask how the big questions and issues that we present to our students for debate and discussion are relevant to the actual decisions that they have to or will have to make in business. How can a discussion of "pollution versus profit" or of Adam Smith's much overtouted "invisible hand" help a busy executive or a harried manager to avoid ethical pitfalls and to make better decisions in his or her company position? And how can a blow-by-blow account of the internal debates among Kantian deontologists, libertarians, and utilitarians provide anything but oversimplification and confusion where ethical decision is required? A large part of the problem is the rather extravagant emphasis on questions of *policy* in current business ethics debates and the philosophers' long-established tendency to peddle their own wares—*theories* of ethics instead of a more *personal* and personally *practical* approach to ethics. We now know from experience that our favorite academic disputes have a way of sinking faster than a heavy metal zeppelin in business circles, and the practical problems involved in most policy disputes are those in which few of us and even fewer of our students have any real say. The chairman of the board may have a real and tangible interest in discussing and resolving large policy issues, and so too the members of this or that governmental commission. But policy disputes don't have very much to say to the ordinary manager or, for that matter, the ordinary executive. What is missing from too much of business ethics is an adequate account of the personal dimension in ethics, the dimension of everyday individual decision making.

It is in this light that I defend business ethics as akin to the humanities, rather than as a forum for debating public policy, a piece of specialized philosophy, or a value-laden by-product of the social sciences. Business ethics is a kind of "understanding," but it is also a practice, or a set or practices, in which we cultivate certain kinds of personal character to fit into certain kinds of institutions and a certain kind of society (archaically called "capitalist"). Here as elsewhere, however, the supposed line between theory and practice turns out to be virtually nonexistent, for to understand the nature of one's role (in the company or the community) is both essential to and often sufficient for the proper performance of that role. This is not to say, of course, that managers who know what they are doing won't cheat or that knowledgeable executives won't deal under the table. (It has always been hard to swallow the Socratic suggestion that it is impossible to do wrong knowingly. Short-term profits, even when seen beyond, still have the temptation of immediacy.) My hypothesis is that a good deal of wrongdoing in business is due to a faulty conception of business life or a lack of adequate understanding, rather than to greed or wickedness as such. It comes from a failure to see the "big picture," a kind of moral myopia, and an inadequate sense of the role of the self and its dignity, which get eclipsed by the urgency of goals, ambitions and demands. Business ethics so conceived is social self-awareness writ large, a clear sense of purpose, of honor, and of the virtues in business. It is a personal—although not in the sense of private or subjective—rather than a policy approach to business ethics. It might well be called—and I will call it here—an Aristotelian approach to business ethics. Quite literally, it is part of the humanities, but it is the essential core of business too.

BUSINESS AND THE HUMANITIES: ETHICS AND ARISTOTLE

Humanism and the Humanities

The humanities is an often overindulged and oversold commodity, especially in the hands of liberal arts college presidents and some recent secretaries of education. The relationship between the humanities and business is complex. It is even present in the architecture of universities. At Harvard University the business school is separated from the rest of the university by the Charles River. The symbolism is unmistakable and is expressed with some vengeance on both sides. At the University of Texas, through accident rather than through wisdom, the Business-Economics Building is less than thirty feet or so from Waggener Hall, which houses the humanities departments and philosophy in particular. And yet, for the amount of commerce between them, they might as well be at opposite ends of the state. It could easily be argued that the two have never gotten along all that well together, but what has changed is that the separation of business and the humanities has been institutionalized, reflected in our educational policies and in the divisions in our schools. The average business student is so steeped in finance and management courses that he or she rarely gets the chance to take more than one or two (usually required) liberal arts courses, and, of course, the typical liberal arts student wouldn't be caught dead in the business building. The result is a sort of social schizophrenia, a fragmentation of sensibilities that all too often gets recognized only in the unflattering terms of mutual abuse that each side throws (from a safe distance) at the other. Needless to say, it is from such a separation that business ethics, in particular, suffers. As a subject, it is part philosophy, part business, and the philosophers teach it as philosophy and the business professors teach it as business. The twain shall meet only briefly, at examination time, and then it's back to business (studies) as usual. Humanities students need to appreciate the dynamics of business and business life—which is where many of them will find their careers—and business students need to be more "humanitized." Today, not knowing what G.N.P. means or what a leveraged buyout is suggests a cultural illiteracy just as embarrassing as not knowing that Sophocles wrote *Oedipus Rex*.

But the gap between business ethics and the humanities isn't just a pedagogical issue. Our current notion of the humanities is inherited from Cicero's concept of *humanitas*, which did not focus just on literacy and education but was concerned also with the cultivation of the virtues and with being a good, "humane" person. We face a question of not only what types of courses we should teach and how but also what sort of people our business students should be. The humanities don't merely comprise a series of subjects, literary and philosophical, to be studied in school. It represents, in several senses, a way of life, and not only for students and professors lucky and leisurely enough to indulge in them. Humanitas is an ancient notion, derived (although the derivation is in some dispute) from the Greek *anthropismos* or *philanthropia*. Humanism itself, of course, has become a matter of considerable controversy; accusations of cultural and intellectual imperialism abound in academic circles, and outside academia humanism has been accused of being a kind of pagan religion. But we should note that the idea actually emerged from the twelfth-century church, with its new emphasis on learning and on individual sensitivities, and the precise term has been around, according to Bruno Snell, only since the early nineteenth century.[3] But the ancient conception(s), as well as our modern version, need not involve any clash between the secular and the divine. The term simply accords some preferential dignity to human beings and to an emphasis on "humane affairs."

In the ancient world, humanitas also referred to the abyss between

persons and beasts and (typically) between Greek citizen and barbarian. In other words, it was selective and more than a bit chauvinist.
In Cicero's writings in particular, however, the term emphasized excellence and achievement and celebrated the virtues of education
and eloquence. Humanitas was not just learning but *wisdom*. Aristip-
pus anticipated humanitas when he said, "I had rather be a beggar
than a dunce; the beggar has no money, but the dunce has no humanity *[anthropismos]*." And Thales, the first philosopher, expressed
a similar sentiment when he said, "I'm glad I am a man and not a
beast." (I would elsewhere protest on behalf of the beasts.)

Snell points out that our modern sense of humanity can first be
seen in Euripides' *Medea*, where a mere barbarian excites our pity.[4]
It is the human that moves us, not just the plight of our kin. Thus,
the meaning of humanitas was extended to encompass the *humane*,
a sense of compassion and kindness, a concern for persons as such.
Humanitas, Snell tells us, means that we are better than the beasts
and have an obligation to *capitalize* on this advantage (the word is
Snell's, but I find it particularly appropriate for our subject here). In
the context of business ethics, we all know what this means: beyond
selfishness and mere survival. From the time of Cicero onward, humanitas has meant the combination of "the humane with the humanistic, a blend of unself-conscious ease and gracious affability paired
with study of the classical authors."[5] Humanitas involves playfulness,
eloquence, personal elegance, and the personal virtues, and not just
a B.A. degree in literature or philosophy. Humanism is, in short,
bringing out what is best in us.

The Aristotelian Approach

Long before Cicero, the philosopher best known for espousing this
view and for an emphasis on the cultivation of the virtues was Aristotle. But Aristotle and business ethics? True, he was the first economist, and he had much to say about the ethics of exchange. But
Aristotle distinguished two different senses of what we call economics, one of them *oecinomicus*, or household trading, which he approved of and thought essential to the working of any even modestly
complex society, and *chrematisike*, or trade for profit. Aristotle declared the latter activity wholly devoid of virtue and called those who
engaged in such purely selfish practices "parasites." Such was his
view of what we call "business." Indeed, Aristotle's attacks on the
unsavory and unproductive practice of usury and on the personal
vice of avarice held force virtually until the seventeenth century and
are still evident at the end of the twentieth. Only outsiders on the
fringe of society, not respectable citizens, used to engage in such
practices. (Shakespeare's Shylock, in *The Merchant of Venice*, was such

an outsider and a usurer, although his terms were certainly extraordinary.) It was with Aristotle that the history of business ethics as a wholesale attack on business and its practices began.

Even today representatives of business offer up such Pyrrhonian arguments as "business is akin to poker and apart from the ethics of everyday life"[6] and "the [only] social responsibility of business is to increase its profits."[7] It is just this schism between business and the rest of life that so infuriated Aristotle, for whom life was supposed to fit together in a coherent whole. The very idea of separating, as we do so readily, the personal from the professional life, the idea that "business is business" (not really a tautology but a throwaway excuse for acting inhumanely), he would have thought to be unthinkable. A person had to think of him- or herself as a member of the community, the polis, and strive to excel, to bring out what was best in ourselves and our shared enterprise. There were no corporations in those days (indeed, there wasn't much corporate life even in the days of Adam Smith), but Aristotle would certainly have known what I mean when I say that most people in business now identify themselves—if tenuously—in terms of their company affiliation. Their ethics, at least in the office and on the job, are inevitably identified with the values of their corporation and the industry, however vigorously one might protest and distinguish his or her personal morality from these. Corporate policies and corporate codes of ethics are not enough to constitute an ethics. Corporate and, therefore, personal ethics are a product of what has recently (but too loosely) been called "corporate culture." What we need to cultivate is a certain way of thinking about ourselves in and out of the corporate cultural context. The Aristotelian approach to business ethics begins with the idea that it is individual virtue that counts; good corporate and social policy will follow. But it is the good corporation that cultivates individual virtue, and so the Aristotelian chicken presupposes a Platonic republican (not Republican) egg.

With what is this Aristotelian approach to be contrasted? First of all, I want to contrast it with the emphasis on public policy that has preoccupied our subject. In many business schools, traditional administrations cannot quite give themselves over to the idea of a business ethics course, so business ethics is given as a public and social policy course. There is nothing wrong with policy studies, of course, and I don't for a moment suggest that they be replaced or discarded. But policy decisions aren't usually made by folks like us. We rarely even get to vote or speak for them. For the ordinary line manager and even most executives, policy questions are, for the most part, something to debate over lunch, usually by way of reaction to some fait accompli. And there is something missing from policy decisions that is absolutely central to ethics on virtually any account, and that is personal responsibility. The question of responsibility pervades every corporation. It is not at all unusual to find many volunteers for available praise, but there is almost always a dearth of volunteers for blame. Of course, there are always a great many candidates for blame, so long as they are to be found elsewhere, but then there are far too many and the locus of responsibility is often too hard to find. This is why corporate America today is so often shaken and undermined by the mindless elimination or replacement of entire departments—chief executives do not know who to blame (and of course do not blame themselves), and so (as the Nazis did) they blame and punish everyone. At the top of too many corporations the proverbial buck that is supposed to stop "here" turns out like a bad check to be made of rubber, and responsibility bounces back and forth along the chain of command to end up nowhere in particular. Blame is placed on "the system" or on current policies that then become the focus of a seemingly endless debate. What gets left out and becomes the main point of business ethics, accordingly, is the recognition that decisions (and their consequences) are one's own, the knowledge that ethics is not just a subject for executive boards, planning committees, and government overseers but for all of us, in the details as well as in the larger dramas of our everyday lives.

The Aristotelian approach is also to be contrasted with that two-hundred-or-so-year-old obsession in ethics that takes everything to be a matter of *rational principles,* morality in the strict Kantian sense of obedience to the moral law. This is not to say, of course, that Aristotelian ethics dispenses with rationality or, for that matter, principles. But Aristotle is quite clear about the fact that it is cultivation of character that counts, long before we begin to "rationalize" our actions, and the formulation of general principles (in what he famously but confusingly calls his practical syllogism) is not an explicit step in correct and virtuous behavior as such but rather a philosopher's formulation about what it means to act rationally.[8] However obvious the principle, it is its interpretation and application that count in practical matters, and these require experience and judgment, not just rationality. They require sensitivity and a sense of responsibility, not just an ability to reason abstractly. Immanuel Kant, magnificent as he was as a thinker, has proved to be a kind of disease in ethics, providing a rationalization of dogmatic and insensitive management or what we more clinically might call anal-compulsive behavior, pushing questions in ethics away from existential matters of personal decision and responsibility. Instead, we get a priori prohibitions, abstract principles, the "categorical imperative" and its various formulations. It's all very elegant, even brilliant, until a person walks into the seminar room with a dozen or so bright, restless corporate managers, waiting to hear what's new and what's relevant to them on the business ethics scene. And then we tell them: don't lie, don't steal, don't cheat—elaborated on and supported by the most gothic noneconometric construction ever allowed in a company training center. But it's not just the impracticality of the Kantian approach and the fact that we don't actually do ethics that way; it is, more important, that the Kantian approach shifts our attention away from just what I would call the inspirational matters of business ethics, the emphasis on excellence (a buzzword for Aristotle as well as for Tom Peters and his millions of readers) and turns the focus from the critical importance of thinking of oneself as a multidimensional person occupying an important role in a particular organization to an overly academic obsession with an abstract conception of role-transcendent morality that necessarily finds itself empty-handed when it comes to most of the matters that we have all heard so much of in corporate seminars.

The Aristotelian approach is also to be contrasted with that rival ethical theory that goes by the name of utilitarianism. Utilitarianism, in its most familiar business usage, is the philosophy of cost/benefit analysis, expanded beyond the limited interests of the company to consider all involved parties as well. It is no accident that such a philosophy achieved prominence coincident with the rise of business culture in eighteenth- and nineteenth-century England or that the most easily quantifiable units of utility should turn out to be pounds, marks, and dollars. In fact, I would argue that too much of contemporary utilitarianism displays a technocratic vulgarization that eclipses the humanistic focus advocated by John Stuart Mill. For now, however, I just want to point out that utilitarianism shares with Kant that special appeal to anal-compulsives in its doting over principles and rationalization (in this case calculation) and its neglect of individual responsibility and the cultivation of character.[9] Indeed, I can imagine a good existentialist complaining quite rightly that the ultimate point of all such "decision procedures" in ethics is precisely to neutralize the annoyance of personal responsibility altogether, appealing every decision to "the procedure" rather than taking responsibility for it oneself. Of course, I am not denying the importance of concern for the public good or the centrality of worrying, in any major policy decision, about the number of people helped and hurt, but not all of the concerns of business ethics are policy decisions, and there are considerations that may, in many cases, be more basic than public utility—if only because, in most of our actions, the impact on public utility is so small that it becomes a negligible factor in our deliberations.

I would also distinguish the Aristotelian approach to business ethics from all of those approaches that primarily emphasize *rights,* whether the rights of free enterprise as such, the rights of the em-

ployee, the customer, or the community, or even civil rights. Again,
I have no wish to deny the relevance of rights to ethics or the centrality of civil rights, but I think that we should remind ourselves,
first of all, that this now pervasive social concept has only a very
recent history—since the seventeenth century or so—and, second,
that the multiple abuses of this concept (e.g., the so-called right of a
citizen to purchase and possess a semiautomatic assault rifle) now
threaten to undermine its virtues. What is wrong with the language
of rights is that it is a language that too readily pretends to transcend
all particular contexts and any concern for the larger public good,
as if a right, to be respected, must be able to trump all other claims
and concerns.[10] But the language of rights also presupposes a context and a very special notion of society that is often neglected in
rights talk, and it can be argued that the primary right is not as such
an individual right but the right of everyone to a just and reasonably
secure society. The language of rights presupposes the totality of a
(recent) tradition and a particular social context that places a pre-
mium on individuality and respect for private property. It is not just
a problem for technical philosophers that the concept of rights has
had so much trouble getting "grounded" (as opposed to "appearing
out of thin air"—an interesting juxtaposition of metaphors). The
problem is that rights cannot be viewed as always trump and considered or defended apart from a concern for society that is at once
both larger and more particular. Within such a larger and more particular context I have no difficulty at all with the idea that we have
rights to all sorts of things, in the workplace in particular (a fair
wage and fair treatment, safety, freedom of speech and beliefs, respect as a person, credit for what one has accomplished). But it is
not entirely clear that all of this could not just as well be expressed
by saying that there are all sorts of things that we should and
shouldn't ever do to people and that the violation of a right is always
first of all a failure of respect and responsibility.[11] Would we need
the language of rights if we had an adequate language (as Aristotle
did) of virtue and responsibility? Then again, Aristotle accepted
without challenge the institution of slavery. Would the language of
rights—which was, after all, adopted by the Continental Congress
while slavery was still an acceptable institution in this country—have
made the difference? I would not be surprised if the notion of human rights turns out to be indispensable for business ethics, but the
language of rights provides not the substance of ethics but what
some authors have called "side constraints" for social behavior, or,
perhaps better, fallback positions that allow us to insist, no matter
what the particular context, that some ways of treating human beings will not be tolerated.[12] Nevertheless, the substance of ethics lies

elsewhere, not in side constraints or fallback positions but in the cultivation of the virtues and in personal responsibility.

It may be evident to many readers that I am arguing—or about to argue—for a version of what has been called "virtue ethics," but I do want to distance myself from much of what has been defended under that title. First of all, I want to reject those versions of ethics that view the virtues as no more than particular instantiations of the abstract principles of morality. This is an analysis that has been argued at some length, for instance, by William Frankena and Kurt Baier, both distinguished defenders of "the moral point of view."[13] If, for example, being an honest man or woman is nothing other than obeying the general Kantian-type principle "do not lie," if being respectful is a conscientious application of the "ends" formulation of the categorical imperative, if one's sense of public service is an expression of the utilitarian principle, then this is emphatically not what I have in mind, nor did Aristotle. To be witty or magnificent (two Aristotelian virtues not taken seriously enough by our contemporaries) is surely not to express or apply certain principles, but neither is to be courageous, temperate, or even just. Our good existentialist here can be heard saying, presumably in French, that one's personal judgments precede rather than follow one's abstract ethical pronouncements. Of course, this isn't exactly Aristotelian (Aristotle was no existentialist), but, modified, it makes a good Aristotelian point: choice and character get cultivated first, philosophical ethics—if one is lucky enough to study in the right academy—afterward.

I also want to distance myself from some of the now familiar features of what is being defended as virtue ethics, in particular the rather dangerous nostalgia for "tradition" and "community" that is expressed by Alasdair MacIntyre and Charles Taylor in philosophy and Robert Bellah in sociology, to name the best of them.[14] Of course, the Aristotelian approach does presuppose something of a sense of community (as both MacIntyre and Taylor point out at great length), and in business ethics, it is the sense of community that I particularly want to emphasize. But there is a difference between the more or less homogeneous (and very elite) community that Aristotle simply took for granted and the nostalgic (I think purely imaginary) communities briefly described by virtue ethicists, with their religious solidarity and their emphasis on communal consensus. What is so often *wrong* with corporations (and some small communities) is precisely such an unhealthy hegemony of ideas, an intolerant conformity that stifles creativity and punishes just those eccentricities that often lead to progress. No adequate theory of ethics today can ignore or wish away the pluralistic and culturally diverse populations that make up almost every actual community, including even the most conformist corporations. Nevertheless, many modern corporations would seem to be ideal representations of the "community" in this Aristotelian sense—with their shared sense of telos (not just "making money") and an essential emphasis on mutual loyalty, teamwork, and excellence.

Finally, I want to distance myself from some feminist writings— including the work of some of my own best students—who have drawn a polemically sharp contrast between the good, warm, feminine virtues of caring and concern and the oppressive, impersonal, war-mongering masculine principles of justice and duty.[15] I certainly agree with the shift in emphasis from abstract Kantian justice and an overly game-theoretical criterion of utility to compassion and caring, but it is not my intention to supply one more weapon in the perennial war between the sexes, and it seems to me that Aristotle— certainly no feminist—has much to say about the virtues that in substance has little or nothing to do with the (admittedly not unimportant) fact that one is a male or a female.

From Polis to Phronesis

So what is the Aristotelian approach to business ethics? What are its primary ingredients? A deontological approach to the subject would highlight such terms as "rational principles," "consistency," "obligation," and "duties." A utilitarian approach would rather emphasize "interests," "preferences," "consequences," and "help and harm." Libertarians would no doubt emphasize the notion of "rights." So, too, the Aristotelian approach has its distinctive vocabulary and characteristics. I want to list a half dozen of them, which I will describe here only briefly. (I think that the point will soon become obvious— if it isn't already.)

Community (polis). The Aristotelian approach begins with the idea that we are all members of an organized group, with something of a history and established practices governing everything from eating and working to worshiping. To be sure, communities in the contemporary "Western" world are anything but homogeneous or harmonious, but the claim I am making here is more metaphysical than nostalgic, and that is that what we call "the individual" is him- or herself socially constituted and socially situated. The philosophical myth that has grown almost cancerous in many business circles, the neo-Hobbesian view that "it's a jungle out there" and "it's every man [sic] for himself," is the direct denial of the Aristotelean view that we are all first and foremost members of a community and that our self-interest is for the most part identical to the larger interests of the group. As the Greeks used to say, "To live the good life, one must live in a great city." To my business students today, who are all too likely to choose a job on the basis of salary and start-up bonus alone, I always say, "To live a decent life, choose the right company." In business ethics the corporation is one's community, but, of course, the corporation is itself a part of a larger community—as diverse as that may be—without which it would have no identity, serve no purpose, and sell no products. Quite the contrary of the cynical business "wisdom" that preaches "every man [sic] for himself," the truth is that every business activity, from the small-time hustler to the giant corporation, presupposes and itself incorporates a community, a polis in which the virtues of mutual trust and cooperation are taken for granted (even in their intentional breach).

Excellence. The Greek *arete* is often translated as either "virtue" or "excellence," and, unlike the rather modest and self-effacing notion of virtue that we inherited from our Victorian ancestors (indeed, even Kant used the term), the dual translation by itself makes a striking point. It is not enough to do no wrong. "Knowingly do no harm" *[primum non nocere]* is *not* the end of business ethics (as Peter Drucker suggests).[16] The hardly original slogan I sometimes use to sell what I do, "ethics and excellence," is not just a tag-along with Peters and Waterman. Virtue is doing one's best, excelling, not merely (from top to bottom) "keeping one's nose clean" and "toeing the line." The virtues that constitute business ethics are, above all, the virtues of doing business, and these should not be conceived of as if business ethics were nothing other than the general application of moral principles to one specific context (among others), primarily as an inhibiting force or a set of side constraints, rather than the underlying set of rules and expectations that make the practice of business possible in the first place. The word "quality," though much overused in advertising, defines the bottom line of business competition far better than "profits," which readily follow. The virtues of self-respect and integrity, far from being antagonistic to long-term success, form its very precondition. (Which is not to say, of course, that slimeballs don't succeed; it is just to point out that they are, nevertheless, still slimeballs.)

Position. Much has been written (e.g., by Norman Bowie, in his good little book *Business Ethics*) on the importance of "role morality" and on "my Position and its duties."[17] It is the situatedness of corporate roles that lends them their particular ethical poignancy, the fact that an employee or an executive is not just a person who happens to be in a place and is constrained by no more than the usual ethical prohibitions. To work for a company is to accept a set of particular obligations, to assume a prima facie loyalty to one's employer, to adopt a certain standard of excellence and conscientiousness that is

largely defined by the job itself. There may be general ethical rules
and guidelines that cut across most positions, but, as these get more
general and more broadly applicable, they also become all but useless in concrete ethical dilemmas. Robert Townsend's cute claim that
if a company needs an ethical code, use the Ten Commandments,
is not only irreverent but ultimately irrelevant.[18] The Aristotelian
approach to business ethics presumes concrete situations and particular people and their place in organizations. There is little point to
an ethics that tries to transcend all such particularities and embrace
the chairman of the board as well as a middle manager, a secretary,
and a factory worker. All ethics is contextual, and one of the problems with all of those grand theories is that they try to transcend
context and end up with vacuity.

Holism. It more or less follows from what I've said that one of the
problems of traditional business thinking is our tendency to isolate
our business or professional roles from the rest of our lives, a process that Marx, following Friedrich Schiller, described as "alien-
ation." The good life may have many facets, but they are facets and
not mere components, much less isolated aspects of a fragmented
existence. We hear more and more in managerial circles that a manager's primary and ultimate concern is *people.* It's gotten trite, but as
I watch our more ambitious students and talk with more and more
semisuccessful but "trapped" middle managers and executives, I become more and more convinced that the tunnel vision of business
life encouraged by the too narrow business curriculum and the daily
rhetoric of the corporate community is damaging and counterpro-
ductive. Good employees are good people, and to pretend that the
virtues of business stand isolated from the virtues of the rest of our
lives—and this is not for a moment to deny the particularity of either
our business roles or our lives—is to set up that familiar tragedy in
which a pressured employee violates his or her "personal values"
because, from a purely business point of view, he or she "didn't really have any choice."

Nobility. This is a word, like "honor"—its close kin—that seems all
but archaic in the modern business world, part of an elitist world
that we have all (happily) left behind. These are concepts that we
greet with suspicion, for example, when Richard Nixon, on two very
separate occasions, declared "peace with honor" as he retreated from
Vietnam and "the nobility of work" when he declared a wage-and-
price freeze during one of his several economic crises. But hypocrisy
and abuse aside, these are concepts that did not die out with the
passing of the Greek polis and the French aristocracy in flight from
the revolution. It is our overly individualistic thinking that keeps us
from appreciating the importance of a sense of honor, which presupposes our embeddedness in a community, and the significance of

a notion of nobility that refers not to a social class and the rituals and pretensions thereof but to a certain mode of behavior and self-respect, a sense of "being above" not other people but certain forms of selfish and otherwise vulgar behavior. There is indeed the "nobility of work," but this phrase, which makes a serious effort to counter residual prejudices against work, has as much to do with ethics as that self-serving defense of the Protestant ethic that would pretend that lousy jobs are just as desirable as good jobs.[19]

Judgment (phronesis). Against the view that ethics consists primarily of general principles that get applied to particular situations, Aristotle thought that it was "good judgment," or *phronesis*, that was of the greatest importance in ethics. Good judgment (which centered on perception, rather than on the abstract formulation and interpretation of general principles) was the product of a good upbringing, a proper education. It was always situated, perhaps something like Joseph Fletcher's still much referred to notion of a "situation ethics," and took into careful account the particularity of the persons and circumstances involved. But I think the real importance of *phronesis* is not just its priority to ethical deliberation and ratiocination; it has rather to do with the inevitable conflicts of both concerns and principles that define almost every ethical dilemma. Justice, for example, may sound as if it were a monolithic, hierarchically layered, and almost mechanical process (especially in the writings of some philosophers). As I have argued elsewhere, however, there are a dozen or more different considerations that enter into most deliberations about justice, including not only rights and prior obligations and the public good but questions of merit (which themselves break down into a variety of sometimes conflicting categories) and responsibility and risk.[20] I won't go into this here, but the point is that there is *no* (nonarbitrary) mechanical decision procedure for resolving most disputes about justice; what is required, in each and every case, is the ability to balance and weigh competing concerns and come to a "fair" conclusion. But what's fair is not the outcome of one or several preordained principles of justice; it is (as they say) a judgment call, always disputable but nevertheless well or badly made. I have often thought that encouraging abstract ethical theory actually discourages and distracts us from the need to make judgments. I have actually heard one of my colleagues say (without qualms) that, since he's been studying ethical theory, he no longer has any sense of ethics. If this sounds implausible, I urge you to remember your last department or boardroom meeting and the inverse relationship between the high moral tone of the conversation and the ridiculousness of the proposals and decisions that followed.

BUSINESS MYTHS AND METAPHORS:
VICES PARADING AS VIRTUES

It is not as if business life and business talk are devoid of philosophy, needless to say, nor are they devoid of any conception of the virtues. But as has so often been commented on and criticized, the philosophy that makes its rounds over business lunches and onto the business pages of many local papers is appalling, and those virtues most often cited as business virtues belong in a locker room, if not in a treatise on Darwinism. The business world is described as a jungle, as a battle, as a money machine in which individuals are dispensable cogs in the insatiable pursuit of profits. But not all bad philosophy and dangerous metaphors are vulgar or naive, and business ethics has also been hampered by some remarkably sophisticated, sometimes even brilliant theorizing that begins with a set of assumptions that make much of business into a game, if not like poker, then perhaps like chess. What lies at the basis of all such images haunting business ethics is still, I think, the one that Richard De George called the myth of amoral business.[21] It is the view that business transactions take place in a moral and social vacuum in which "anything goes" and only profits are of concern. It is a myth that persists not only among the suspicious public and some socialist-minded philosophers but among many businesspeople themselves, who thus degrade and misunderstand their own world and its significance. A defense of Aristotelian thinking in business thus requires a purging of these vulgar, naive, and sometimes downright disgusting images that pervade all too much talk about business, not only in the arguments of its detractors but in the words of its enthusiastic defenders and promoters. The first task of business ethics is to clear the way through incriminating and dangerous myths and metaphors that obscure rather than clarify the underlying ethos that makes business possible and make any talk of "virtue" sound merely quaint and naively idealistic.

Every discipline has its own self-glorifying vocabulary. Politicians bask in the concepts of "public service" while they pursue personal power, lawyers defend our "rights" on a handsome contingency basis, and professors describe what they do in the noble language of "truth and knowledge" while they spend most of their time and energy in campus politics. But in the case of business the self-glorifying language is especially unflattering. For example, executives still talk about what they do in terms of "the profit motive," not realizing that the phrase was invented by the last century's socialists as an *attack* on business and its narrow-minded pursuit of the dollar, the mark, and the pound to the exclusion of all other considerations and obligations. To be sure, a business does aim to make a profit, but it does so only by supplying quality goods and services, by providing jobs, and by fitting in with the community. To single out profits rather than productivity or public service as the central aim of business activity is to ask for trouble. And profits as such are not the end or the goal of business activity: profits get distributed and reinvested. Profits are a *means* of building the business and rewarding employees, executives, and investors. For some people, profits may be a means of "keeping score," but even to those degenerate cases, it is the status and satisfaction of "winning" that is the goal, not the profits as such. It was for good reason, whatever else we might think of his prejudices, that Aristotle scorned the notion of profit for its own sake, and even Adam Smith was clear that it was prosperity, not profits, that constituted the goal of the free-market system, whether or not the individual businessperson thought of this at the time.

A more sophisticated but not dissimilar executive myth states that the managers of a business are bound above all by one and only one obligation—to maximize the profits for their stockholders. We need not inquire whether this is the actual motive behind most upper management decisions in order to point out that, while managers do recognize that their own business roles are defined primarily by obligations rather than by the profit motive, that unflattering image has simply been transferred to the stockholders (i.e., the owners). But it is true that investors/owners care *only* about the maximization of their profits? Do *they* not think that there are all sorts of values and virtues to be considered along the road to dividends and share-value increases? And if some four-month "in-and-out" investor does indeed care only about increasing his investment by 30 percent or so, why should the managers of the firm have any obligation to him, other than to avoid intentionally frittering away or wasting that money?

This is how we misunderstand business and lose our Aristotelian orientation: we adopt a too narrow vision of what business is (e.g., the pursuit of profits) and then derive unethical and divisive conclusions. It is the inexcusably limited focus on the "rights of the stockholders," for example, that has been used to defend some of the very destructive and certainly unproductive hostile takeovers of major corporations in the last few years. To say this is not to deny the rights of stockholders to a fair return, of course, or to deny the fiduciary responsibility of the managers of a company; but these rights and responsibilities make sense only in a larger social context, and the very idea of the profit motive as an end in itself—as opposed to profits as a means of encouraging and rewarding hard work and investment, building a better business, and serving society better—poses a serious obstacle to understanding the rich tapestry of motives and activities that make up the business world.

Among the most damaging myths and metaphors in business talk are those macho Darwinian concepts, such as "survival of the fittest" and "it's a jungle out there." The underlying idea, of course, is that life in business is competitive, and it isn't always fair. But that obvious pair of points is very different from the "dog-eat-dog," "every-[man]-for-[him]self" imagery that is routine in the business world. It is true that business is and must be competitive, but it is not true that it is cutthroat or cannibalistic or that "one does whatever it takes to survive." However competitive a particular industry may be, it always rests on a foundation of shared interests and mutually agreed upon rules of conduct, and the competition takes place not in a jungle but in a society that the industry in question presumably both serves and depends on. Business life is fundamentally *cooperative*. It is only within the bounds of mutually shared concerns that competition is possible. And despite the "every animal for itself" jungle metaphor, business almost always involves large cooperative and mutually trusting groups, not only corporations themselves but networks of suppliers, service people, customers, and investors. Competition is essential to capitalism, but to misunderstand this as "unbridled" competition is to undermine ethics and misunderstand the nature of competition.

Similar to the Darwinian metaphor but slightly more in tune with the corporate nature of most competition is the familiar war metaphor that one hears in so many corporate boardrooms. It has often been pointed out that the hierarchical structure of most corporations not only resembles but is modeled after a military chain of command. Employees are referred to as troops, and courses of action are called campaigns. Cash reserves are dubbed war chests, and doing business is a described as battle. But even if all were fair in love and war (it's not), it is clear that doing business isn't like going to war but presupposes mutual trust and cooperation and the honoring of contracts, not just winning at any cost, in any way possible.

Business competition leads quite naturally to an emphasis on winning, but lately we've gotten somewhat more civilized in our competitive imagery. A person wins (or loses) wars, but a person also wins (or loses) games, and games are a lot more fun than wars. (The game metaphor came to the fore in the sixties, when life itself was commonly viewed as a game.) Business was no longer described bloodthirstily as a life-and-death endeavor but was seen as something voluntary, thrilling, and challenging. Thus the sports and team imagery of much recent business talk, similar in some senses to military imagery but without the violence and much more aware of the underlying mutual interests and rules of fair play. The problem with the sports metaphor, however, is that it makes business too self-enclosed, too merely coincidentally connected with productivity, service, and prosperity. Business for most people is not or is no longer a game within life, to be played if one wants for the challenge and the excitement. The business world encompasses and affects everyone. Of course, most people in business don't see it as a game at all but rather as a way to make a living.

There is, however, a far more sophisticated conception of business as a game, derived from utilitarianism and currently the source of a number of technical disciplines, such as social choice theory. This model, so dear to the hearts of econometricians, is generally based on what has been called, since the pioneering work of von Neumann and others, game theory. Except for an occasional piece of jargon (e.g., "zero-sum game"), this model has not infiltrated business as such nearly as thoroughly as it has come to define much of business ethics and social philosophy. Game theory begins with a set of dubious, anti-Aristotelian presuppositions about business and human decision making, in particular the uncritical notion that people tend to act in their own self-interest to maximize their "utility preferences." Sometime this is presented as merely a worst-case scenario; occasionally it is couched in the more neutral terms of rationality such that the theory is uncommitted to the nature of ends (whether self-interested or altruistic).[22] A frequent paradigm is the so-called prisoner's dilemma, in which rationality seems to require that cooperation is antithetical to prudence, an extremely dangerous paradigm for business practices.[23] In game theory, however, as in the more vulgar game metaphor, the model is too self-contained, too cut off from the larger social picture, and at the same time too negligent of the intrinsic rewards of participating in a practice where, contrary to some versions of the metaphor, winning isn't the only thing. In other words, the appealing idea of individual players presumes what is not the case, that business is essentially competition, whether lawful or warlike, between isolated individuals whose interests (as winners or losers) are either antagonistic or independent of those of the other.[24]

This most persistent metaphor, which seems to endure no matter how much evidence is amassed against it, is atomistic individualism. It is this, more than anything else, that makes the Aristotelian approach to business ethics seem so odd, so suspicious. We assume, whether or not we say so, that business is "every man [sic] for himself" and then find it hard to agree on any place for the virtues, at least, any virtue over and above rational prudence. The resulting idea, that business life consists wholly of mutually agreed upon transactions between individual citizens (avoiding government interference), goes back beyond Adam Smith and the philosophy that dominated eighteenth-century Britain and France. But it has always been a false view of human nature, whether in the "state of nature" or in society, and most of business life too consists of roles and responsibilities in cooperative enterprises (whether they be small mom-and-pop businesses or gigantic multinational corporations). Government and business are as often partners as opponents (however frustrating the labyrinth of regulation that connects them may sometimes seem). But atomistic individualism is not only a bad theory of human nature and wholly inaccurate in the face of the corporate complexity of today's business world; it is also naive in its supposition that no institutional rules and practices underlie even the simplest promise, contract, or exchange. Business is a social practice, not an activity of isolated individuals. It is possible only because it takes place in a culture with an established set of procedures and expectations, and these are not (except in the details) open to individual tinkering.

Accordingly, it is a sign of considerable progress that one of the dominant models of today's corporate thinking is the idea of a corporate culture. As with any analogy or metaphor, there are, of course, disanalogies, but it is important to appreciate the virtue of this metaphor.[25] It is social and rejects atomistic individualism. It recognizes the placement of people in the organization as the fundamental structure of business life. It openly embraces the idea of ethics. It recognizes that shared values hold a culture together. There is still room for that individualistic maverick—the "entrepreneur"— but he or she is possible only insofar as there is a role (an important one) for eccentricity and innovation. The problem with the "culture" metaphor, however, is that it also tends to be too self-enclosed. A corporation is not like an isolated tribe in the Trobriand Islands. A corporate culture is an inseparable part of a larger culture, at most a subculture (or a sub-subculture), a specialized organelle in an organ in an organism. Indeed, it is the tendency to see business as an isolated and insulated endeavor, with values different from those of the surrounding society, that characterizes all these myths and metaphors. It is illustrative that one of the most widely read articles in the field is the *Harvard Business Review* essay by Albert Carr defending the implausible thesis that business is a lot like poker and, as such, tolerates unethical behavior that would not be tolerated in the larger society.[26] The interesting point I want to question is not whether business is like poker (or whether, as Carr misleadingly argues, bluffing is akin to lying) but why such a morally bankrupt thesis should have received any attention at all. Breaking down this sense of separation between ethics and business ethics has to be one of the first tasks of business ethics, on a par, perhaps, with appreciating what is so special about business.

To this end, perhaps, we should advance a new metaphor, one that (like all metaphors) displays certain mismatches but that, unlike the brutal and frivolous metaphors that now rule conversation, is flattering and inspiring to businesspeople. That is the metaphor of the manager as a professional, a designation that is already finding its way into the titles of some business schools and winning favor (not surprisingly) with many managers themselves. The professional, unlike the mere entrepreneur, openly recognizes his or her role in the community, rejects the idea that everyone is out for his- or her-self, and accepts the claims to expertise and public service that are part and parcel of the very idea of a professional.[27]

BUSINESS ETHICS IN AN ARISTOTELIAN PERSPECTIVE: THE VIRTUES OF CORPORATE LIFE

The bottom line of the Aristotelian approach to business ethics is that we have to get away from bottom-line thinking. What is essential to a good life in business is not just results and accomplishments as measured by financial gain but what is above (not beyond) the bottom line, the whole package of cooperative as well as competitive effort, personal integrity as well as contribution to the community. Wanting too much without regard to one's character or reputation is a myopic form of stupidity, evident in Midas-like individuals throughout history, no doubt, but peculiar as a generally approved consciousness in our time. Aristotle saw quite clearly that greed (or "grasping," *pleonexia*) was a kind of pathology, a defect of character so serious that it was beyond redemption. Not that he was against wealth and comfort (no ascetics, those Athenians), but in the quest for the good life it was at most a favorable precondition, not something worth worrying about at the expense of one's soul. To this we might reply, of course, that in Athenian society aristocrats and their favorite philosophers didn't have to worry about such matters, but we do. Socrates provides a clear counterexample, however, and Aristotle, like almost all philosophers, recognized the nobility of Socrates' virtue even in his poverty. The point is not that Americans should stop worrying about money or that we can or should try to discourage our students from their current career-obsessive paths. It is a question of proper perspective, and the truth is that our concept of happiness is a lot more Aristotelian than we would think. Students and job-hoppers (and, let me say, even professors of the humanities) who accept positions on the basis of salary alone and then hate their jobs (and often their luxurious lives, as well) miss the obvious: what makes for happiness is not money to spend but a respected place in a decent and prosperous community and time in which to enjoy it. Success is not salary but respect and love and admiration. As John Steinbeck wrote in *East of Eden*, "A living, or money. . . . Money's easy to make if it's money you want. But with a few exceptions peo-

ple don't want money. They want luxury and they want love and
they want admiration."

What the Aristotelian approach to business ethics demands is that
we enlarge this common-sense observation and apply it not only to
people in their so-called personal lives (even that notion is the symptom of an enormous sociological problem) but to business and people in business, for much of the problem of business ethics and its
faulty myths and metaphors has to do with the artificial and problematic walling off of business practices and business life from the
larger arena of people, communities, and society. (The new and wel-
come concept of the "stakeholders" in a business, which pointedly
includes community and the larger society, still tends to retain too
much of the cloistered business imagery even while expanding the
scope and vocabulary of social responsibility.) The Aristotelian approach to business ethics ultimately comes down to the idea that,
while business life has its specific goals and distinctive practices and
people in business have their particular concerns, loyalties, roles, and
responsibilities, there is ultimately no business world but only people
working in business as part of their life in society. It is an obvious
point, perhaps, but to read much if not most of what gets written
about business and to listen to managers and executives on the job
talk about what they do is to realize that it is a point readily lost in
the obsessive pressure to satisfy the bottom line. That line, after all,
is only a measure, and what it measures—often falsely or misleadingly—is the quality and efficiency of an organization and its output,
which in turn is the product of hundreds or thousands of individuals
and how well they work together.

The Aristotelian approach is not antibusiness and certainly not
antisuccess but only anti-*pleonexia,* antigreed. Aristotle's central ethical concept is "happiness" (more accurately, *eudaimonia,* perhaps better translated as "flourishing" or "doing well"). "Happiness," therefore, has what we would call "success" built into it, and success in a
consumer society necessarily entails a certain level of financial success. Let's remember, however, that we "consume" art and music,
books and ideas, as well as cars and kitchenware, and the dollar costs
of such consumption may not be considerable at all. What Aristotle's
conception excludes is mediocrity and isolation—especially the
mean-spirited competition that too many people in business abstractly confuse with free enterprise. Moreover, it is not enough to
be a subjectively contented or even blithe failure; it is what one actually accomplishes, with and for others as well as by and for oneself,
that counts.

It would be a crass vulgarization to suppose that doing well is to
be understood, in our society, as just a matter of "making it." Most
Americans, when not engaged in business conversation, would

rather readily admit that the only bottom line that counts is how happy we are, as individuals, as families, as employees, as a people. Happiness may include success, but it is not wholly defined by success, and while an excellent company will almost always do well in the market, it is not doing well that makes them excellent. Tom Peters's incessant insistence on the "satisfied customer" and the "contented employee" highlights an extremely important Aristotelian measure. The rather banal equation between happiness and having fun too readily blinds us to the idea that our work ought to be satisfying and rewarding (only occasionally "fun"). The familiar image of the harried manager, on the other hand, is a symptom of something very wrong, in a career, in a company, in the market itself. Happiness (for us as well as for Aristotle) is a holistic concept, and it is one's character, not one's bottom line, that is the ultimate determinant and beneficiary of happiness. This is equally true, I want to insist, for giant corporations as it is for the individuals who work for them.

I want to use Aristotle to attack a popular misconception of what this notion of character and the related notion of social-mindedness entails. One of the worst philosophical dichotomies to have worked itself through the ranks of the hoi polloi is the false antagonism between selfishness on the one hand and what is called altruism on the other, but for the properly constituted social self the distinction between self-interest and social-mindedness is all but unintelligible and what we call selfishness is guaranteed to be self-destructive as well. And altruism is too easily turned into self-sacrifice, for instance by that self-appointed champion of selfishness, Ayn Rand. But altruism isn't self-sacrifice; it's just a more reasonable conception of self as tied up intimately with community, with friends and family who may, indeed, count at times for more than we do. What the Aristotelian approach to business ethics demands isn't self-sacrifice or the submerging of oneself to the interests of the corporation, much less voluntary unhappiness. What it does say is that the distinctions and oppositions between self and society that give rise to these wrongheaded conceptions are themselves the problem, as well as the cause of so much unhappiness and dissatisfaction.

To get beyond the bottom line is not just to give up an overly narrow conception of the good or, at least, the good in business. It is also to reject a certain kind of "hard-headed" thinking, so evident in the sophisticated games of game theory and in much of the discussion of ethics and business ethics. It is that obsession with quantification, with precise comparisons of options and strategies. Aristotle famously commented at the beginning of his *Nicomachean Ethics* that a person should not demand more precision of a subject than it is capable of providing. He might have been warning us against late-

twentieth century ethics. Somewhere along the line, we lost sight of
ethics as one of the humanities and got into our heads the idea that
it was one of the social sciences. Granted, there is no paucity of candidates to shoulder the blame, especially among the various defenders of *Wissenschaft* in the last century. And there are some rich sociological accounts of this transformation, as one would expect in the
annals of the social sciences plotting their own progress. But when I
ask my philosophical students and colleagues who is to blame or
praise for this atomization of business thinking (no pun intended),
the name that comes up most frequently is Adam Smith. I think that
Smith is innocent of the charge. I would rather point the philosophical finger at the particularly utility-minded ethics, rendered ever
more refined and sophisticated by decision theory and the social sciences, called utilitarianism. But the charge of bottom-line thinking
seems to me as unfair to the leading proponent of utilitarianism,
John Stuart Mill, as it is to Adam Smith. Given the current climate,
however, these claims require a long defense, which I will not attempt even to summarize here.[28]

The virtue of the Aristotelian approach to business ethics, I have
argued, is its focus on the character of the individual and not just
on impersonal policies and abstract principles and theories. A related virtue, however, points us in just the opposite direction, toward
the enlargement of the self as a thoroughly social self and not an
isolated Hobbesian or Lockean self whose place in society is up for
negotiation. The Aristotelian approach must be understood in terms
of a certain concept of self, an expanded self that is constituted by
and identifies itself with the larger community or society. The self is,
as I have argued elsewhere, first of all a matter of emotions, and so
one might suspect that a special set of emotions will be particularly
concerned with this enlarged sense of self. Too often it is assumed
without argument or discussion that the emotions are merely personal, whether this means that they are merely subjective, exclusively
of concern to the emotee, or merely physical and of no real importance. But emotions can be "about" all sorts of things and of varied
significance to both the individual and the society. Some emotions
are not only "about" society (as their "object") but involve society in
the very identity of their subject. They are emotions that would be
unintelligible without this larger sense of self. I should like to end
this brief essay, therefore, with an even more brief outline of a few
of the emotional virtues that it is the aim of the Aristotelian approach to business to cultivate.

Of particular interest here is a mixed set of emotions that, with
the rise of radical individualism and the loss of a sense of Aristotelian virtue, the emphasis on policies and principles and the neglect
of the person, has all but dropped out of business ethics. They in-

clude *loyalty, honor,* and a sense of *shame.* (Guilt is quite different from shame and is not part of the set.) All three emotions tie into the central notion of *integrity,* the first two by way of definition, the latter in the breach. Loyalty is a kind of integrity, not within oneself (conceived of as a self-sufficient, integral whole), but rather with oneself conceived as a part of a larger self, a group, a community, an organization or institution. As Josiah Royce wrote in his *Philosophy of Loyalty,* "Loyalty has its domestic, its religious, its commercial, its professional forms, and many other forms as well. The essence of it, whatever forms it may take, is . . . this: Since no man can find a plan of life by merely looking within his own chaotic nature, he has to look without, to the world of social conventions, deeds and causes."[29] Business ethics too often ignores loyalty in favor of the more abstract and universal concepts of rights. It is as if to say that, so long as we respect contracts, we need not be concerned with a superfluous and perhaps childish emotion like loyalty. Of course, loyalty (like patriotism, one special variant of it) can be a refuge from responsibility or a forum for venal self-righteousness, but it does not follow—as many people seem to think it does—that it is an emotion that has lost its place in the corporate world and that one's loyalties should always be first and foremost to oneself, to one's conscience, or to some set of "higher" standards. Every employer wants the loyalty of the employees, of course, but the objection to such loyalty is that the employees will thereby lose sight of their own best interests and perhaps find themselves bound to plans or policies that they find unethical or even illegal. The argument here, however, is not against loyalty but rather in support of the need for critical self-awareness of one's loyalties. It is not an argument against loyalty any more than the dangers of love are an argument against love. (Loyalty would not be wrongly conceived as a variety of love, appropriate to groups and institutions as well as to individuals.) Against the recent "work-for-hire" approach to employer-employee relations, I want to argue that an Aristotelian emphasis on loyalty—and that means loyalty in both directions—has a lot to offer to business ethics that too often gets dismissed with the usual stories of uncritical loyalty and gross corporate malfeasance.[30]

Honor is a second grand emotion of the Aristotelian self, an essential ingredient in integrity (some people would equate the two) and another emotion that is an endangered species in radical individualist thinking. Honor, when we use the term at all, usually means pride—a very different emotion—or even vanity, a very different and hardly flattering emotion indeed. As Hume argued in his *Treatise,* pride has mainly to do with a sense of personal accomplishment. Its focus is typically the individual self, but through loyalty and affiliation it can be expanded to encompass one's community and corpo-

ration. Pride, however, tends to be too personal and too concerned
with accomplishment. Honor, by contrast, need not involve accomplishment at all (although it certainly may and often does), and it
makes very little sense as a purely personal notion. (That is why,
when people say that they are defending their honor but are obviously nursing their pride, we find such behavior not only foolish but
pretentious as well.) Honor requires a sense of belonging, a sense of
membership, a sense of self that incorporates one's corporate identity. It also involves living up to the expectations of the corporation,
whether these are spelled out as a code of honor or set of moral
rules or are simply implicit in the practices and goals of the group.
(It is not obeying moral rules that makes a person honorable, however; it is obeying the rules because they are the rules of his or her
corporation—very un-Kantian). A person's honor, in other words, is
never his or her honor alone. It is the honor of the community or
corporation that he or she represents, and standing up for honor
necessarily entails defending it as a representative of that community
or corporation. In business ethics, this sense of honor helps clarify
both the role of the individual employee or executive in the corporation and, even more important, the role of both the individual and
the corporation in society. (Tragedy in business ethics, one might
add, does not usually consist of a conflict of interests but a rather a
conflicting sense of honor, a sense of being torn between one membership and another—as an employee of the company, as the friend
of one's immediate supervisor or as the member of the greater community.)

Honor should not be thought of as a set of personal constraints
defined by membership in a group. The notion of constraints is appropriate rather to a group of which one is not a member or, perhaps, is a member only by chance or because one was a member
even though one now desperately wants to extricate oneself. One's
sense of honor is, if not voluntary, at least personally acceptable,
part and parcel of one's sense of self. It is, in this sense, a species of
merit, but this is very different from any sense of desert or what one
has achieved. Merit in the context of honor has to do with who one
is—namely, a member of the group in good standing—and not particularly with anything that one has done (or not done) except insofar as such acts are part of one's membership in the group. So, too,
there is a natural affinity between honor and self-esteem; one's self-
esteem depends on one's sense of honor (though not vice versa), and
one's standing in the group becomes the criterion of self-esteem.
One cannot be much of a member if one can be humiliated in the
group and nevertheless have a solid sense of self-worth. So, too, the
contemporary idea that one's main objective after public humiliation
is to "get over it" makes impossible any sense of honor—which pre-

supposes that one doesn't just "get over it." One might note that one symptom of our collective loss of honor is the fact that no one seems to believe in the concept of a "ruined life" anymore. One just moves to another town or gets another job or sets up another company and "starts over." In practical terms, what this means is that the business community is notoriously poor in sanctioning its own rules and punishing even the most flagrant offenders of those rules. Business failure is neither adequate nor sufficiently dependable as a measure or a punishment for unethical business practices. It is a person's sense of honor that must be put into play, and for those who don't understand or who scoff at this notion the old tribal practice of exile (federal minimum security prisons will do) serves an extremely necessary function in the survival of the business community.

The opposite of honor is *shame*. Aristotle lists, with some discomfort, shame as one of the virtues, not because it is good to be ashamed but rather because, as in that Ethiopian proverb, "where there is no shame, there is no honor." Thus, John Rawls is not entirely wrong when he insists that shame is the opposite of self-esteem, since honor can be the criterion for self-esteem. Not all societies are honor societies, however, and not everyone's self-esteem is tied to a sense of honor. Shame is not, as Rawls says, failing to live up to one's potential; it is, much more specifically, failing to live up to the standards of the group through which one gains one's self-identity and one's standards. Shame is, in other words, a loss of integrity, a breach of the commitments or principles one accepts and knows that one should accept.[31] Of course, in the Aristotelian approach to business ethics, failing to live up to one's potential may well be equivalent to failing to live up to the standards of the group, perhaps because one has made a commitment that cannot be kept or set a goal that cannot be met. But personal achievement and failure as such are not essential and often not relevant to honor and shame. What one fails to *be* is acceptable to the group and, accordingly, acceptable in terms of one's own essential sense of identity. To feel shame (not quite the same as "being ashamed") is quite literally to fail oneself, but only in the context of one's larger self.

It is in this sense that shame is contrasted to guilt, for it is guilt, not shame, that defines the appropriate attitude in our nonhonor society. Shame is always defined in a group context; guilt is borne by one alone. It is not surprising that the Scriptures talk mainly of sin and guilt when discussing an individual's wrongdoing before God. Guilt is an emotion that permeates the personal self, but other people, one's peers, play no clear role in its workings. We feel guilty, not shamed, for failing to live up to our own goals and standards. We feel guilty, not shamed, for breaking the rules or committing a moral infelicity. Guilt is appropriate to isolated individuals; shame is possible only in groups. Guilt ties in nicely with the traditional concept of the individual soul; shame is essentially a tribal emotion. It has often been said (by Nietzsche and Freud most famously) that there is too much guilt in our society. I would like to suggest that, while this is probably true, there isn't nearly enough shame. Indeed, the payoff for public humiliation in current-day America seems to be a fat book advance and profitable public appearances, not repentence, apology, and retribution. We may have more guilt than we ought to have, but part of the reason may be that we don't have enough room for honor—or shame.

What all of this amounts to is the idea that business ethics is at once more personal and more social than it is usually thought to be. It is not enough to teach principles and policies, much less the theories of the great, dead, mostly white male philosophers. Business ethics requires the cultivation of the civic virtues, not something possible in an isolated business ethics course—on this, at least, the critics are correct—but nevertheless, as Aristotle himself surely would have argued, something absolutely necessary for the health and well-being of the business world itself. What business ethics does and what business ethics courses do is not to "teach" ethics to business students and managers. Instead, they remind us all that there are standards and virtues at issue in business without which an enterprise (no matter how "free") will not and does not deserve to survive.

It is in the humanities that the personal dimension of ethics gets cultivated (not inculcated, perhaps—that comes long before), but the current myths and metaphors of business convince me that most of the obstacles to ethics in business are not the result of inadequate upbringing but rather of corporate cultural illiteracy and moral myopia. Business students are steeped in business lore and too rarely exposed to those broader human issues and concerns that are the stuff of literature and philosophy. They learn the ins and outs of game theory and strategic planning but are taught to think very little about their lives or the values they are pursuing with such enthusiasm. They learn techniques of finance, theories of management, and maybe even some public policy, but they get little chance to exercise their imaginations or their emotions, much less to experience (one can hear them scoffing) their "humanity."

I have argued elsewhere that the subjects and disciplines of the humanities—in particular, reading books—are essential and not merely marginal in the cultivation of the moral imagination and emotions.[32] It is a tragedy—albeit one that can be easily explained and rationalized—that business and the humanities have drifted so far apart. The price of the resulting gap between them is not only uncultivated executives and unworldly scholars; it is an enormous gap in business ethics, not just the study but the actual ethics of business. So long as ethics gets deferred and appealed to government policies, so long as ethics remains formalized in rules and codes and abstract principles and isn't taken seriously and personally by the individual businessman and -woman, it will continue to appear as something foreign, something imposed on if not opposed to the aims and ambitions of business. The humanities, whatever else they may be, are serious and personal. The great books allow us to get involved in and to live vicariously through the difficulties and dilemmas of life, and those difficulties and dilemmas are, to a large extent, ethical quandaries, predicaments of loyalty and honor, or occasions for shame. The tragedies of *King Lear* and *Macbeth*, the comedies of Molière and Tom Stoppard, the rude advice of Rousseau and Machiavelli—these may not contain the precise situations faced by every middle manager and executive, but it takes very little imagination to see how those grand tragedies, farces, and philosophical essays stretch the mind and open up our awareness for the more pedestrian dilemmas that we do face daily. Humanitas is ultimately not a subject matter but a certain attitude toward life, an attitude of "humanity" and a broad perspective in which it is the whole of life that comes into focus, not just the office problem of the moment, in which the whole of community and even the whole of humanity is within our scope, not just the boardroom or the stock report or one's immediate superiors and subordinates. It is, in other words, just that larger sense of self that Aristotle talked about so long ago. The Aristotelian approach to business ethics is, ultimately, just another way of saying that people come before profits, and before a great deal of what is often called ethics, too.

NOTES

1. Michael Levin, "Ethics Courses: Useless," *New York Times*, November 27, 1989, p. 23. Levin is a professional philosopher who specializes in scandalizing the profession on public issues such as torture and feminism. Here he takes a perfectly obvious Aristotelian premise (that ethics involves training, not just reflection) and wrongly concludes that ethics courses are "pointless."

2. Mark Pastin, *The Hard Problems of Management* (San Francisco: Jossey-Bass, 1986).

3. Bruno Snell, *The Discovery of the Mind: The Greek Origins of European Thought,* trans. T. G. Rosenmeyer (Oxford: Basil Blackwell, 1953), p. 246.

4. Ibid., p. 250.

5. Ibid., pp. 254–55.

6. Alfred Carr, "Is Business Bluffing Ethical?" *Harvard Business Review* 46 (January–February 1968): 143–53.

7. Milton Friedman, "The Social Responsibility of Business Is to Increase Its Profits," *New York Times Magazine,* September 13, 1970, sec. 6, p. 32. Friedman elsewhere insisted, in response to the ample criticism of this article, that he was "not pro-business [but] pro-free enterprise." For some reason this statement did not dampen his following among business executives.

8. There is some dispute about this. See, e.g., G. M. E. Anscombe, *Intention,* 2nd ed. (Ithaca, N.Y.: Cornell University Press, 1976), pp. 57–63. But see also John M. Cooper, *Reason and Human Good in Aristotle* (Cambridge, Mass.: Harvard University Press, 1975), pp. 56–57.

9. Psychologist-philosopher Michael Green has written a devastating diagnosis—unfortunately unpublished—of just this philosophical syndrome.

10. Alasdair MacIntyre, *After Virtue: A Study in Moral Theory* (Notre Dame: Ind.: University of Notre Dame Press, 1981), pp. 64–67.

11. Elizabeth Wolgast, *The Grammar of Justice* (Ithaca, N.Y.: Cornell University Press, 1987).

12. Robert Nozick, *Anarchy, State, and Utopia* (New York: Basic Books, 1974), pp. 28–29. See also Tara Smith, "Rights, Friends, and Egoism," *Journal of Philosophy* 90 (March 1993): 144–48.

13. William Frankena, *Ethics,* 2nd ed. (Englewood Cliffs, N.J.: Prentice-Hall, 1973), pp. 113–14; Kurt Baier, *The Moral Point of View: A Rational Basis of Ethics* (Ithaca, N.Y.: Cornell University Press, 1958), chap. 5.

14. MacIntyre, *After Virtue;* Charles Taylor, *Sources of the Self: The Making of the Modern Identity* (Cambridge, Mass.: Harvard University Press, 1989); Robert N. Bellah et al., *Habits of the Heart: Individualism and Commitment in American Life* (Berkeley: University of California Press, 1985).

15. Cheshire Calhoun, "Justice, Care and Gender Bias," *Journal of Philosophy* 85 (September 1988): 451–63.

16. Peter Drucker, *Management* (New York: Harper and Row, 1974), chap. 28.

17. Norman Bowie, *Business Ethics* (Englewood Cliffs, N.J.: Prentice-Hall, 1982), pp. 1–16.

18. Robert Townsend, *Up the Organization* (New York: Alfred A. Knopf, 1970), p. 147. See also Townsend, *Further Up the Organization* (New York: Alfred A. Knopf, 1984), p. 176.

19. See Joanne B. Ciulla, *Honest Work,* forthcoming.

20. Robert C. Solomon, *A Passion for Justice* (New York: Addison-Wesley, 1989), esp. chap. 4.

21. Richard De George, *Business Ethics,* 2nd ed. (New York: Macmillan, 1982), esp. chap. 1.

22. See, e.g., John Rawls, *A Theory of Justice* (Cambridge, Mass.: Harvard University Press, 1971), p. 144.

23. See, e.g., Nicholas Rescher, *Unselfishness* (Pittsburgh, Pa.: University of Pittsburgh Press, 1975): "[T]he paradox is that if both players make the rational choice . . . both lose." Anatole Rapaport, "Escape from Paradox," *Scientific American* 217 (1967): 51; Edward McClennen, "Foundational Explorations for a Normative Theory of Political Economic," unpublished manuscript.

24. I have attempted to argue this at greater length in another volume in

this series; see Robert C. Solomon, *Ethics and Excellence: Cooperation and Integrity in Business* (New York: Oxford University Press, 1992).

25. But see Pastin, *The Hard Problems of Management,* for some doubts about this.

26. Carr, "Is Business Bluffing Ethical?"

27. On this point see Walter P. Metzger, "What Is a Profession?" *College and University* 52 (1976): 42–55, which is discussed in Norman Bowie, "Business Ethics as a Discipline: The Search for Legitimacy," in R. Edward Freeman, ed., *Business Ethics: The State of the Art* (New York: Oxford University Press, 1991), pp. 17–41.

28. I attempted to provide such a defense in my previous volume in *Ethics and Excellence.* In my reading of Adam Smith, I have particularly benefited from Patricia H. Werhane's *Adam Smith and His Legacy for Modern Capitalism* (New York: Oxford University Press, 1991).

29. Josiah Royce, *The Philosophy of Loyalty* (New York: Macmillan, 1908); quoted in Bowie, *Business Ethics,* p. 14.

30. For a good philosophical discussion of loyalty, see Andrew Oldenquist, "Loyalties," *Journal of Philosophy* 79, no. 4 (April 1982): 173ff.

31. By far, the best discussion of integrity and its violations I know is Lynne McFall, "Integrity," *Ethics* 98 (October 1987): 5–20.

32. Robert C. Solomon, "Business Ethics, Literacy, and the Education of Emotions," in Freeman, ed., *State of the Art,* pp. 188–211.

Virtue and Rules: A Response to Robert C. Solomon

Edwin Hartman

Robert C. Solomon's essay "Business and the Humanities: An Aristotelian Approach to Business Ethics" advances business ethicists' understanding of the importance to our field of the concept of virtue, and in particular of Aristotle's treatment of it. Solomon laments our tendency to overlook, for example, the dangers created by oversimplification in discussions of utility and rights and the significance for organizational ethics of our communal nature.

Not only does Solomon show us what we have slighted; his discussion has implications of fundamental importance for the status of business ethics. His criticisms of utilitarianism and similar approaches form the basis of an answer to the (usually snidely posed) question "What is business ethics other than ethics with examples from business?" That question presupposes just the sort of abstract account of moral action that Solomon gives reason to reject.

The criticisms that follow do not undermine Solomon's approach so much as find its limits. Much the same could be said of Solomon's criticisms of the approaches he does not like, although Solomon does not say it. Instead, he finds the areas in which those disfavored approaches work least well, while parading the Aristotelian approach primarily in contexts in which it works. Consider his treatment of game theory.

IN DEFENSE OF THE USE OF GAME THEORY

Solomon is not wrong in identifying possible pitfalls in game theory, but he gives little reason to believe that a recreational user of game

76

theory in discussions of pollution control and other commons issues will necessarily develop a craving to take it too literally or will become so dependent on it as to ignore each individual's stake in other people's welfare or to strive for more precision than the subject matter permits. Applied modestly, the story of the commons in particular teaches some extraordinarily important lessons, including lessons about life within the organization. Solomon's complaints seem not to apply to Mark Pastin's use of commons arguments or to Freeman's and Gilbert's use of game theory.[1] Still less do they apply to Robert H. Frank's use of game theory to introduce a destructive attack on standard views about rational self-interest and an updated theory of moral sentiments.[2] An advantage all these users' accounts share is that they accommodate talk of civic virtue without raising hard questions about collectivism by bringing in something called the common good.

Solomon might have found in the commons argument some good reasons for acting with the interests of the community in mind, for that form of argument shows how unrestrained individual greed may not be in one's best interests even if one is so selfish as to perceive no stake in others' welfare.

It does not, however, assume that people really are that way, as Solomon rightly argues they are not. Philosophers need not fall into the fallacy for which economists are known: the inference that, because useful models rest on the assumption that people are selfish, rational, perfectly informed, and so on, people are in fact that way. Pragmatists especially are subtler than that; some even hold that there is nothing wrong with using incompatible theories for separate tasks. Even Aristotle himself is quite ready to accept some of his opponents' assumptions for the sake of an argument that will finally defeat them dialectically, as in *Metaphysics* IV.[3]

VIRTUE, *PHRONESIS*, AND REAL MORAL PROBLEMS

Solomon prefers virtue talk to anything that admits of calculation. Virtue talk is indeed often appropriate in discussing the sort of issue that most individuals face in most organizations, and utilitarianism and justice, for example, are more useful in the discussion of public policy issues. Nonetheless, students who will be managers making more than seventy-five thousand dollars a year need some guidance on how to deal with external stakeholders who speak in many voices. What Solomon thinks will help them is *phronesis*, or practical wisdom. Sharpening our students' *phronesis*, which Aristotle regards as a necessary and sufficient condition of virtue but not identical with it, is part of the point of giving them case studies. The doctrine of *phrone-*

sis is today often invoked to adjudicate among incommensurable ways of calculation or incompatible systems of rules; so, for example, Bernstein.[4] But the first intention of the doctrine is not to minimize the importance of calculation or rules; on the contrary, it includes calculation, and universals as well as particulars are within its ken.[5] The emphasis is on the necessary role of intelligence in guiding virtuous action. If it is true that virtue generates good corporate and social policy, as Solomon claims, it can only be because virtue includes intellectual virtues such as *phronesis* as well as moral virtues. Aristotle would never claim that managers (or others, for that matter) should love virtue and do as they please.

Just mentioning *phronesis* does not, in any case, solve any actual moral questions. There is a great deal in Aristotle's ethics about what is involved in being a good person, but not much that helps guide action given that one is or wants to be good. One thinks of the turn-of-the-century Oxford satirical piece entitled "Aristotle on Golf": "For the good golfer is he who hits the ball truly and well and as the professional would hit."[6]

In truth, there is no reason to believe that any one approach to ethics, whether it focuses on rules or attitudes or kinds of person,[7] addresses all the ethical problems we have or investigate or accounts for even most of our shared intuitions. We can use any of these approaches as "a tool for understanding" rather than a "prescription" if we are careful.

And how do we decide which method or methods to use in a particular case when there is a conflict? Let us grant that there could be no rules for determining whether a case permits a rule-based approach and that experience and intelligence are necessary conditions of reliably moral behavior. But utilitarians and game theorists too have a right to invoke *phronesis*. As R. Edward Freeman has written, ethics is no more about virtue than about the interests of others.[8] We require conversation between those two views of what ethics is about, which are at the very least logically independent. Aristotle is careful not to concentrate on the personal aspect of virtue to the exclusion of others' interests: he claims that virtue encompasses dealing justly with others.[9] Solomon downplays the tension here in part by arguing that one's self-interest involves the interests of others in the community. This is true as far as it goes, and faithful to Aristotle, but it does not eliminate the conflicts.

These considerations do not show that an Aristotelian, virtue-based approach to business ethics is wrong; the point is only that one need not exalt virtue at the expense of rules, as Solomon seems to do more than Aristotle. I do want to argue now that Aristotle's particular brand of virtue ethics is deficient because it is parochial, in a way in which Solomon's is not.

ARISTOTLE'S VIEW OF THE NATURAL

Aristotle's great strength, as well as his great weakness, is his confidence about what is natural. Although he seldom claims to find rules that sharply circumscribe anything, including moral behavior, he does believe in nature as a constant and in its categories as fixed and external to our minds and our purposes in a way in which many philosophers nowadays do not. He thinks man is an animal whose nature it is to live in a polis, to which we might respond, "That's right: in a community." There is, however, good reason to think he means a polis, not just any old community; he is that parochial. This is after all the philosopher who claims that the great-souled man, the one who cares about honor above all else, has a dignified gait and speaks in a bass voice.[10]

This is also a philosopher who countenances slavery. We should now recall that brilliant passage in *Huckleberry Finn* in which Huck wrestles with his conscience, which tells him not to assist the runaway slave Jim in his escape. "After all, what has Jim's owner ever done to Huck to make him treat her so mean?"[11] He gives in finally to his moral weakness because he isn't man enough to obey the clear promptings of his better self, in part because he lacks the appropriate moral education. It is not clear that Aristotle would see the irony.

For Aristotle the paradigm of what is natural—virtually synonymous with essential—cannot be otherwise, but Aristotle extends the concept beyond its paradigm case and calls natural what can in fact be otherwise, although with more self-consciousness than later philosophers have shown in taking as analytic what can be otherwise. Aristotle takes the borderline between essence (which he sometimes calls nature) and accident to be possibly fuzzy but not changeable, and very important. That position makes a great deal of sense in morality: for example, we see a fuzzy line between a dolphin's soul and that of a profoundly retarded human, but we honor that line and do not suppose we can readily move it or cross it. It matters to Aristotle and to us that humans are by nature rational, even if this human is not. But on ethical issues Aristotle shows his narrowness when he gives the strong impression that, while the Athenian gentleman may not be the only person who is in any way virtuous, no one who is very unlike the Athenian gentleman could be virtuous.

Aristotle takes virtue itself to be natural, and rationality, too. Solomon adds some reasons for linking nature, happiness, community, and morality. But the conceptual connections—no community without morality, and not even a linguistic community without rationality—leave more leeway for irrational behavior than Aristotle admits in his discussion of weakness of will and are consistent with bad behavior in one's own interests within a community.[12] *Pace* Aristotle, one can be vicious and happy;[13] and it may be in one's best interests to be selfish. What is impossible is that this should be the case generally. Of course sympathy is not necessarily an artificial state; of course the economists' standard talk about rational egoism is wrong or trivially right. It is a great mistake, however, to underestimate the extent to which businesspeople in particular live happily as players in a game that is at best zero-sum—if that is a permissible use of game theory language.

TRUE HAPPINESS

But can Gordon Gekko really be happy? Let us begin by stipulating, in favor of Aristotle and Solomon and against crude utilitarianism, that one's happiness depends greatly on one's community. The forms of pleasure that humans, unlike animals, can have involve other people in various ways: consider not only honor and shame but success, friendship, love, respect and hence self-respect, and similar states near the top of the Maslow hierarchy. Consider humiliation, than which there are few forms of unhappiness keener: it is almost entirely community-dependent.

But what if "empty greed" animates you, and pointless acquisition makes you happy? What if, as a true amateur, you want to win just for the sake of winning? The objection to talk about false happiness is a familiar one: one thinks of the child who says, "I'm glad I don't like spinach, because if I did, I'd eat it, and I hate it." For the same reason Solomon is glad he doesn't like money-grubbing. We are to pity or despise yuppies because they want all that money but do not stop to think what they will buy with it or why they want a BMW. But money is what they use to keep score. Surely we would not pity or despise an Olympic athlete who has trained for years to win a medal or ask, Why do you want the medal? What will do you with it? Aristotle seems not to despise boxers who take heavy punishment to win a little garland.[14] Noble as he thinks it is to die for one's country in war,[15] could he give good grounds for disapproval of the trader who selflessly accepts a jail sentence for the sake of Drexel, Burnham?

Aristotle does show some feeling for this issue when he discusses whether honor is the good and then appears to disqualify it as being too dependent on the opinions of others, whereas a good is one's own possession and not easily taken away.[16] He says that one who fears ill repute is decent and has a sense of shame and one who does not is shameless.[17] He does not want to put a person's well-being into the hands of others, but to some extent he must: he cannot deny that others' views on what is correct behavior have some legitimate influence on how one behaves.

Solomon implies that yuppies do not know who they are thereby suggesting that some pleasures are in harmony with human nature while others are not; in that he clearly follows Aristotle. There is much value in Aristotle's definition of happiness as necessarily involving one's rational faculties and in Solomon's suggestion that one is not free to be or desire just anything, but I am not aware of any actual arguments to show that competitiveness, for example, is irrational or otherwise unnatural.

One might object on Solomon's behalf that what counts as happiness for such people is culturally conditioned, but so is virtue, according to both Aristotle and Solomon. Even before starting the M.B.A. program, one begins to learn what counts as courage, decency, resourcefulness, and loyalty to one's community as surely as did the Homeric heroes from whom generations of Greeks learned what virtue was. Solomon is in no position to use that criticism, since he permits no conception of human happiness abstracted from one's community. How Solomon deals with this problem is interesting, not least because he goes beyond Aristotle in doing so, although he is too modest to admit it. But there is a bit more to be said about the problem itself.

COMMUNITIES AND COMMUNITY-NEUTRAL MORALITY

If we reject Aristotle's parochialism but agree about the importance of community, then at the very least we have a problem about distinguishing good communities, including organizations, from bad ones. Aristotle does address this problem in the *Politics,* often wisely, as one would expect, but in a way that raises doubts about whether he thinks anything unlike Athenian democracy would do.[18] Certainly one could do worse; he has good reason to consider politics inseparable from ethics and legislative ability a manifestation of *phronesis* at its best.[19] Starting with a plausible but not narrow view of human nature, one could construct an argument that a certain form of democracy is the best breeding ground for virtue.

There is a particular problem about people who live in many different communities, as a good many people nowadays do. Consider courage, for example. In most organizations courage is highly admired, but the criteria for it differ from one culture to the next, even from one organizational culture to the next. Is a courageous person, sensitive to honor and repute, supposed to act differently from one community to the next?[20]

One way to avoid making morality radically relative to its community setting, which in turn cannot be evaluated, is to argue that you can find a way of defining moral terms by a utilitarian calculus that transcends all communities. That is how utilitarianism is supposed to resolve moral conflicts; it should adjudicate between virtues in somewhat the way conceptual considerations mediate between theories. Aristotelians might object that different communities may have different criteria of happiness, as I argued earlier, but Aristotle himself did not deal with this problem at all. Neither a utilitarian nor anybody else who asks "What is courage?" in a way that invites a translation from some other language into utility talk or some other community-neutral language will get a satisfactory answer. There is no utility talk that is community-neutral, because there is no happiness that is community-neutral.

The problem is not simply about utilitarianism. There are no community-neutral rules that fully define either morality or happiness. A Rawlsian approach, for example, is of little help, since it is hard to make sense of choosing among conceptions of happiness while not knowing which conception is consistent with one's own. Fairness too is hard to define in a community-neutral way, for different communities differ hugely over what counts as a relevant difference.

Aristotle's doctrine of the mean, which is meant to include fairness, has the same problems. He seems confident about his doctrine as an action-guiding device, in spite of his recognition of exceptions and his warning that the circumstances have a bearing on the appropriateness of an action. The third, fourth, and fifth chapters of Book V of *Ethica Nicomachea* exhibit in their calculative talk of proportion and justice some of the worst features of Bentham and Richard Posner and not much understanding of the problems with the concept of fairness. Aristotle does concede that context is important and that *phronesis* is not calculation alone, but he goes further in quantifying virtue than would most utilitarians.

What the doctrine of the mean does not do and is not intended to do is function as a community-neutral device for calculating what one ought to do. The conception of courage in any organization will be compatible with Aristotle's definition of it as the mean between the extremes of cowardice and foolhardiness, but that is just the problem, not a solution. Aristotle's definitions of the virtues as means between extremes presuppose and are meaningful within a community in which each person shares views of virtues and vices—for example, cowardice and foolhardiness—sufficiently to be able to gain some further understanding from seeing how they stand with respect to each other. It is as though the community members all speak the same language, or at any rate enough to permit conversation. In such a case there is agreement about the references of common words, and you can enlighten people by defining some terms by the use of others. If, however, you are outside the linguistic/moral community that shares certain conceptions of cowardice and foolhardiness, you will not learn much about courage just from being told that it is the mean between those other two. There are no common reference points from which to triangulate.[21]

In this respect the mean is similar to the categorical imperative, the hedonic calculus, the veil of ignorance, and other devices intended to enable us to calculate what is the good thing to do. Aristotle differs from, say, Kant in his ready admission that one needs *phronesis* to use the device correctly, but he patently does not hold that if you are *phronimos* you do not need the device at all—still less that principles are not significant in ethics.[22] We do need something other than calculation to apply Aristotle's and Kant's and Bentham's and Rawls's rules and devices usefully; why is this a point to Aristotle? He is just a bit more modest than the others.

It is not a point to Aristotle that he fails to see his doctrine as a way of dealing with moral conflict, because he does not see moral conflict as a problem. If you believe that moral behavior is natural, as Aristotle does, then you may have difficulty in giving an account of tragedy—that is, conflict between virtuous or at least conscientious people whose conceptions of duty clash. Aristotle's way with tragedy is to take it as a sign that somebody has made a mistake.[23] How could two gentlemen disagree on a serious matter of duty? No stakeholder-sensitive manager would take that position, which simply ignores the possibility that noble and loyal people might differ in part precisely because they are so noble and loyal. In fact, stakeholder-sensitive managers will experience the clash within themselves.

Utility and other devices promise to deal with the problem from a standpoint free of the values associated with any particular community. According to crude utilitarianism, you add up the points to determine which side is right; according to Rawls, you conduct a certain kind of thought experiment. There is reason to believe that these devices do not solve the problem. But Aristotle not only does not solve the problem; he does not see it.

All of this suggests what we would not like to have to conclude—that communities themselves must be beyond any possible moral judgment. How, in the absence of any community-neutral moral device, do we distinguish good communities from bad ones?

THE PROBLEM OF BAD COMMUNITIES

There are corporate and other cultures that encourage and reward very bad behavior by people who think themselves and are thought by their peers to be courageous, honest team players. Most of us know at least one organization that is an ongoing Zimbardo experiment. We encourage our students to avoid getting sucked into a bad corporate culture. We tell them that they should be able to step back from their workplace situation and assess it, and what it seeks to impress on them, from the standpoint of their own values. It is a moral catastrophe to have one's desires, values, beliefs, personality—in short, one's self—entirely molded by the community one's employer has created. But what do we want our students to step back to, if there is no community-neutral standpoint or device?

One solution that won't do, according to Solomon and Aristotle, is that of the Cynics: against Aristotle's social self, which from their point of view would amount to the end of the autonomy that the Cynics so highly prized, they argued for a self detached from the effect of any community. Bravely, they drew the conclusion that the autonomous self could achieve neither happiness nor unhappiness through satisfaction of its desires: its goal was *apatheia,* which I take it Solomon would find difficult to distinguish from death and which by implication Aristotle rather curtly dismisses.[24] For the Cynics, then, the yuppie's pleasure is a snare and a delusion, but so is everybody else's.

According to Aristotle, one should not abjure pleasure but instead derive it from how one learns to behave in a good community, that is, virtuously. To that end, he advocates that one find a good polis and stay there—advice he probably should have taken himself. In that case one need not step back and ask oneself whether one is being brainwashed against one's interests. But then the study of politics, which enables one to distinguish the good community from the bad, must itself be a matter of stepping back from all possible communities and choosing the best. It is not surprising that in effect he advocates living in a polis that an Athenian gentleman would consider good.

Yet we should not miss what is important and quite possibly correct in Aristotle's position. Freeman follows Aristotle as well as Rorty in suggesting that ethics reflects politics.[25] We are inclined to ask ourselves what justifies politics, but we might also ask ourselves whether the foundationalism presupposed by that question is appropriate. Plato believes there is a rock-bottom justification for the good state; Aristotle is not so sure. That difference in itself helps explain why Aristotle is something of a democrat and Plato is not.

A few Cynics and some of their Stoic successors advocated broadening one's experience and thought and becoming a citizen of the universe—a cosmopolitan. Solomon adopts their view: he wants students to become acquainted with Antigone and Billy Budd and Huckleberry Finn; then they can step back and assess any corporate or other cultural situation from a point of view that goes beyond any single polis or institution in which they will spend part of their time. But there is no offer of a neutral, objective standpoint from which one can choose one's values or the kind of happiness one reasonably and virtuously wants. This position, clearer in Solomon than in Aristotle, seems not a wholly satisfactory solution to problems about the communal nature of morality and of true happiness: among other things, the notion of reflecting on one's preferences seems to invite an infinite regress. But it may be the best we can do.[26]

It does not follow, however, that Kant and Rawls have no useful suggestions to make about what morality would look like in nearly any community. If we were to find a community in which the word usually translated "moral" had in its application to people and acts nothing to do with human fairness or rights or anything we could imagine as happiness, then we would have good reason to question the usual translation.[27] I do not believe the doctrine of the mean is as essential to morality as are fairness, rights, and happiness.

None of this implies that we should embrace Kant and Rawls and reject Aristotle. All three have a great deal to teach us about morality. One thing they collectively teach us is that morality is far too rich and complex to admit of only one approach.[28]

NOTES

1. Mark Pastin, *The Hard Problems of Management* (San Francisco: Jossey-Bass, 1986); R. Edward Freeman and Daniel R. Gilbert, Jr., *Corporate Strategy and the Search for Ethics* (Englewood Cliffs, N.J.: Prentice-Hall, 1988), chap. 5.

2. Robert H. Frank, *Passions Within Reason: The Strategic Role of the Emotions* (New York: Norton, 1988).

3. Aristotle, *Metaphysica*, ed. W. D. Ross (Oxford: Clarendon Press, 1924), bk. IV.

4. Richard J. Bernstein, *Beyond Objectivism and Relativism: Science, Hermeneutics, and Praxis* (Philadelphia: University of Pennsylvania Press, 1983).

5. Aristotle, *Ethica Nicomachea*, ed. I. By-water (Oxford: Clarendon Press, 1894), bk. VI, 7 41b14ff. and elsewhere (hereafter cited in text as *EN*).

6. It is possible that a contemporary criticized Aristotle along these lines, for he says that, of course, it is unhelpful to say that one should aim at the mean according to right reason, as though one were to give medical advice by telling a patient to apply whatever medicine medical science recommends and as the medical professional would apply it; his account of morality must define right reason adequately. Ibid., bk. I, 1 1138a27ff. This essay's criticisms of Aristotle are meant to raise questions about that account, which includes the doctrine of the mean, but the criticisms should not be taken as assuming that some account of how morality rests on right reason is possible.

7. Aristotle says virtue is primarily concerned with emotions and actions. Ibid., bk. III, 1 *ad init.* But, as I shall argue later, the notion of principle does play a significant role in his theory.

8. R. Edward Freeman, Review of *Executive Integrity: The Search for High Human Values in Organizational Life,* by Suresh Srivastva and Associates, *The Academy of Management Executive* 3 (1989): 78–80.

9. *EN,* bk. V, 1 1129b27ff.

10. Ibid., bk. IV, 3 1125a12ff; cf. 1123a5.

11. Mark Twain, *Adventures of Huckleberry Finn,* ed. Charles Neider (Garden City, N.Y.: Doubleday, 1985), pp. 108–9.

12. *EN,* bk. VII.

13. Aristotle's *eudaimonia* is a broader state than happiness. John M. Cooper, for example, translates it as "flourishing" (*Reason and Human Good in Aristotle* [Indianapolis, Ind.: Hackett, 1986], p. 89). He points out that Aristotle holds that the fate of one's children after one is dead affects one's *eudaimonia. EN,* bk. I, 10 1100a22ff. Large and difficult issues lie close at hand, but it is safe to say that the difference between Aristotle's concept of happiness and ours betokens something far more substantive than a semantic issue, and that therefore his conception is itself not beyond criticism. It is less safe to say that someone who libels me after my death is seriously injuring me.

14. *EN,* bk. III, 9 1117b2ff.

15. Ibid., bk. III, 7 1115a28ff.

16. Ibid., bk. I, 5.

17. Ibid., bk. III, 7 15a12ff.

18. Aristotle, *Politica,* ed. W. D. Ross (Oxford: Clarendon Press, 1957).

19. *EN,* bk. VI, 8 1141b24.

20. Aristotle would join most ancient Greek authors in holding that virtue is and ought to be dependent upon one's proper function and that of the organization of which one is a member. Presumably, in different organizations there are different things one should reasonably fear. But this does not address the problem of cultures that are themselves irrational and therefore dysfunctional about what one should fear.

21. Some professions are communities in just this sense; their ethical codes define the virtue of, say, medicine. It is hard to argue with the prevailing conception of morality in medicine because the technical vocabulary and the moral vocabulary of the profession overlap. Think of the way the word *care* is used, for example.

22. See, for example, *EN,* bk. VI, 7 1141b14ff., where Aristotle claims that *phronesis* deals with universals as well as particulars; see also bk. X, 8 1178a16ff., where *phronesis* is said to be about *principles* of virtue, and bk. X, 9 1189b8ff., where Aristotle notes that one cannot teach virtue without knowing its rules (surely he is right). Exactly what Aristotle means by rules (literally, "common things") is not altogether clear. They might be rules of thumb or precedents; what is clear is that Aristotle thinks they cannot be both detailed and unexceptionable.

23. See, for example, Aristotle, *De Arte Poetica,* ed. Rudolf Kassel (Oxford: Clarendon Press, 1965), 13, 1453a7ff.

24. *EN,* bk. I, 3.

25. R. Edward Freeman, "Let's Disband the Academy of Management," Division Chairperson's Address, Social Issues in Management Division, Academy of Management, Washington, D.C., 1989. A number of commentators have found reason to believe that Aristotle permits not only his ethics but his psychology and his biology to be influenced by his political views. For instance, Aristotle holds that a woman's soul is deficient because the part concerned with acting on reason is by nature ineffective. It appears the closest Aristotle can come to a basis for this view is that women are not supposed to be free to do as they wish without some male's say-so. See Aristotle, *Politica,* bk. I, 13 1260a12f. Rhoda H. Kotzin has reviewed the scholarship on this point; see her article "Aristotle's Views on Women," *American Philosophical Association Newsletter on Feminism and Philosophy* 88, no. 3 (1981): 21–24.

26. In not invoking some Platonic foundation of morality, Solomon follows Aristotle. But Aristotle is far more confident than Solomon could or should be that people are inclined by nature toward certain preferences and that reflection according to correct reason will reveal their real preferences to them. In believing that there is such a thing as the good life for humans and that ethics is about promoting the good life rather than just any old pleasure, Aristotle is not clearly wrong.

27. Consider Homeric society. The position I am taking implies that the *Illiad* represents a view of virtue different from our own, but it is not clear that it takes a different view of morality, for the Homeric hero's virtue is so different from what we understand moral virtue to be that one might well hesitate to call that virtue moral. Yet it does at least contribute in some way to the well-being of the community.

28. In addition to the works already cited, the following source was also consulted: Alasdair MacIntyre, *After Virtue: A Study in Moral Theory* (Notre Dame: Ind.: University of Notre Dame Press, 1981), pp. 64–67.

Responsibility and the Moral Role of Corporate Entities

Peter A. French

Robert C. Solomon's essay "Business and the Humanities: An Aristotelian Approach to Business Ethics," is a breath of fresh air in what is in danger of becoming a very stuffy field: ethics. I wholeheartedly agree with so much of what Solomon is doing that it is tempting simply to heap on the praise. I'm going to resist that temptation, however, because I want to raise issues that I believe Solomon has overlooked, but none of what I will discuss is intended to abort the campaign on which he has embarked. I hope he may see that I am about the business of carrying matters a step or two further.

Solomon is right on target in his attack on the miserable state into which the academic discipline of ethics has descended. Most contemporary ethical theory bores students and those with serious practical ethical concerns because its favored theories have abstracted the individual actor almost off the stage of meaningful moral decision making. Only a trace of a human person remains, and this framework cannot be fleshed out without doing serious damage to the theories, ironically often of justice, on which it depends. The twin plagues of atomistic individualism and the doctrine of individual rights, both traceable to the fifteenth-century Protestant reformers' insistence on the priesthood of all believers, have left for those confronted with moral concerns little more than interchangeable, game-theoretical selectors (chess played with nothing but free-floating pawns) with which to identify. Full-blooded human beings are not to be found. Nor are the organizations in which they exist and make their livings. It is notable that this dehumanization has resulted from a revolution intended to put forth the claims of the individual against the tyranny of institutions. Such are the fortunes of a good idea!

What makes us individuals, the people we are rather than other people, is not any abstracted element that can be plugged into a hedonic calculus, computed in a decision-theoretic formula, pinpointed on a game matrix, or idealized as a transcendental ego subjected to a categorical imperative. It is our association with others and with institutions and corporate bodies that in large measure defines our identities, which are derived from and dependent on those relationships. One of Solomon's strongest points is his insistence on the personal dimension in ethics, which he rightly identifies as the Aristotelian approach. When applied to business ethics, this translates into a concern for personal decision makers *within* complex, usually corporate, settings, molding their characters as they make their business choices and, I will add, corporate entities forming their personalities synergistically with the decision making of those employed by them.

Solomon, again correctly, argues that both Kantians and utilitarians have a "special appeal to anal-compulsives."[1] Both traditional ethical points of view, so often the centerpieces of collegiate ethics courses, focus on the transcendence of place in society or in organizations. Yet it is place that gives meaning, definition, and identity to moral persons. The spatial element is crucial to understanding the moral world. F. H. Bradley's devastating criticisms of both Kant and Mill[2] on just this point are vaguely echoed by Solomon.

The moral world may be profitably compared to a city. The buildings in a city mesh to form neighborhoods. A particular building can be isolated in thought from all the rest and questions raised about its design, its use of stone, glass, ornamentation, and so on. But something very important will then have been left out: the building's place on a street, in the neighborhood, among the other buildings. If it does not fill its space well and does not cohere with its neighbors, it may be regarded as an architectural failure. The very features that are praised in isolation may be the reasons for its negative appraisal. It may be seen to be "out of place," inappropriate, an eyesore, ugly. To see the building in its full-bodied sense, to evaluate it aesthetically, one must study it in its space, which is marked by its relations to other things. And there is yet another element that must be considered namely, its purpose. Is it in the right place to serve the purposes for which it is constructed? (This was a problem with Brasilia.) Is it suited to those purposes? It is to questions akin of this spatial sort with respect to persons that the standard ethical theories are systematically silent. Yet in the spatial dimension of society are found the entities that most closely resemble everyday people. Solomon is bringing us back to the spatial, the relational, and the teleological in ethics. The teleological, as in Aristotle, is not so much a temporal end state as a matter of perfection: excellence achieved by "a multi-dimensional person occupying an important role in a particular organization."[3]

Having touched on what I regard as my general agreement with Solomon, I wish to turn to a central issue about which, I suspect, we may differ. Nevertheless, things he says toward the end of his essay about expanded selves and the emotions that would be unintelligible without them suggest that we may, in fact, be closer than most of his emphasis on the personal aspect of ethics would lead one to assume. Certainly his discussion of shame as requiring a group identity is very close to what I want to say, although my way of coming to say it may be notably different from his and may be perceived as more radical.

I want to argue that what is wrong with most attempts to talk about business ethics is that the central players in the game (a metaphor that Solomon will not like) are ignored or misrepresented due to the set of biases that Solomon identifies: those related to the adoption of atomistic, reductionistic individualism. The entities in question are, of course, corporations (or corporate bodies).

Otto von Gierke argued that the theory that a corporation is just a legal fiction (results from a "desire to safeguard Natural Law as the supreme source of right and obligation."[4] Because natural legal theory bestows rights and duties only on natural persons, all collectivities must be nothing but the products of contractual arrangements between natural persons. Any corporate will or personality or culture that might show up in ordinary experience and discourse is nothing but a coordination of the activities and objectives of natural persons.

There is something pathological in adhering to the legal fiction theory in the face of experience, other things being equal. It is rather like insisting that one's playmate is imaginary even after he or she has just hit one over the head with a hammer and stolen all the ice cream. Even the most committed of the atomistic individualists deal regularly and willfully with corporate entities and think nothing of it. They read newspapers that accuse oil companies of pollution of the waterways, watch television shows in which corporate giants urge the purchase of their products, pay the monthly bill to the gas company, and protest the dumping of toxic wastes by manufacturing plants. A convinced individualist once talked to me after I'd presented a paper on corporate liability. He said that he always believed that corporations were just fictions but couldn't rationally explain the fact that he had spent many days protesting against Dow Chemical for its manufacture of napalm during the late 1960s.

He fully realized that he was protesting against the company and not its executives, for there had been a full-scale managerial change during the period of his protest. He wondered if he was suffering from a serious mental problem, perhaps induced by other chemicals in his system. In any event, he despised Dow.

I think the reason most writers on business ethics fail to identify the moral standing of the corporate entity in the moral community is that they do not appreciate the multitiered topography over which the concept of responsibility operates. Looking through the glasses provided by the atomistic individualist, they are prevented from seeing any more than one type of entity as a proper subject of moral responsibility ascriptions. Hence, when they hear ordinary discourse using responsibility ascriptions in reference to other types, they perform corrective reductions to tell the ordinary folk "what they really mean." Maybe ordinary folk mean what they say—that the structure of those responsibility ascriptions needs to be examined to see if it is really as exclusive as some philosophers say it must be.

Responsibility ascriptions, whether made for the purposes of identifying targets for punishment or those to be held liable to compensate injuries or those whose character is being evaluated, are sensible only if at least two sets of conditions are satisfied. One set might be called the input conditions and the other, the output conditions.

The input conditions appear in the formula for responsibility ascription sketched by Edmund Pincoffs: "A imputes C to B on account of D, in light of E, and in the absence of F."[5] C is an event, typically an untoward one, D is an activity or action, E role requirements, and F a defense (usually an excuse). All of those are important aspects of a responsibility ascription, but the whole business is sensible only if A and B are persons. The input conditions then contain a metaphysical doctrine of personhood (as well as an action theory).

The output conditions depend on the existence of the practices, noted earlier, that supply a purpose to responsibility ascribing. In other words, the output conditions are satisfied if there are reasons to punish, hold liable to restitution, or blame a person for the untoward event (C) for which that person is responsible. Although there are important issues regarding all of the input conditions in the formula, personhood is certainly primary. The formula tells us that as long as we can access a person in a description that is true of an event under moral scrutiny, the other conditions in the formula having been satisfied, a moral responsibility ascription will be in order. Imagine any event and the different levels or types of descriptions that could be given of the event. We could start with descriptions on an atomic or subatomic level, where the use of responsibility ascriptions (at least of the full-blooded moral sort schematized by Pincoffs) are senseless. Imagine, next, that we layer on more and more descriptions (or conceptual levels) until a responsibility ascription becomes sensible. According to the formula, that will happen only when we arrive at a descriptive level in which personhood is attributed. The layering of descriptive levels is not an arbitrary process. Access to higher or more complex levels is gained by use of a ticket for (or license of) redescription. ("Higher" is probably not a good term, for it implies that there is a basic or primary description on which the others are layered. I don't think any descriptive level is more basic in that sense. It is the movement from one level to another that is important.) Simply put, there needs to be a basis for describing an event in one way rather than another and a means of ensuring that the same event is the subject of the second description. What is needed is a linking device between descriptions. The contraction of the muscles of a hand may be redescribed as "the pulling of the trigger of a gun" and that as "the murdering of a hostage" only if certain conditions with respect to the event have been met. For one thing, the description that says it was a murder is allowed only if the subject is properly classed as a person. Trees can kill people, but they cannot murder people. Generally, it is an attribution of intentionality that signals a person. That attribution is the ticket to the redescription we seek.

Most moral theorists within the natural law tradition block redescription with respect to moral evaluations when a human person emerges in the process. For them, "person" is bound to a specific type or level of redescription. It is restricted to the descriptive level at which the intentional actions of individual humans are a part of the descriptions. Any account of collective action, for them, can only be a shorthand for a conjunction of descriptions about the actions of individuals. They regard the attribution of personhood to entities that appear only at more complex levels of description as fictive. But why should "person" be restricted only to descriptions of the actions of individual humans? I have shown elsewhere that the actions of corporations can be understood as redescriptions of the actions of humans and that Corporate Internal Decision Structures (CID Structures) provide the licenses for such redescription.[6] Corporations can do a number of things that are not sensibly reduced to the actions of those associated with them. They can join cartels, manufacture automobiles, enter bankruptcy, set the price of goods and services, and so forth. In a number of places I have elaborated on the ways corporations act and how they manifest corporate intentionality. The personhood input conditions for moral responsibility ascriptions are met by corporate entities. Ordinary discourse abounds with instances in which corporations are held responsible and liable for untoward events. A cursory reading of a newspaper will provide evidence enough.

The output conditions for moral responsibility are also applicable to corporate bodies. Put simply, there is a point to blaming corporations if in doing so we are keeping a kind of moral ledger on them—note the way most people responded to the Exxon Valdez oil spill in Alaskan waters. There is also good reason to hold them liable for compensatory damages when they cause injury. Again, the Exxon oil spill is a case in point, but any number of tort cases, especially those concerning product liability, would do just as well. Furthermore, punishment is appropriate and can be exacted from corporate entities. Clutchability of corporations is achieved via a number of strategies that need not be discussed here.[7]

Corporations satisfy both the input and output conditions for moral responsibility. They make decisions, have rights and duties in law, carry on nonlegal relationships with other corporations and with human persons; in short, they participate in the whole spectrum of activities and relationships we associate with persons. Importantly, they are historical entities with births, lives, and deaths. They flourish and decline, succeed and fail. Roger Scruton has pointed out that they can "even be the leading character in a drama (as in Wagner's *Die Meistersinger.*)"[8] I want to argue that not only are corporations persons in a full-fledged moral sense, but that corporations are essential elements of the moral world. Solomon hints at this when he writes that "business is a social practice, not an activity of isolated individuals."[9] He goes on to say that it can take place only in "a culture with an established set of procedures and expectations" that are not open to tinkering by individual human beings.[10] The maintenance of the business culture is, according to Solomon, a prerequisite for the prosperity of a nation and, he sometimes says and sometimes implies, of the happiness, in the Aristotelian sense, of the individual members of the society. The corporate culture's existence and character are clearly central to Solomon's conception of the good life. They are also not, he assures us, the product of an invisible hand operating to our benefit unbeknownst to or unintended by any of us. In this regard Solomon stands against the procedural bent of modern ethics that is dependent on the concept of individual rights and rarefied rationality. I can stand with him, but there is much more to be said about the relationship between the corporation and the individual.

Rousseau, Hegel, and Bradley provide a perspective different from the one offered by the individualists on the place of corporatelike entities (in using "corporatelike" I mean to include not only business firms but any institution that operates in CID Structural

Ways) in relation to human (or natural) persons. Even those individualists who are willing to acknowledge that corporations may be persons (or quasi-persons) will, like Rawls,[11] maintain that there is an
ontological priority that must bias us in favor of individuals. Whatever moral personality corporations are granted exists by virtue of
the moral personality of their members. If IBM is a good corporation or a good citizen, it must be because the people who work for
IBM are good citizens. Of course, the standard view is reductionist
in the sense that human persons can exist in the absence of corporate entities, but corporate entities are dependent on the existence
of persons for their existence. It is against such a view that the alternative perspective is set, and, I suspect, Solomon may be persuaded
to join with me in this band of contras.

What the writers mentioned suggest, each in his own way, is that
in nature humans are only potential persons. To achieve full moral
personhood, humans must associate with corporate institutions that
forge relationships between their members and also between their
members and the larger corporate units. Gaining moral personhood,
in effect, involves finding a place in a corporatelike institution. In
my *Collective and Corporate Responsibility* I maintained that Rousseau
and Bradley were the forefathers of the theory of the corporation
as a moral person.[12] For Rousseau civil union is essential, not only
for civil liberty and rights, but for moral freedom, "which alone
makes man the master of himself."[13] In his view, although individuals can exist outside the corporate union of the state, they cannot
achieve completeness as moral persons in its absence. The political
machine is required for moral freedom and so for realization of true
human personhood. It converts humans from mere animals to noble, moral entities: "His mind is so enlarged, his sentiments so enno-
bled, and his whole spirit so elevated that . . . he should . . . bless
the happy hour that lifted him forever from the state of nature and
from a narrow, stupid animal made a creature of intelligence and
a man."[14]

Bradley's position is even stronger, for he does not admit to the
sense of talking about the individual outside corporate-like relations.
"What we call the individual man is what he is because of and by
virtue of community. . . . [C]ommunities are thus not mere names
but something real."[15] To have a moral personality, even to have
rights and duties, is for Bradley to have a station, a place, in an
institution. To be a natural person is to be a member of a corporate
person. The child at birth, to use one of Bradley's favorite examples,
is born into "a living world . . . which has a true individuality of its
own."[16] For both Rousseau and Bradley, the dependency relationship moves in a direction opposite that described by the individualists. Corporatelike entities provide the context in which individual

human persons not only develop but flourish. Scruton writes: "Such an individual comes into existence . . . already marked by the ties of membership, and without those ties, which compel him to recognize and to honour the personality of institutions, he would not possess the autonomy that is necessary for any contractual undertaking."[17] In short, without the existence of corporations (or corporatelike entities), the freely contracting person of game theory and rights-based political theory does not come into existence.

Individualists are likely to argue that even if corporations are required for the full development of the moral human person, they still need not ontologically precede human individuals. Scruton suggests—and I think he is right—that a Hegelian like Bradley can argue that ontological priority is of no metaphysical significance:

> It is *logically* possible for the parts of an organism—the cells—to persist without the organism and not logically possible for the organism to persist without its parts. Nevertheless (a) the organism is a real existent *in addition to* its parts and (b) the parts owe their existence, not just empirically, but also metaphysically, to their participation in the whole which nurtures them.[18]

The argument just says that ontological priority has no moral significance because it makes no metaphysical difference. I make a similar argument from a base in identity theory to show that the identity of a corporation is independent of the aggregate identities of those associated with it at any particular time, even though its operations at any time require that there be persons associated with it.[19]

The crucial Hegelian point,[20] loudly echoed by Bradley, is that the isolating and abstracting of the individual, required by Kantians and utilitarians alike, leaves the characteristics of the individual that are needed to generate the preferred notions of duty and rights at a level of description that is lost. The baby is thrown out with the bath water! According to Scruton, "Agency is the greatest irrationality, until tempered and guided by a sense of value."[21] Value, however, comes not from isolated individuals but from associations. That was one of the central points of Rousseau's theory; surprisingly, it also can be teased from Hobbes's description of the state of nature.

The Hegelian argument for the necessity of corporatelike entities to the moral life has also a distant relative in Aristotle. Solomon notes that Aristotle argued that we are all members of organized groups or communities and that, for the Greeks, "to live the good life, one must live in a great city."[22] The idea, I think, is that it is not possible to live a good life if a major element of your identity is shameful. I once spoke to a group of banking executives, many of whose institutions had entered bankruptcy due to bad management, including outright criminal activity. Most of those bankers were financially secure in their comfortable homes and enjoyed rewarding familial relations. But when I asked them how the failure and disgrace of their institutions had affected them, they all said they felt unhappy and ashamed (one or two used the term "dirty"), even though none had personally been responsible for the mismanagement. They felt that their lives, no matter how successful otherwise, could not be good until their institutions had been restored to their former status and respectability in the larger community.

There is yet another reason for admitting corporations into the moral realm. It may be the most crucial of all, as it involves a unique and irreducible element of corporations. A great deal is currently made in moral philosophy in general and in business ethics about our long-term obligations. Solomon talks about the flourishing community, its creation and maintenance, continuing associations, and ongoing practices. Certainly one of the dominant general issues in business ethics involves the treatment of populations that will make up that community into the distant future. The environment, and its protection, is a factor of considerable import, but it is so in large part because of views we have about our obligations to protect it for the enjoyment and use of future generations. We may have similar views with respect to our obligations to preserve the creations of the past. In short, there is a widespread belief in the general population and among moral philosophers that the dead and the unborn have claims on us that should be honored. Establishing a relationship on which such claims can be based between those currently living and those long dead or those to be born in the distant future requires incredibly obtuse links if we are restricted only to human persons. No individual human now living can enter into a personal obligation with the long dead or with future persons. But the protection of obligations in both temporal directions is crucial to our sense of place and culture and so to our moral personhood. It is also essential to the explication of social roles and model identities that are used to set moral expectations.

Corporatelike entities solve the problem. They endure through many generations, even centuries. The moral relationships to the past and the future can be sustained in and through them. Hence, they can be the conduits for the projection of duties to both the past and the future. The protection of civilization and the environment for future generations can be made a meetable obligation for those entities that will survive long enough to have genuine relationships with us and with those now unborn. Our individual intentions to preserve the best of the past and to ensure the well-being of the generations of the future, although noble-sounding, are generally impotent. Corporatelike entities, on the other hand, bridge generations and so are in the best position to bear consistently the obligations of culture while also providing, as Solomon notes, the enduring standards and role model expectations on which a powerful morality of shame can operate.

NOTES

1. Robert C. Solomon, "Business and the Humanities: An Aristotelian Approach to Business Ethics," in Thomas J. Donaldson and R. Edward Freeman, eds., *Business as a Humanity* (New York: Oxford University Press, 1994), p. 53.

2. F. H. Bradley, *Ethical Studies* (Oxford: Oxford University Press, 1876), Essays III and IV.

3. Solomon, "Business and the Humanities," p. 53.

4. Otto von Gierke, *Natural Law and the Theory of Society,* trans. Sir Ernest Barker (Cambridge: Cambridge University Press, 1934); quoted in Roger Scruton, "Corporate Persons," *Proceedings of the Aristotelian Society,* in press.

5. Edmund Pincoffs, "The Practices of Responsibility-Ascription," *Proceedings and Addresses of the American Philosophical Association* 61, no. 5 (June 1988): 825–39.

6. Peter A. French, *Collective and Corporate Responsibility* (New York: Columbia University Press, 1984), esp. chaps. 3, 4, and 12.

7. See Peter A. French, "Enforced Corporate Responsive Adjustment," *Legal Studies Forum* 13, no. 2 (1989): 115–33.

8. Scruton, "Corporate Persons."

9. Solomon, "Business and the Humanities," p. 64.

10. Ibid.

11. John Rawls, "Justice as Reciprocity," in Samuel Gorovitz, ed., *John Stuart Mill: Utilitarianism* (Indianapolis: University of Indiana Press, 1971).

12. French, *Collective and Corporate Responsibility,* chap. 7.

13. Jean-Jacques Rousseau, *The Social Contract,* trans. Maurice Cranston (Baltimore, Md.: Penguin Books, 1968), p. 65.

14. Ibid.

15. Bradley, *Ethical Studies,* p. 166.

16. Ibid., p. 171.

17. Scruton, "Corporate Persons."

18. Ibid.

19. French, *Collective and Corporate Responsibility,* chap. 2.

20. This point is made in G. W. F. Hegel, *The Philosophy of Right,* trans. T. M. Knox (Oxford: Clarendon Press, 1952), pp. 122–26; and in Hegel, *The Phenomenology of Spirit,* trans. Parvis Emad and Kenneth Maly (Indianapolis: Indiana University Press, 1980), pp. 136–40.

21. Scruton, "Corporate Persons."

22. Solomon, "Business and the Humanities," pp. 56–57.

Moral Character
and Moral Reasoning

Patricia H. Werhane

At a symposium on financial ethics, the chairman of a large New York bank asked why it is that the moral character of managers has declined in recent years. The chairman complained that younger managers exhibit none of the virtues that characterized good management in earlier decades; they care little about the bank, they have no notion of social welfare or the public interests, and they are concerned primarily with themselves, their future, and their own contributions. Robert C. Solomon's complex and fascinating essay "Business and the Humanities: An Aristotelian Approach to Business Ethics" addresses such concerns directly. Solomon argues that we have lost what William Ophuls in another context calls a sense of "civic virtue."[1] This loss is due in great measure to a neglect of the personal dimension in ethics caused by an "obsession in ethics . . . with rational principles," a neglect Solomon would remedy with an Aristotelian approach to business ethics.

Solomon is particularly critical of what he correctly identifies as standard approaches to the subject matter of business ethics. Many ethicists in the field begin with an exacting and often abstract analysis contrasting various forms of deontology, utilitarianism, rights theories, and a social contract approach. Yet seldom are the differences between these theories resolved, even in their subsequent application to business practice. The obtuse nature of the analysis and the lack of resolution produce a twofold negative result. First, as Solomon points out, such approaches are too abstract and "neglect . . . individual responsibility and the cultivation of character."[2] I shall return to that point later in the essay.

Second, the character of traditional ethical theories, while interesting to the philosopher, does not easily lend itself to practice, and often such theories obstruct or confuse practitioners. Traditional ethicists often disagree among themselves as to the proper procedure for ethical decision making and as to which principles, if any, are to be the standards by which to judge the rightness or wrongness, the good or evil, of a particular decision or action. Those not intimately familiar with the nuances of ethical theory have trouble sorting out the various points of view and even more difficulty deciding how to apply what appear to be conflicting approaches to practical dilemmas that require resolution. The importance of such application is crucial, since the focus should be on the resolution of ethical dilemmas in the decision-making process. In the "real world" of business, medicine, law, or the professions one must make choices and act, and not making a decision is itself an action that often produces serious consequences.

Solomon presents a model for approaching business ethics, a model derived from Aristotle, Smith, and Mill, rather than from Kant, Nozick, and Rawls. This model emphasizes the personal dimension of business ethics: the cultivation of excellence in moral character. In brief, Solomon's framework positions what he calls the social self, with its civic virtues of loyalty, honor, and shame, against six Aristotelian ingredients for business ethics: community, excellence, public identity, holism, nobility, and judgment. The aim of the model, its "bottom line," is the common good: the well-being of society.

What Solomon has done is to lay out a matrix for personal moral excellence and to suggest that the development of moral character is a necessary condition for good businesspeople and, therefore, for ethical excellence in business. The strength of this framework is its focus on personal character and moral excellence in a social setting from which the individual cannot be isolated. Solomon is correct that to a large extent we have neglected this kind of approach to business ethics, just as, according to Allan Bloom, we have neglected the development of moral character in all aspects of education. The question is, however, why this neglect is peculiar to *business* ethics and not, as Bloom contends, endemic to our whole educational system. This does not exonerate business ethics from its alleged failures, but it raises the following question: What is unique to business ethics as distinct from theoretical ethics, education, or, even more broadly, character development and civic virtue? In what follows I shall suggest that while personal moral excellence is a necessary condition for business decision making, what is peculiar or even unique to applied ethics, of which business ethics is a part, are the kinds of moral dilemmas faced in concrete settings. Solving the kinds of dilemmas that often confront individuals in institutional and market contexts requires moral reasoning skills, skills that are not merely a matter of character but that take into account precedents and precedent-setting standards that entail impartial generalizations transcending a particular business situation. What is unique or at least interesting about business decision making is that it is inherently contextual and utilitarian, while at the same time it demands the application, or set-ting out, of more general principles or rules.

To put the point more concretely, the development of moral ex-cellence provides the individual with the character and backbone to face moral dilemmas and to take stands. Does it, however, prepare the businessperson to engage in moral decision making and to solve everyday moral dilemmas in business? I raise that issue because many of the moral dilemmas in business are problems endemic to or built into Solomon's six ingredients for business ethics. The busi-nessperson needs some way to work through such dilemmas that does not presuppose the very ingredients out of which the dilemmas arise. Strength of moral character and concern for the public good are essential to problem solving, but working one's way out of a moral maze requires viewing the maze from a distance so that one's judgments are not merely determined by a specific context or set of values. Let me illustrate by briefly suggesting some of the kinds of problems that develop within the context of Solomon's six Aristote-lian ingredients for business ethics.

The notion of community is crucial in business decision making, but it is better thought of in the plural, as *communities.* The average manager must balance the interests of various communities: employ-ees, customers, the corporate culture, shareholders, societal interests, and the everpresent, ever pressuring community of the market. While it may appear that the well-being of society should be the guideline for business decisions, in real life it is difficult to translate "well-being of society" into objective or measurable elements. More-over, the problem often lies not in the fact that various communities are not considered but in the conflicting demands made on business by these various communities. For example, to oversimplify a very complex case, one of the reasons Union Carbide built a plant in Bho-pal, India, was to provide pesticides that are absolutely essential for India's economic survival. The goal of fostering Indian well-being may have tainted the business judgment of Union Carbide manage-ment, and distracted it from recognizing the difficulties inherent in building a plant for the manufacture of dangerous chemicals in a culture where the company's safety standards could not be enforced.

Conversely, the E. F. Hutton case is a good illustration of a situa-tion where corporate and market interests outweighed a view of soci-etal good. E. F. Hutton was until recently a large New York brokerage firm. During the early 1980s, when interest rates ran as high as 18 percent, one-third of Hutton's offices engaged in a massive overdrafting scheme, earning interest on the "float" between the time checks were deposited and cleared. The most successful offices at Hutton earned more on interest than on brokerage commissions, and were rewarded accordingly by the firm. Moreover, in the Hutton case loyalty, honor, and doing well—all virtues in the proper context—interfered with good moral judgment. In the Hutton case, too, what Solomon calls "public identity" in the form of role morality is at issue, because what was needed in this case was a challenge to the expected norm of the role model expectations at Hutton. The ingredient of holism should have rescued the E. F. Hutton manager from her predicament. But a sense of holism, at least in this case, conflicted with other senses of communities and with role morality. It is these conflicts that the manager must be aware of and confront. And could holism have prevented the Bhopal decision?

Solomon would rescue his manager from these difficulties with excellence and nobility, a sense of not merely not causing harm but of emulating the best sort of character in concern for the public good. The business community has traditionally not been helpful in this regard. Business seldom punishes or blackballs its recalcitrant members unless they fail or are caught. Here Solomon's suggestions on the role of shame should be taken most seriously, because unless the business community polices its own morality one cannot expect the average manager to do more than emulate his or her colleagues. But because the term "excellence" in business is broadly defined to include both moral and market excellence, the businessperson faces the challenge of how to do good and do well. The market community places pressures on excellence that cannot be oversimplified, and the dilemma of how to do good while doing well, or the reverse, raises acute problems in business decision making.

Turning to the ingredient of judgment, I suggest that judgment requires not merely working one's way through a particular situation but appealing to, or setting precedents for, other moral decisions. Just as the development of moral character cultivates excellence in moral behavior, moral reasoning helps the manager to step back, evaluate a particular situation, and work his or her way out of dilemmas, some of which are created out of conflicts arising from the very ingredients of business in which moral character flourishes. Such moral reasoning in business involves not merely taking general principles and applying them to particular contexts. Rather, such reasoning entails a process of decision making that is both contextual and impartial. Solomon has made a good defense of contextuality. Why, then, impartiality? Impartiality is crucial because unless one can disengage oneself from the context of a particular decision, one's notions of loyalty, honor, community, excellence, and even personal identity are parochially embedded and are likely to result in the very kinds of business decisions that Solomon criticizes. Moreover, whether or not the decision maker means to, such contextual decisions set precedents that other managers follow out of loyalty, identity, and community. Again, the E. F. Hutton case is a fine example of how unwritten corporate policy set a model for achievement that those loyal to Hutton were to follow as a matter of honor. It therefore matters what one decides, because of the kind of example that decision sets.

But if an Aristotelian approach has its shortcomings in the practical process of decision making in business, how can one remedy those shortcomings without reverting to the abstract debate between deontology and utilitarianism? To get a perspective on this question, let us look at how the eighteenth-century economist and philosopher Adam Smith approached ethical decision making. Smith's notion of the impartial spectator is particularly helpful in this regard. Smith envisioned the impartial spectator as the average person who disengages him- or herself from a particular situation in order to make a moral judgment about it. In moral decision making Smith's impartial spectator asks (1) whether a particular judgment is the kind of judgment society deems appropriate for that kind of situation, (2) whether it is the kind of decision others should make, all things considered, and (3) whether the decision embodies a rule that could serve as a general rule for other, similar cases.[3] Translating Smith's scheme for making moral decisions and moral judgments into contemporary terms, one may ask, (1) is this a decision that would ordinarily be agreed upon as appropriate by rational agents? (2) Does the decision pass the television or "60 Minutes" test? (3) Is the decision "legislatable," that is, does it set a precedent that could be followed in other similar contexts? Interestingly, Smith's impartial spectator, like a manager in the middle of a decision, must make a choice. Like all moral decisions, the choice is both contextual, solving a particular problem, and precedent-setting. As we shall see, Smith also recognizes, too, that most moral choices have utilitarian components.

With Smith's analysis as a model and taking what I find to be some common elements in procedural approaches to ethical decision making, one can use Smith's outline and these elements to develop a framework for ethical decision making to which one can appeal in making practical choices. Such a framework provides a general matrix for decision making such that the decision reached will be one that most rational agents could agree upon. The ideal, of course, would be consensus, but that is probably not realizable. This framework should apply not merely to individual decision making but to decision making involving institutions such as corporations and to public policy. It should take into account both the precedent-setting character of moral decisions and the necessity for positive economic outcomes in business choices.

The approach I shall propose takes what I shall call "axioms for moral decision making," a formal procedural framework that characterizes decision procedures, and views it against what I shall call "moral minimums," those negative standards beyond which ordinarily one would agree no action should be undertaken without very good and justifiable reasons.

1. Morality is a public system; it has to do with relationships between individuals or between individuals and institutions. Whether Robinson Crusoe on his desert island exhibits moral behavior or not is irrelevant, since no one can observe his behavior and no one is affected by it.

2. Moral decisions are normative decisions. They have to do with what one should do, all things considered, with what is right or wrong, good or bad, not with what, in fact, any of us will do or hold to be good in a particular instance.

3. Because a moral decision is a normative decision involving human relationships, a moral decision must be impartial. That is, it must reflect what, on balance, an impartial reasonable person would decide is right. The term "rational agent" is a controversial notion in philosophy, and a debate about what that term means or would mean would take us far afield from this short essay I have used the term "reasonable person." While that term also has its philosophical difficulties, it seems intuitively acceptable to say that an impartial decision is a decision acceptable to most disinterested, sane (i.e., not irrational) adults when they are not involved in or affected by the particular decision. One can also say that a decision by an irrational agent would not be acceptable as either impartial or applicable to anyone other than that agent.

4. A moral decision is "legislatable," that is, it sets a precedent for what one thinks should be rules applying to everyone in a particular set of contexts. In more colloquial terms, a moral decision must past the television or "60 Minutes" test, that is, it should be the kind of decision one would not mind being aired on television or dissected by Mike Wallace.[4]

5. It follows from (2) and (3) that a moral decision should be one that would be acceptable to other impartial agents, because moral rules and moral judgments apply to everyone and to everyone equally. If they do not, then a moral rule is simply something I make up that applies to me at a particular moment.

6. Moral decisions are also contextual. A moral decision must therefore take into account the peculiar circumstances of the situation

at hand, the personalities and the social histories of the participants, the context of the decision, and the historical and cultural
precedents that preceded the situation and the decision.

Notice that so far I have talked not about principles but about
precedents. I have suggested that one work from the specific case to
generalizations, rather than the reverse. But there is a "bottom line,"
one Solomon himself recognizes when he says that the overall well-
being of society counts as most important. In other words, there is
some basic principle or standard or ideal that moral virtue and
moral decision making presuppose or to which they aspire, and this
standard must be taken into account in the moral process. Since I
am not sure what "well-being" is, and because Solomon's bottom line
is a maximal ideal that seldom can be achieved, I prefer to talk about
moral minimums, a reversed bottom line that sets minimums for
moral decisions such that any decision that challenges these minimums can do so only for justifiable reasons, that is, for reasons acceptable to an impartial, reasonable person as precedent-setting for
future, similar decisions.

Like "well-being," what should count as a moral minimum is subject to philosophical debate. Adam Smith took as moral minimums
(1) not harming another or oneself, (2) engaging in fair play and not
engaging in activities that are unfair to certain individuals or groups
of individuals, and (3) not engaging in conduct that violates basic
rights that apply to everyone equally and whose violation requires
redress.[5] The following represent formulations of these moral minimums in terms more amenable to contemporary ethical and economic analysis.

1. A decision and any subsequent action should not "better one's
   situation through interaction that worsens the situation of another"[6] or oneself unless each party to the interaction is fully informed and equally competitive. In any case, one should try to
   find a solution that compromises or reduces harms. Ideally, too,
   the decision should aim at increasing economic well-being.
2. A decision should not be unfair to individuals, groups of individuals, or to those who would be affected by similar decisions.
3. The action should not violate basic rights, those rights to which
   every person unquestionably has claim, while recognizing from
   (2) that rights claims also carry a recognition of the requirement
   to respect equally the rights of others.

When a moral decision challenges one of these minimums, it must
justify itself on the basis of another minimum and for good reasons,
that is, reasons an impartial agent would acknowledge as setting the
proper precedents in that particular set for situations.

Given this scheme, the decision maker should ask herself the following questions:

1. Who is affected by the decision (e.g., one individual, a group of individuals, stakeholders, an institution or set of institutions, the public, society)?
2. What are the consequences of this decision for the individuals involved? For the institution? For multinational constituents? For society and public policy?
3. Is this the kind of decision a disinterested, reasonable person would make, all things considered?
4. What kind of precedent would this decision set? Would I mind if my decision was discussed on television? Does this decision apply only to this particular case or does it apply to all cases like it? To all subjects (e.g., persons, institutions, or society) in similar situations?
5. Does the decision meet moral minimums? If not, can I justify the fact that it does not?
6. What kind of institutional structure, accountability procedure, constraint, or absence of constraint might have contributed to the dilemma for which a decision is required? Are there societal or legal factors that must be considered? How might one change any of these factors to try to avoid similar dilemmas in the future?

Notice that, in applying this framework, one must take into account the subject of the decision and the kind of setting in which it takes place. This framework should be applicable to the three subject areas of greatest concern in business ethics—individual, corporate, and public policy decisions—and it should be translatable to multinational settings.

Have I, however, fallen into Solomon's trap? Have I reverted to abstract moral reasoning, "doting over principles and rationalization," and thereby neglecting "individual responsibility and the cultivation of character"?[7] If Solomon is right, in the past we have engaged in abstract moral rationalizations that neglected the cultivation of moral character. An opposite pitfall, I suggest, would be to dwell on moral character without placing it in the larger context of moral precedent. These two aspects of business ethics need to be melded, the aim being to develop responsible decision-making and problem-solving processes in which the development of virtue and moral reasoning play equal roles in both good character and good decisions, as well as in the cultivation of the civic virtues and their precedent-setting practices in business and business decision making.

NOTES

1. William Ophuls, "The Scarcity Society," *Harpers Magazine* (1974); rpt. in Thomas J. Donaldson and Patricia H. Werhane, eds., *Ethical Issues in Business* (Englewood Cliffs, N.J.: Prentice-Hall, 1988), p. 381.

2. Robert C. Solomon, "Business and the Humanities: An Aristotelian Approach to Business Ethics," in Thomas J. Donaldson and R. Edward Freeman, eds., *Business as a Humanity* (New York: Oxford University Press, 1994), p. 53.

3. Adam Smith, *The Theory of Moral Sentiments*, ed. A. L. Macfie and D. D. Raphael (Indianapolis, Ind.: Liberty Classics, 1982), II.i–ii.

4. See Bernard Gert, *Morality* (New York: Oxford University Press, 1988), esp. chaps. 1 and 4. Gert would not formulate the framework in the way I do, but his work has influenced my analysis, as has the work of Ronald Green, particularly his essay "The First Formulation of the Categorical Imperative as Literally a 'Legislative' Metaphor," in press.

5. See *The Theory of Moral Sentiments*, II.ii., and Smith, *Lectures on Jurisprudence*, ed. R. L. Mcck, D. D. Raphael, and P. G. Stein (Indianapolis, Ind.: Liberty Classics, 1982), *(A)* i.9–15.

6. David Gauthier, *Morals by Agreement* (New York: Oxford University Press, 1986), p. 205. See also James Buchanan, "The Gauthier Enterprise," in Ellen Paul et al., eds., *The New Social Contract* (New York: Basil Blackwell, 1988), pp. 88–93.

7. Solomon, "Business and the Humanities," p. 53.

III

Management Education: Seeing the Round Earth Squarely

Clarence C. Walton

The very act of selecting titles for their essays forces writers to come to grips with their purposes. Are the tracts designed to inform? Intrigue? Stimulate or provoke? Since elements of each are part of this author's goal, it is seemly to provide a note on the title's source.

The round earth concept derives from a tale told about Cambridge University Professor I. A. Richards, whose favorite teaching device was forcing students to give explicit meanings to artfully crafted poems. One of Richards's favorite poems was John Donne's "At the Round Earth's Imagined Corners." Students having no knowledge of the scriptural story of the Last Judgment found the title meaningless.[1] Awareness of the implications that the global economy has for management education provides insight into the round earth meaning.

The round-and-square motif was suggested by Bonaventure in the thirteenth century when he was teaching at the University of Paris. Although less well remembered than his illustrious faculty colleague Thomas Aquinas, Bonaventure gave more explicit attention to the goals of education—in his case, the relationships between theology and philosophy. He sought to have the Paris faculty read the world right and squarely by keeping theology in a preeminent position.[2] Squarely facing up to the challenges of an economically and culturally connected globe is a difficulty that is rarely confronted by pioneering business faculties at Wharton; nor is it identical to the educational problems created by the separation of ownership and control that Berle and Means described over a half century ago.[3] Finally, it is not the same as the challenge spawned by the more

109

recent revolution in electronics, which made management information systems so important. To these earlier revolutions—financial, marketing, management, and electronics—is added this new global revolution.

It is the contributor's thesis that the coming of the global economy requires managers to see the *oneness* of world economies. Skill acquisition must be complemented by knowledge/wisdom acquisition, and the humanities are very well suited for this purpose. Partnerships will not be welcomed by a potential participant who feels that the other participant is part of the "hostile elite" that Schumptere spoke of before World War II.[4]

The new times call for new attitudes. To begin to get at the opportunities *and* problems, I intend to (1) describe briefly the kind of economic world business school graduates enter; (2) review the paradigms in classical economics that business students are taught; (3) note the already stated educational needs by leaders in management education; (4) *concentrate on the obstacles that business and humanities faculties face* in defining materials considered most useful to managers, business faculties, and students; (5) provide a tentative outline of courses as well as unifying themes from the humanities that could be useful to managers; and then (6) duck!!!

THE ECONOMY

When earthtone hues of umbrae and siennas define the landscape of an artist's canvas, it is often difficult for untrained eyes to know whether the scene is early spring or late fall. If spring, the promise is seedtime for summer's flowering and growth; if waning autumn, it is the eve of winter's sleep and chill. The question of the season of society has special relevance to the thousands of business school graduates who, as the poet wrote, annually walk "alone and unafraid into a world they never made." Unlike grandparents (and even parents) who quickly learned to use such buzzwords as expansion, growth, and progress, today's generation joins organizations whose leaders speak of constriction, downsizing, and survival. In the face of competition from abroad and takeovers at home, organizations become leaner and meaner; like the "undying organization that was the Church in France, the undying organizations of the corporate world look more and more fragile."[5]

If indeed some firms are in fact terminally ill, is it because the larger economy in which they operate is itself morbid? The experts are widely split over the answer: critics deplore the basic budget deficits of the 1980s—deficits of unprecedented magnitude and persistence, averaging a colossal 3 percent plus of the nation's gross national product.[6] They note that the United States, which in 1980 was the world's largest creditor nation, became the world's largest debtor nation only three years later: "We have been selling the farm and the ship to foreigners, selling U.S. public debt, office buildings, and lately big-company common stocks and bonds, branch plant installations."[7] Of its top twenty trading partners in 1988, the United States had trade imbalances with seventeen—outselling only the Netherlands, Belgium, and Australia.

In physics, what goes up must come down; in economics, what goes down may keep going down. And the United States, say the critics, is definitely on the way down—a tragedy that has occurred because American managers have not faced the challenge but simply checked it through restructuring techniques that involved, more than anything else, the abrogation of the social contract that labor, management, and government had slowly but surely constructed over the past half century.[8] If true, the results are far-reaching; economic prospects for the average American will worsen. The current standard of living of American workers is already in serious trouble; debt of $2.6 trillion is mind-boggling.[9]

In an economy battered by debt, a first reaction might be to leave the logic of syllogism for the language of paradox, a belles lettres form particularly well suited to describe responses to difficult problems. Debt, for instance, was a favorite subject of Renaissance paradoxists largely because the landed gentry were having a beastly time with the new cash economy. Needed, perhaps, is a new band of paradoxists to show the illogic of logic—all of a standard epideictic type.

Paradox, however, is irrelevant to those who see the national canvas in brighter hues:[10] per capita real GNP has grown at an annual rate of 2 percent, its pattern since 1870; the country's unemployment rate of 5.7 percent should be compared to the 19 percent rate of Spain, currently western Europe's fastest-growing economy; the budget deficit is not a Keynesian policy deficit designed to spur consumption but a consequence of an unanticipated 1981–82 recession as well as a sudden collapse in inflation that wiped out $2.5 trillion of taxable gross national product during the 1981–86 period. In reality, budget deficits and imbalances in foreign trade are a blessing, according to Nobel economist Milton Friedman, who insists that trade deficits are signs of the economy's substantial improvements during the past six years. As growth companies borrow money, so do growth countries; to Friedman "the accounting counterpart of the current account deficit is the capital account surplus and the realistic question is to ask whether Americans would prefer to see capital lined along its borders trying to get in or lined up trying to get out."[11] Because foreigners have provided the United States with those real resources essential to increase output, employment, and productivity, the trade deficit is not a problem but has been a solution.[12]

What does the American canvas really show? And what do young entrants into the business world really face? "Confusion," responded Michael Blumenthal, UNYSIS CEO and former secretary of the Treasury in the Carter administration;[13] "relative decline" was Harvard historian Paul Kennedy's answer;[14] "disintegration," responded University of Maryland economist Mancur Olson.[15]

Entrants to the business world might conclude that they confront one of three options: doom and gloom, prosper and rejoice, or watch and wait. Of the three, the first is worst and, happily, the young are not like either the New England social reformer Theodore Parker (1810–1860) or the Russian communist leader Nikolai Bukharin (1888–1938). On his deathbed, the first said, "When I see the inevitable I fall in love with it."[16] And Bukharin, convicted of a crime of which his accuser, Stalin, knew he was innocent, wrote on the eve of his execution that only "vanity in the last remarks of pride came to me: Die in silence, say nothing, or die with a noble gesture, with a moving swan song on your lips; pour out your hearts and challenge your accusers. That would have been easier for an old rebel, but I overcame the temptation."[17] The Parker-Bukharin paradigm is outlandishly ill suited to the American temperament as a whole and much less to the young in particular.

But there are problems for the young; important as are the challenges, the attitudes of the young are equally so. If they and their mentors could be persuaded by Alfred North Whitehead's soaring rhetoric, then that ingrained optimism in the American character would be reawakened and, as a consequence, their imaginations fired. Here is what Whitehead wrote:

> [T]he intellectual adventure of analysis . . . must precede any successful reorganization. In a simpler world, business relations were simpler, being based on the immediate contact of man with man and on immediate confrontation with all relevant material circumstances. Today business organization requires an imaginative grasp of the psychologies of populations engaged in differing modes of occupations, of populations scattered through cities, through mountains, though plains; of populations on the ocean, and of populations in mines, and of populations in forests. It requires an imaginative grasp of conditions in the tropics, and of conditions in temperate zones. It requires an imaginative grasp of the interlocking interests of great organizations, and of the reactions of the whole complex to any change in one of its elements. It requires an imaginative understanding of laws of political economy, not merely in the abstract, but also with the power to construe them in terms of the particular circumstances of a concrete business. It requires some knowledge of the habits under diverse conditions. It requires an imaginative vision of the binding forces

of any human organization, a sympathetic vision of the limits of human nature and of the conditions which evoke loyalty of service. It requires some knowledge of the laws of health, and of the laws of fatigue, and of the conditions for sustained reliability. It requires an imaginative understanding of the social effects of the conditions of factories. It requires a sufficient conception of the role of applied science in modern society. It requires that discipline of character which can say "yes" and "no" to other men, not by reason of blind obstinacy, but with firmness derived from a conscious evaluation of relevant alternatives.

The universities have trained the intellectual pioneers of our civilization—the priests, the lawyers, the statesmen, the doctors, the men of science, and the men of letters. . . . The conduct of business now requires intellectual imagination of the same type as that which in former times has mainly passed into those other occupations; and the universities are the organizations which have supplied this type of mentality for the service of the progress of the European races.[18]

With an enthusiasm equal to Whitehead's, the sage of contemporary business scholars, Peter Drucker, wrote: "Rarely in human history has any institution emerged as fast as management or had as great an impact as quickly. In less than 150 years, management has transformed the social and economic fabric of the world's developed countries. It has created a global economy and set new rules for countries that would participate in that economy as equals. And it has itself been transformed."[19] Drucker went on to say that management and modern corporations could not exist without the knowledge base that developed societies have built: "But equally, it is management and management alone that makes all this knowledge and these knowledgeable people effective. The emergence of management has converted knowledge from a social ornament and luxury into what we now know to be the true capital of any economy."[20]

That the manager's knowledge, the true capital in Drucker's formulation, needs to have Whitehead's "imaginative grasp" is not an arguable proposition when new challenges have already come from Pacific Rim countries and the United States of Europe.[21] The adjective *global* is the word to be reckoned with.

A harbinger of things to come was the 1988 invitation by Harvard's business faculty to one hundred world-class managers "to discuss *worldbusiness* in Boston. . . . New business practices are penetrating international boundaries with increasing ease and speed, outdating many of the tactics of multinationalism, creating the need to make international business decisions with a view to world *oneness*."[22] *Oneness* touches our common humanity before it touches our common economy; *oneness* impinges more on what we think in common than the language used to convey it; *oneness* requires each of the parts to identify the role that its own culture may play in the totality. Such a conception of *oneness* can then deal with the plurality of values. In all of these things humanistic studies play a part: they invite us to consider, in ways that economics and political science do not, the totality of the human journey as defined for each person by four sets of encounters: the *individual* (the I), the *bilateral* (the I-Thou), the *communal* (the We), and the *sacral* (the We-Thou).[23] Classical economic theory (the self-interest maximizer) starts with the first, bargaining theory with the second, political science the third, and theology the fourth. But the humanities—philosophy, literature, and history—embrace all. It is, therefore, necessary to ask what priority, if any, the humanities hold in professional business education. The question, in turn, leads to consideration of current programs in business schools.

MALPRACTICES IN EDUCATION?

That the intellectual fare provided in typical institutions of higher learning is of poor quality is the thesis advanced by Allan Bloom, William Bennett, and others of their persuasion.[24] But psychologist Barry Schwartz and sociologist Amitai Etzioni have directed the fire of their ire against classical economics, a staple in business education.[25] The basic paradigm of economics is that individuals seek to maximize their material self-interest. When choices are made between good and goods, the latter invariably precedes the former. English-speaking theorists have found their inspiration in the writing of Adam Smith, David Ricardo, and John Stuart Mill.

But French economists have claimed—and with a large measure of truth—that their pathfinders—Condillac (1715–1780), Turgot (1727–1781), and Say (1767–1832)—were the first to see fully the revolutionary implications of the paradigm. Condillac's 1776 tract *La Commerce et le gouvernement considérés l'un relativement à l'autre* stated more briefly and more explicitly than Adam Smith's *Wealth of Nations* (which appeared in the same year) that there were large lessons to be learned from the economist's model: in business, individuals work to promote their own self-interests; in politics, interest groups work to advance their own causes; in international relations, countries use diplomacy and war to increase their powers. While Condillac may not have gone as far as his followers, he helped to establish a mindset that made the political corollaries to his basic thesis acceptable: self-interest was *the* ethic.

Before many caught the full flavor of the revolutionary nature of classical economics, a few continental thinkers (with little-known names like Henry Pesch and Goetz Briefs) sounded alarms.[26] They saw classical economics as a system designed to support capitalism that led to a logical and natural progression from individualism to vested interests to pluralism and, ultimately, to statism.[27] Were he alive today, Emerson would join Orwell in warnings against Big Brother.

Less clearly, perhaps, but no less realistically, Condillac's emphasis on self-seeking as a law of nature proved useful to evolutionary biologists. The theory, generally associated with Edward Wilson of Harvard, holds that humans are products of their genes.[28] More interesting is the work of Richard Dawkins, with his idea of the "blind watchmaker."[29] Writing with more force and passion than his famous predecessor, Dawkins said that the full significance of Darwinism had been too long delayed from being recognized, and that it was high time to redress its neglect because the theory of natural selection has overwhelming importance to the way societies are organized, the way individuals behave, and even the way people worship. Humans are to be seen for what they are, namely, the result of very, very long sequences of unplanned—but adaptive—changes. And while early evolutionary biologists tried, Condillacian-like, to dance around the problem of natural evolution and divine ordering, Dawkins said that party is over: God is not dead—He was never born! While it may seem farfetched to believe that the same blind forces that carved out mountains could produce the bat's radar, the hawk's eye, and the human mind, such simple processes in Dawkins's paradigm, in fact, did generate "prodigies of apparent miracles."

Flowing from the formal paradigms in economics and evolutionary biology, according to Dawkins, are consequences of no mean significance to liberal learning: group survival is more important than individual liberty; inexorable struggle determines the fittest; and an individual's worldly journey, while short, rocky, and complicated, moves in a predetermined, irreversible way. Implicit was a sharp criticism of "the humanist social science which never sought to explain how social rules come into existence, why rules are violated, or why unintended social consequences attend political decisions."[30] The pretensions, both petty and imperialistic, of some of our influential theorists, however, threaten a major theme of the humanities, namely, that people are rational *and* emotional, predictable *and* unpredictable, joy-giving *and* sorrow-bearing, fathomable *and* unfathomable. To ignore the connections is to miss what humans are and what the humanities are about.

Fear of missed connections may have prompted Lionel Trilling, shortly before his death in 1975, to write that in American society "there are few factors to be perceived, if any at all, which make it likely that within the next quarter-century there will be articulated in a convincing and effective way an educational ideal that has posi-

tive and significant connection with the humanistic educational traditions of the past."[31] The concern must now be rephrased into a new
question: Is there a chance today to introduce into management education *"significant connections with humanistic tradition"*? Our response
is a positive one: the times are propitious!

WINDS OF CHANGE

Of the many calls for curriculum reform in business, only two will
be noted. The selection is governed by an important reality, namely,
both come from very influential groups in the Western world: the
European Foundation for Management Development (EFMD) and
the American Assembly of Collegiate Schools of Business (AACSB).
The two joined forces in 1975 to issue a report that has been too
long neglected by educators. Especially pertinent to the humanities
are their observations regarding theories of self, society, and
thought.[32]

1. *Theory of Self.* Modern man has been profoundly influenced by Adam
   Smith's definition of the person as one primarily concerned with en-
   lightened self-interest. Without denying the importance of this view,
   however, . . . fulfillment of the self necessitates fulfillment by others—"anything done to diminish another diminishes me."
2. *Theory of Society.* Certain theories of society that gained ascendancy in
   the last three centuries were drawn from a view of society built on
   adversarial relations: businessmen relied on competition, politicians on
   partisan rivalries, lawyers on adversarial techniques. . . . While an adversarial society has provided substantial gains, it lacks elements that
   give cohesion to life.
3. *Theory of Thought.* It is a gross oversimplification to suggest that one
   man has defined the nature of the "modern mind". . . . If one dared
   to suggest a candidate, certainly high on the list would be René Des-
   cartes. . . . From the Cartesian revolution flowed swift (empirical)
   currents to carry forward man's understanding. . . . There is now a
   concern that a redress is in order and that matters not so readily measured or quantified are important: ambition, self-respect, creativity,
   community, compassion, sacrifice.

Of equal importance to the humanities is the very recent AACSB-
sponsored report. Of its six recommendations, three should be summarized.

1. Business schools should emphasize the importance of a broad education and avoid the specification of increased business course requirements and electives at the expense of opportunities for enrichment
   elsewhere in the university.

2. Business schools need to strike a better balance between the attention focused on the operational effectiveness of firms—the "internal" environment—and outside influences (governmental regulations, societal trends, legal climate, international developments and the like) by increasing their relative curriculum emphasis on the latter.

3. Business schools need to increase considerably the globalization of the curriculum, and the corporate community should apply pressure on business schools to incorporate a more thorough and rigorous global perspective in the education of students in all areas of the curriculum.[33]

The two reports raise issues related to the roles of liberal and professional education in business. Combining the two strikes some as "a significant departure" from the tradition of liberal learning, a departure that "bears careful scrutiny lest it transform liberal education's autonomous rationality into purely instrumental rationality."[34] Much earlier, Santayana issued the same warning when he said that "insofar as thought is instrumental, it is not worth having . . . except for its promise; it must terminate in something truly profitable and ultimate change, being good in itself, may lend value to all that led up to it. . . . Thought in no way is instrumental or servile; it is an experience realized, not a force to be used."[35]

Professional faculties are not likely to buy into this view, arguing that learning should prepare for doing. Perhaps participants in the debate have become overexercised by a dispute that, upon fresh examination, may be less serious than supposed. Large ideas lead to large, practical consequences.[36] Surely the meaning of liberal education could be expanded to include the view expressed long ago by an unidentified writer who said: "To each species of creations has been allotted a peculiar and instructive gift. Galloping comes naturally to horses and flying to birds. To man only is given the desire to learn"[37]—and, one might add, the desire to work. More to the point, if the assumption that classical education is independent of society's values is illusory—and it has been so argued[38]—then the real question is less about academic provinces and more about how the humanities can best be used to provide the imaginative grasp Whitehead correctly said was so necessary.[39] As the cooperative effort moves slowly, one can hope for a new Enlightenment to emerge from the colloquy between business and humanities faculties. Nevertheless, prudence suggests that if discussions are marked by excessive enthusiasm, a great moment in higher professional education may pass with lamentations for what might have been. So it is well to begin any initiative with an outsider's assessments of problems the humanities themselves pose.

THE HUMANITIES IN PROFESSIONAL EDUCATION: CAUTIONS AND PRECAUTIONS

What do the humanities offer? One answer has come from the American Council of Learned Societies, which has said that "the humanities are to remind us of, and to act as witnesses for, the American belief in the profound connection between education and democracy, between an alert mind and the exercise of civic virtue."[40] The purpose explains why the humanities continue to:

1. take with the utmost seriousness their responsibilities to the past and to include those who have hitherto remained on the margins of history: the powerless, the illiterate, the dispossessed;
2. encourage the free discussion of human values
3. protect and celebrate languages—verbal and visual, in poems and paintings, novels and films, and also in nonfiction writing and in artifacts. But protection and celebration do not mean inflexible affirmation of past structures; rather, they entail a rigorous self-consciousness about the structure and operations of languages as they change throughout history
4. investigate the way meaning is created, how we determine what is true or false, how we interpret and define "reality"
5. encourage and investigate the uses of the imagination in its creation of alternative worlds through language and the arts.[41]

To declare goals is not the same as to meet them. If, therefore, the goal of those who favor an infusion of more humanities into the business curriculum is to be reached, three problems must be addressed: (1) the problem of contemporaneity, (2) the problem of complexity, and (3) the problem of compatibility. An impressionistic look at each illumines the larger issue of the humanities' relevance to management.

The Problem of Contemporaneity

As used here, contemporaneity relates to the quantity of books and tracts now flooding the reading public. In times past, Jefferson profited from a well-stocked library, but Lincoln could prepare himself for leadership by reading a few canonical texts such as the Bible and Shakespeare's plays. In Elizabethan times, the "riffraff" joined the elite at Shakespearean productions and, in later centuries equally diverse American audiences crowded theaters in large cities. For example, in the first quarter of the nineteenth century Philadelphians were able to see twenty-one of Shakespeare's thirty-seven plays—and Shakespeare was welcomed because no one told people that he was good for them.[42]

Today the presses pump and pump. Students and their mentors are so overwhelmed by sheer numbers of books that the prince of pessimism, Arthur Schopenhauer, would have applauded critic Bruce Bawer's denunciation of today's trend-happy publishing industry.[43] Schopenhauer himself wrote:

> [I]n looking over a huge catalogue of new books, one might weep at thinking that, when ten years have passed, not one of them will be heard of. . . . Nine-tenths of the whole of our present literature has no other aim than to get a few shillings out of the pockets of the public; and to this end author, publisher, and reviewer are in league. . . . [T]hey have succeeded in getting the whole of the world of fashion . . . all trained to read in time, and all the same thing, viz., *the newest books;* and that for the purpose of getting food for conversation in the circles in which they move. . . . Hence, in regard to reading, it is a very important thing to be able to refrain. . . . [L]imit your time for reading, and devote it exclusively to the works of those great minds of all times and countries, who o'ertop the rest of humanity, those whom the voice of fame points to as such. These alone really educate and instruct.[44]

If, in reading, it is "important to refrain," it becomes even more important to know what to contain. Precisely at this point a new problem appears. Assuming Schopenhauer is half-right, those who press for more humanities in management education face a formidable challenge: agreeing not only on what is permanent and what is ephemeral but on what of the permanent is most likely to contribute to the preparation of political and business leaders.[45] This calls attention to the importance of unifying themes. In the 1930s Robert Maynard Hutchins asserted that the "study of truth for its own sake is not precise enough to hold a university together. Real unity can be achieved only by an ordering which shows us which are fundamental and which subsidiary, which significant and which is not."[46] The unifying principle for the Greeks was philosophy; for medieval universities it was theology (God's philosophy of perilous optimism). Are we at the point where liberal education can be so defined that it more meaningfully contributes to enlargement of the moral imagination of managers? Would Schopenhauer's maxim *"know the great minds* of liberal learning" provide the starting point?

The Problem of Complexity

One place to begin is with a review of the current state of certain fields within the humanities that have particular potential for management education: political theory, history, and literature. The first is chosen because, while it deals with the goals, methods, and leadership qualities appropriate to large public organizations, it provides useful instruction on the goals, methods, and leadership qualities of large private organization.[47] History is chosen for its importance in instructing managers how business corporations influenced—and were influenced by—the larger society. Literature rounds out the picture because it contributes to those special managerial skills acquired less through inquiry than through moral imagination.[48]

Political Theory. The range of one political philosopher's influence is suggested by the experience of English social theorist L. T. Hobhouse. Recalling a summer day in 1917 when he was in the garden reading Hegel and German zeppelins bombed London, Hobhouse wrote: "In the bombing of London I had just witnessed the visible and tangible outcome of a false and wicked doctrine, the foundations of which lay, as I believe, in the book before me."[49] Before 1914 Hegel was the great expositor of metaphysics; after 1918 he and the field itself were jettisoned as useless intellectual baggage. Not only Hegel but a host of political philosophers (from Plato and Aristotle to Aquinas and Bellarmine and on down to the archdemon Hegel) were denounced. People like Karl Popper and Bertrand Russell led the assault because they firmly believed that in old traditions were found the enemies of all open, tolerant, diverse, and pluralistically democratic societies.[50] Now a point of curiosity to humanists is a theme found so often among the revisionists: *whatever is not science is nonsense.* Emigrés from a European group known as the Vienna Circle taught eager American students that judgments reached in ethics, aesthetics, and theology were puny expressions of overheated emotions.[51] Coming under particularly heavy attack were political philosophers as different as Thomas Hobbes and John Locke because they saw in the state an organization necessary to protect private property and other institutions of a civilized community. To those of Popperian leanings, democracy was to be explored not through ambiguous principles such as "consent of the governed" but through the answer to a practical problem: Can the government be gotten rid of without bloodshed?[52] High priests of the new approach were popular figures like the American journalist Walter Lippman and the British writer Harold Laski, whose popularity attested to the hold of the positivists on the American mind. Their message was simple: facts and values live in two separate and unequal houses; seek the "grammar of science," not the rhetoric of philosophy.

The message to higher education was important: restrain and restrict the study of political philosophy while concentrating on the quantitative development and study of empirically derived data. Traditional studies in ethics were banished; quantitative analyses replaced qualitative speculation; voter reactions were more important than political reflection. The sad part of the story is that what philosophers lacked in the past, namely, rigorous empirical study, should have been met not by complementarity but by conquest.[53]

The power of Karl Popper is still seen in the works of scholars such as Josef Schumpeter, Edward Shils, Daniel Bell, and Seymour Martin Lipset. Those outside the new tradition were philosophical systematizers like Yves Simon, Daniel Aron, and Bertrand de Jouvenel, who saw the value element in politics as critical to the resolution of the age-old conflict between public authority and private liberty. Simon, for example, after joining the faculty of the University of Chicago, produced a series of books that advanced an old Aristotelean premise that civil society is natural to man and not the necessary evil outlined by the new class of theorists.[54] The rise of the antistate ideology that Yves Simon and Raymond Aaron detected was perceived by only a few novelists—and the one who did perceive it, George Orwell, was pilloried by editors and publishers from both the left and the right.[55]

Lest the point in this treatment of political theory be lost, it is necessary to cite two examples of a positivistic approach to the study of politics and business. The first was the old but enormously popular text on American government by Frederick Ogg and Orman Ray, a text replete with description of government agencies, congressional enactments, and court rulings but unconcerned with the philosophical ideas that gave meaning to the American experiment.[56] Minimal use was made of the themes from Hobbes or Locke, the philosophical differences between Jefferson and Adams, the influence of Montesquieu, or the moral overtones of the Lincoln-Douglas debates. Ogg and Ray told students about government "like it is," while withholding views on what made the "is" possible. A second example comes from some texts on business and government: lobbying is described, PACS are paraded, regulations detailed, Supreme Court decisions recounted, and so on. But one often looks in vain for any sort of philosophical and historical explanations for the existence of these phenomena. If political science needs political philosophy and if management needs some formal grounding in political theory, who among the political theorists can entice business faculties to dance at lease one waltz to a humanities tune? Is choice even necessary? And if it is, who will choose whom?

History.   Historians rightly complain about the present sad state of affairs, in which reading about the past seems a lost art. But what the guild itself is doing to provide a synthetic view of world development merits a few observations. To meet Clio is to grapple for her meanings: history can mean concern for the past, records of that past, narratives on the past, methodologies for uncovering the past, the uses to which history may be put. Does "what was" have relevance to "what is" and "what may be"?

Managers, like others in power, cannot be without history, even though they are often confused about what to do with it. Yet what inspires the historian inspires the authentic manager, namely, an almost mystical interest in those who have gone before and in those who have built what we now use and a sense that the legacy should be used responsibly for present and future generations. History was a cri de coeur to Jefferson and to Madison and, except for the Germans, few have used history more than Americans to romanticize the past. Names like Pocohantas and Betsy Ross, Mad Anthony Wayne and Benedict Arnold, Washington and Lincoln, Daniel Boone and Robert E. Lee evoke great dramas played out by a great people.

History has been popular among leaders because it can be used extravagantly to give Americans a sense of destiny. Like the Bayeux tapestry, the American fabric has to be something meaningful. Now a question: Are American historians providing the public with well-written popular histories that provide coherent pictures of the American past? The answer is not encouraging. Spurred by the rise of great historical journals, historians have turned more and more to specialized fields and in the process have neglected the traditions of those who wrote beautifully crafted narrative histories of a country's growth.[57] Specialists write for specialists; historians read other historians. The great masters who sought to weave monumental tapestries of great meaning—Macaulay for England, Ranke for Germany, Bancroft for America—have not been replaced. And when professionals study the "old boys," they do so historiographically, that is, to understand what methods their famous predecessors used, what philosophies they espoused, and what sources they unearthed.

But nonprofessionals read history for quite different reasons. They want to know in rather straightforward ways what Washington, Jefferson, and Lincoln did, why the Civil War was fought, what its consequences were, why management in the twentieth century subscribed to Social Darwinism, why unions were feared by the public, what precipitated the New and Fair Deals, why antitrust laws have caused endless debate, why big business was feared by most Americans. Rich detail is provided for relatively small events, while the larger drama seems to be neglected.[58] There are, of course, splendid stories of particular individuals and firms, but not the kind that would lead students to see both the good and the evil of the market system or the virtue and the wickedness of those who established it.[59] In thinking of history as one of the humanities essential to management education, curriculum architects may face formidable problems.

Literature. Literature presents a quite different picture. Stated in oversimplified terms, if great historical narratives are not being written by historians for students to read, great classics in literature are not being read by today's students, if, indeed, they ever were. The reasons for the neglect are twofold: electronics and literary criticism. Since immediate specifications do not convey the full story, it is helpful to recall the evolution of literature as a distinct academic field in higher education.[60] Although literature was used as a vehicle for instruction in ancient times, it came to the United States only in the late nineteenth century, when universities began to organize the study of literature in a separate department. In preacademic times great books were meant to be enjoyed; now they were meant to be analyzed. The first tradition was associated with Matthew Arnold; the second, scientific component was built on research and has so many children no one knows who the father of the family really is. Tensions between the Arnoldians and the Scientificists were minimized through the age-old trick of "field coverage," which allowed each professor "to do his or her thing." Innovations would be accepted without critical evaluation through the simple device of adding another professor to the department. If intellectual volcanoes seethed between generalists and specialist, between literary scholar and literary critic, outsiders rarely knew.

What is so fascinating about the story of university-based literature departments is that they are microcosms of American universities in general. Institutions of higher learning are built not on a logocentric base but on what is known in literary criticism as a deconstructionist model. The result has been a proliferation of technical "vocabularies that no one can reduce to the common measure of any metalanguage."[61] It is, as a consequence, easy to speak of the humanities as if there is a common understanding of what the word means. What is known of literature is that it is a Gutenberg institution centered on the printed book and dependent on skills in reading and writing. Consequently, what becomes the medium, what affects the reading skills, and what attitudes readers have toward writers have important consequences.

So far as electronics is concerned, it is known that it is "knocking the legs out from under Gutenberg literature," resulting in increasing amounts of illiteracy and television watching.[62] Technology has shaken postindustrial societies to their roots.[63] Members of the general public may not know the degree to which they subscribe to the old Chinese maxim that one picture is worth a thousand words, but they honor it in their daily lives: reading is subordinated to viewing; instantaneous impressions replace incrementally-arrived-at judgments; the screen's momentary flash becomes the mind's sole picture—a picture followed by a two-minute oral commentary, and then on to the next major event. Lost is an important interplay between writer and reader.[64]

Another factor in the neglect of literature is the influence, rising over the past half century, of the literary critic. In 1939 editor John Crowe Ransom used the first issue of *The Kenyon Review* to point out how the age of criticism was taking over: "The living art decays," he wrote, "but the love of it quickens." While the conclusion flowing from the premise is arguable, some do contend that criticisms of Dante and Shakespeare, Goethe and Tolstoy are widely read but that the works themselves gather dust on library shelves.[65] It is, aver the traditionalists, a world indifferent to the classical studies that scholars, from the seventeenth century on, have used to understand not only the texts themselves but the world in which they were written. One traditionalist, Edward Gibbons, lamenting the decline of classical studies in his *Essai sur l'étude de la littérature*, might today never be accepted into the upper reaches of literary scholarship.

Because of its current importance, New Criticism has received attention. It has been generally assumed that relationships between reader and writer were established by the ability of the former to participate meaningfully in the thoughts of the latter. But the New Critics insist that language is a sign system that never corresponds to what the author is trying to convey. The meaning of a literary work, if it exists at all, is found in the rules of language[66]—in linguistic analysis of the kind expressed by Saussure, Derrida, Lévi-Strauss, and Barthes.

The power of New Criticism is not restricted to literature alone. Managers' decisions are profoundly influenced by judges' decisions, and how jurists reason toward their conclusions is important. It may come as a surprise to hear Frank Easterbrook, a federal judge and the editor of a scholarly journal, say that important cases are being decided not by constitutional interpretation but by the canons of literary criticism.[67] Understanding the decision-making process requires comparing the nine Supreme Court Justices to nine chairpersons of English literature departments serving as a board of literary arbiters. According to Easterbrook,

The board would decide by majority vote which interpretations were acceptable. These would be taught everywhere, and any practitioner of literature who disagreed with the decision would be jailed. If a majority concluded that John Bunyan's *Pilgrim's Progress* was really about Buddhism or priestly homosexuality, or that *Moby Dick* was about the environmental problems of whaling (from whales' perspective), this would become dogma.[68]

Yet, insists Easterbrook, this is how judges act and how leading legal scholars like Ronald Dworkin think.[69]

This analysis is restricted to what the literary critics themselves say of their own field and what their pronouncements mean to the humanities-management nexus in education. Two schools of literary criticism tend to dominate literature departments in the country's major universities. One, called deconstructionism, aims to expose contradictions in the written text; if successful, deconstructionists conclude that the text has no meaning. The second, New Criticism, avers that it is the reader, not the writer, who gives meaning to the text. Two writers who illustrate the general views of New Criticism are Jacques Derrida and Harold Bloom. Although neither provides easily isolated sample themes, both seem eager to purge romanticism from every vestige of German idealism.

Derrida thinks that any attempt to identify the self with something greater—nation or church, humanity or God—is a wasted effort.[70] Common sense tells us to stop theorizing about what others say and begin fantasizing, as he does (with heavily erotic overtones), about what can be done by the reader's free associations to the writers' works. Any attempt to devise a theory that seeks to reconcile the individual's private and public worlds is doomed.[71] The new orthodoxy's first article of faith is that poetry conveys a truth of its own, a truth instinctively grasped by poets themselves and "graspable" only in terms unique to the reader.[72] One thing about which Derrida is certain is that texts will always be reconceptualized by the reader's own experiences.

Equally renowned is Harold Bloom, whose book captures in its very title so much of the spirit of New Criticism: *Ruin the Sacred Truths.*[73] Bloom's message is that great literature is good when it is independent of beliefs and great when it triumphs over beliefs. He reads the Torah as man's literature, not as God's word, and the Bible as precursor to Shakespeare and Freud. Poets who assimilate unto themselves the past "greats" of literature will surpass them to become the high priests, the self-reliant creatures that Emerson, whom he greatly admires, extolled. Words are used pragmatically to get things done, not to raise questions about ultimate destinies or ultimate meanings. Good poets, therefore, are children of no creed, no cult, no party. Yet their words are constant reminders of the enormous strength each cultivated person possesses within the self. The creed is neoromanticism; the present takes shape in the past; the word is not flesh but spirit, and the spirit is to be understood in

Freudian terms; there are no right readings, only weak misreadings and strong misreadings.

Not all subscribe to the new dogma. Bloom and his like-minded colleagues have been described as exemplars of a new "trahison des clercs" in their alleged pandering to the quick, the subjective, and the expedient. Nathan Scott of Virginia said: "For the new theorists, whether they march under the banners of the late Roland Barthes or Jacques Derrida or Stanley Fish or J. Hillis Miller or Harold Bloom, are bent on convincing us that, prior to the enlightenment which they bring, all reading was misguided and illusionary—what the New People are concerned above all else to do is to 'de-mean' meaning itself."[74]

What is to be made of all this in terms of relevance to management education? There is, on one hand, a sense that a new Tower of Babel is being constructed by the deconstructionists; when the units of intelligibility conveyed in speech have no independent being, when words have no power to reveal things as they truly are, then speech becomes only self-referential and, finally, unintelligible.[75] There is today a certain restiveness that literature—as well as the other creative arts—has become unhinged and that, as the Cambridge-based critic George Steiner has written:

> [T]here is something to the widespread sentiment that ordinary men and women in their daily existence can no longer draw from the great springs of the imagination on the strengths, the delights, the bracing hopes they once did. Paintings are opaque scrawls; sculptures seem to be lumps of ugly matter; music banishes melody. Modern writing is often autistically demanding.[76]

The fact remains that literature has an almost unrivaled power to contribute to that "imaginative group" that Whitehead perceptively noted was essential to effective management of complex organizations in a complex world.

The Problem of Compatibility

Suppose a few brave souls on business and humanities faculties agree on what can be done to incorporate the humanities into business education. How will the "fit" between humanistic and professional education be perceived by those whose decision is vital to the whole enterprise—the business faculties and the corporate archons?

The first group is likely to be cautious, the second ambivalent. Business faculties rightly perceive themselves as assigned to prepare profession-oriented students. And their students, quick-marched through a demanding two-year graduate program, simply have no time for what they perceive as "luxuries." Furthermore, specialists in each of the functional areas can show convincingly that their respective fields—accounting, marketing, production, and finance—are changing so rapidly that merely keeping current is a never-ceasing challenge. Penetrating the current business program with meaningful doses of the humanities appears to be quixotic. No business school shows any serious inclination to add another semester or two to the current M.B.A. program, which might make the experiment possible. And there is also the nagging fact that liberal arts faculties still have their own problems, even at the undergraduate level where, presumably, they can make their greatest impact. A case in point is the report by a University of Pennsylvania professor, Robert Zemsky. After studying twenty-five thousand student transcripts at thirty colleges, Zemsky concluded that liberal arts curricula are unstructured, fragmented, lacking in depth in the humanities, and almost totally lacking in the natural sciences and mathematics.[77] Even the cultural studies programs (an amalgam of literature, history, anthropology, and media studies), which provide a possible base for enrichment of management education, have been accused of leftist leanings. Given the fragmentation in liberal arts and a perceived official ideology in the one area that offers some promise, the logistics of cooperation will be difficult to develop.

Corporate managers tend to be ambivalent about including the humanities in management education. On the one hand, they have supported humanities programs at institutions such as Dartmouth and the University of Pennsylvania;[78] on the other hand, managers often see poets and playwrights as sharpshooters ready to riddle the first business head to appear above the trenches. *Death of a Salesman* invariably surfaces as the typical example. If this overgeneralization is not enough, business managers often employ overextension—the identification of humanists (particularly novelists and dramatists) with the media—and the media are bad news. For example, Ted Smith III, professor of communications at Virginia Commonwealth University used Vanderbilt University archives to examine the content of nearly fourteen thousand new programs on ABC, CBS, and NBC that dealt with business conditions. Smith reported that when the business performance improved, the news coverage declined: "*In every relevant instance, and regardless of the character of events, stories reporting economic losses or failures outnumbered stories reporting economic gains or successes by substantial, and usually overwhelming, margins.*" News coverage was drastically lopsided and thus distorted. "To be blunt," Smith added, "systematic suppressions of positive information, economic or otherwise, is nothing less than systematic censorship. As such, it strikes at the foundations of the democratic process."[79] The head of the national Chamber of Commerce once wryly noted: "If

Thomas Edison were to invent the light bulb today, the CBS Evening News would lead off with Dan Rather somberly announcing that disaster has just struck the candlestick industry."[80] Adding to the problem is a new wrinkle that casts professors in the role of villain. The argument is that professors are grossly overpaid and grotesquely underworked, that they neglect students to engage in meaningless research, use academic freedom and tenure to defend intolerable behavior, and employ the language of "profspeak" to edify themselves and confound everyone else.[81]

To summarize, to inventory a few fields in the humanities is to encounter some formidable obstacles in incorporating them into a business curriculum. Influential political scientists insist that their field is a science where the nonsense element is value analysis that only gets in the way of understanding; drawn to specialized research, historians write for other historians; influential literary critics deemphasize what the classic texts say and emphasize what they make of them. Yet, for reasons that have been offered, managers of the future need the humanities.

The question then becomes how that need can best be met. Based on an outsider's perception of the current state of the humanities, one reasonable inference is that business faculties should themselves take the lead in deciding the what, when, and how of humanistic education appropriate to the preparation for a demanding career. It is useful to recall Robert Hutchins's words that an "ordering" of subject matter is the first step.[82] Given the deconstructionist organization of American universities, such reordering can best be furthered by constructing unifying themes and selecting courses through which the themes are addressed. In a leap-before-look mood, the writer undertakes a first tentative effort.

CURRICULUM BUILDING: FULTON'S FOLLY RELIVED?

Apposite is the tale of a traveler who stopped at a countryside pub to ask directions to Dublin. The tavernowner, startled by the question, answered simply: "Well, if I were going to Dublin I wouldn't start here."[83] More relevant is the experience of the Pennsylvanian Robert Fulton. Skeptics became enthusiasts when Fulton's steamboat, the *Clermont,* moved slowly upstream against the Hudson River current. No doubt similar skepticism marks any effort to generate steam for a run against the intellectual currents. Nevertheless, all one has to do is recognize the power of such themes as truth or justice or leadership to know that the energy is there. Needed only is synergy.

Unifying Themes

Consider the theme of truth. What does truth mean to a system that daily faces issues involving disclosure, misleading advertising, truth in packaging, intelligence gathering, and the like? A marvelous starting point in literature is Huck Finn at the point when he was trying to help the slave Jim escape from his owner. Huck's will wavered as he pondered the risk. As his boat neared shore and the lights of Cairo were visible, Huck heard Jim singing with joy, unaware that Huck intended to turn him in. And then came the heart-pumping passage when Jim called after Huck, who was paddling off in the boat:

> "Dah you goes, de ole true Huck; de on'y white genlman dat ever kep' his promise to ole Jim."
>
> Well, I just felt sick. But I says, I *got* to do it—I can't get *out* of it. Right then, along comes a skiff with two men in it, with guns, and they stopped and I stopped. One of them says:
>
> "What's that, yonder?"
>
> "A piece of a raft," I says.
>
> "Do you belong on it?"
>
> "Yes, sir."
>
> "Any men on it?"
>
> "Only one, sir."
>
> "Well, there's five niggers run off tonight, up yonder above the head of the bend. Is your man white or black?"
>
> I didn't answer up prompt. I tried to, but the words wouldn't come. I tried, for a second or two, to brace up and out with it, but I warn't man enough—hadn't the spunk of a rabbit. I see I was weakening; so I just give up trying, and up and says—
>
> "He's white."[84]

Relevance of truth? Of course! When Congress, to take one example, cannot define a merger or when a Supreme Court decision confuses executives on the timing of disclosure information pertinent to merger talks, there is a Huck Finn temptation either to talk too openly or to conceal too completely.

Other unifying themes are liberty, leadership, revenge, equality, and justice. Although in the light of this nation's tradition it is likely that Americans will use liberty or leadership as the binding cord, more pressing—because of domestic demands by women, blacks, Chicanos, and Native Americans—is justice. It has been said that in the whole of Western philosophy justice consists of little more than a series of footnotes to Plato, and that Aristotle wrote most of them.[85] The two Athenians' texts and notes are worth exploring.

Even more comprehensive than justice is equity, a term that encompasses fairness, equality, compassion, legal and moral judgment, and resource allocation. The particular value of equity as a unifying theme lies not only in its comprehensiveness but in its reminder that institutionalized law often falls short of justice and that the moral manager must be prepared to address the shortcomings. In this instance, the insurance clerk-turned-novelist Franz Kafka wrote a book, *The Trial*, which has been more widely read than any of Justice Holmes's notable court decisions, the standard fare in economics, marketing, finance, and legal environment courses.

Once unifying themes have been established, it is necessary to see what course could comfortably encompass them. What follows is only a suggestion—meaning that this curricular *Clermont* is unfinished. Nevertheless, it may be ready for a trial run.

Humanities Courses and Business

Explorations in Comparative Jurisprudence
Management Classics
Managers in the Mirror of Religion
Managers in the Mirror of Literature
Social and Intellectual History of the West
Social and Intellectual History of Selected Nonwestern Regions
Political, Economic, and Business History of the United States
Biographies and Autobiographies of American Business Leaders
Integrating Seminar

A comment on the first two may provide a sense of how unifying themes could be used.

Explorations in Comparative Jurisprudence. It is important to note immediately the priority accorded to the word "exploration": the journey's end is not known. Justification for study of comparative legal environments comes from awareness that the globalization of the economy is better understood by those who have some grasp of the legal cultures in which the different national economies operate.[86] Analysis of legal cultures may, for example, take as a paradigm the evolution of American law from a pre-Civil War "age of discovery" about English law to an original and vigorous assertion of how the court system should work. In *Swift* v. *Tyson* (1842), Justice Joseph Story asked the critical jurisdictional question: Are federal courts bound by decisions of state courts?[87] His answer was no. Story's opinion was enthusiastically accepted, and federal judicial opinions became the law of the land. There is now concern that the judicial reach has moved from Chief Justice John Marshall's 1803 *Marbury* v. *Madison* decision establishing judicial review to the decision in *Cooper* v. *Aaron* (1958), which held that judges determine what the law was intended—or should have been intended—to say and that all are bound by the court's opinion whether or not they were party to the litigation.[88]

It is time to speculate about the potential revolutionary implications for the global economy—and for the entire world—if international tribunals were to move along paths similar to the ones marked by American federal courts. Would nations become states with equal standing before an international court of justice? Would the new judicial system eventually tame naked power politics and restrain recourse to military solutions? Would an international court have a new Marshall or a new Story to extend the judicial reach to new, possibly unacceptable, lengths? Our inability to answer these questions does not mean futility.

If efforts to provide a paradigm in the history of American law prove inadequate, the architects of a new course in comparative jurisprudence might find a unifying theme in *The Cheyenne Way*, wherein was advanced the thesis that identifiable legal attributes and functions are common to all systems:[89] churches, universities, corporations—even the Mafia.[90] Every entity has goals, a value matrix, an authority structure, an enculturation process, and a disciplinary system. Analysis of organizations in subcultures might prove worthy of inclusion among the humanities.

A third theme might be revenge. Former Chicago law professor and later federal judge Richard Posner used revenge as a unifying theme to critique masterpieces such as Homer's *Iliad* and Shakespeare's *Hamlet*. The critique showed the inadequacies of social systems based on revenge; the Hatfields and McCoys just kept shooting, never solving. As a matter of fact, Homer's epic story of Troy might be profitably reexplained. Usually seen as an epic of peace (even though Achilles turned a deaf ear to Priam's plea for mercy), the *Iliad* was seen by Simone Weil as an epic poem of force.[91] Other instances of revenge are seen in *The Merchant of Venice* and *Measure for Measure* which, incidentally, also call attention to the tension between the law's explicit rules of justice and morality's less explicit canons of equity.[92]

Reflection on the works just mentioned shows this writer's unconscious parochialism, even arrogance. Instead of asking only what Americans can give, we might also ask what we can learn from the jurisprudential concepts of others—the Swiss or German interpretations of private property or the duties of citizenship, the Japanese idea of social harmony, the English view of the court's powers, the canon law of the Roman Catholic Church,[93] decisions by the World Court, or international arbitration awards. Who knows where the exploration into comparative jurisprudence may take us?

A new chapter remains to be written on how each nation's rights in the world—like each state's rights in America—can be preserved and reconciled with the local needs and the rights of others. Perhaps a new Langdell will appear in the Far East to prescribe how law should be taught, a new Holmes in the Mideast to tell what law should mean, a new Story in Africa to define relationships between national and international systems.[94] All this is to repeat a theme, namely, that the world economy needs a new common law to serve a common humanity.

Management Classics. Drucker's previously noted proposition that management is a child born two centuries ago cannot be taken to mean that thinking about management is something novel. The Greeks had thought about managing their city states; Alexander managed eighty thousand soldiers who conquered an area twice the size of Europe; Caesar Augustus was a management genius who maintained for nearly a century control of most of the Mediterranean, continental Europe, and the British Isles; the British themselves managed an empire over which, it was said, "the sun never sets."

In these large organizations theorists have appeared—Plato and Aristotle, Aquinas and Bellarmine, Hobbes and Locke. Machiavelli, for example, is remembered only for *The Prince,* and not for his essay on Livy, where he offered a more enduring message: organizational stability comes only when there is virtue in the leaders, integrity in the followers, and reason for the organization's existence. It can only be imagined what ambitions are enkindled by Machiavelli's *Prince* and what sobriety is encouraged by his essays on Livy. If leaders were Machiavellian in the higher meaning of the word, there would be less need for regulators, fewer sleazy maneuvers by inside traders, and less damage to the public's trust in economic institutions.

Clearly, city states are no longer dominant organizations. Modern multinational corporations are; they have more resources—human and financial—than most nations. Import theorists have appeared to explain them—Fayol in France, Weber in Germany, Follet in England, Barnard in the United States. The list of classical management writers, while extensive, is, happily, not exhaustive. Also worth noting is the fact that these classics are in the tradition of the humanities, and many have been written by people who themselves have been managers.[95]

If this ambitious vision (or variations thereon) of the relevance of the humanities to management education is taken seriously, three other questions arise: (1) When should managers begin the program? (2) What resources are available? (3) How should it be administered? I hope to start a discussion on these points by offering a comment or two that may engage—or enrage—others.

Timing

Under present circumstances, it is unrealistic to believe that business schools will expand their curricula substantially. More humble expectations, however, may be a disguised blessing. Studies in humanities related to management could begin ten—no later than fifteen—years after the M.B.A. has been granted. At this stage in a person's career the initial emphasis on managerial skills has become modified by a new emphasis on managerial art. And art forms are more appropriately achieved at later levels of career development. Students would set their own pace, but some time limits would be imposed for completion of the work. Examination on demand (EOD) would be available to test competency on substantial portions of each course. Networking could be encouraged by the sponsors so that students could exchange views with fellow students in their own areas.

Resources

If a small fraction of *Fortune* 500 companies would pledge to become involved in practical forms of support (through grants for curriculum development and faculty retraining) and to provide financial support for their more promising managers, a great leap forward would already have been recorded. After all, business itself has the most to gain. And with corporate commitment could come foundation commitment. In 1959 the Ford and the Carnegie foundations helped to revolutionize the business curriculum, and they just might do it again.

Structure

The delivery systems might combine short but intensive residency programs and "distance learning" (off-campus study), an area where technology is already being used quite productively. The sponsoring institution might be a single university, a consortium of universities, or an academy of scholars working outside the mainstream. Given American hunger for credentials, a diploma in humanities and management (DHM) might be awarded. The credential-granting institution could be the sponsor or, as in Great Britain, a national body that does not prescribe the curriculum but that permits institutions to award the diploma according to agreed-upon criteria.[96] The point is that not only can innovative programs be conceived—they have already been born.

CONCLUDING NOTE

Bringing a long survey to a merciful end results, not surprisingly, in mixed reactions. It has been the thesis of this essay that, while providing humanities programs in management education is difficult, the necessity of doing so admits no excuses for failure. The reexamination—as far as we are concerned—leads to the following conclusions:

- Broad education helps to provide the "imaginative grasp" needed by responsible leaders in worldwide business.[97]
- While humanities are a necessary component in professional education, they are marked by their own confusions.
- The first order of business, therefore, is to select unifying themes for courses through which the themes can be exposed.
- Instruction in the humanities is most fruitful after individuals have reached midmanagement levels.
- Whatever delivery system is selected can take advantage of innovative schemes and technologies already introduced in traditional and nontraditional education.
- Multiple approaches to sponsorship of such programs (single university, consortia, independent institute) should be explored.[98]

Exposure to the humanities can help managers maintain a healthy respect for the connections between practical skills and personal values, for what the job entails and what life demands. For everyone, the important question was asked by a character in an Ibsen play:

> *Peer Gynt:* "Who are you?"
> *Voice:* "Myself—Can you say as much?"[99]

If managers have learned to say as much, then, for some lucky people, some professors will have turned office lights into north stars!

NOTES

1. Gerald Graff, *Professing Literature: An Institutional History* (Chicago: University of Chicago Press, 1987), p. 175.

2. Kent Emery, Jr., "Reading the World Rightly and Squarely: Bonaventure's Doctrine of the Cardinal Virtues," *Tradition: Studies in Ancient and Medieval History, Thought and Religion* 39 (1983): 183–218.

3. A. A. Berle, Jr., and Gardiner Means, *The Modern Corporation and Private Property* (New York: Macmillan, 1932).

4. Joseph Schumpeter, *Democracy, Capitalism, and Socialism* (New York: Harper and Row, 1942). See also Clarence C. Walton, "Schumpeter: The Absent Presence," in Richard De George, ed., *The Humanities in Business Education* (Manhattan: University of Kansas School of Business, 1983).

5. Confrontation with seemingly undying organizations is not a new experience in the West. Before 1789 the French revolutionaries were devising ways to expropriate the holdings of an undying organization called the Church. Henry VIII had set a good example much earlier when he "nationalized" monastic properties.

6. A "basic" deficit is different from a Keynsian-type "cyclical" deficit in that after the nation returns to full employment, the basic deficit persists at a level that makes the public debt rise as a percentage of GNP—something not seen in the times of Truman, Kennedy, Johnson, Nixon, Ford, or Carter.

7. Paul A. Samuleson, "Economics and the Oval Office: Advice to the New President and Other CEOs," *Harvard Business Review* 66 (November–December 1988): 65–75. In his latest book, James Fallows proposes that Americans return to the individualism in American culture that helped America become the world's economic leader in the first place. Fallows, *More Like Us: Making America Great Again* (New York: Houghton Mifflin, 1988), chap. 1.

8. Barry Bluestone and Bennett Harrison, *The Great U-Turn: Corporate Restructuring and the Polarizing of America* (New York: Basic Books, 1988), p. 7.

9. *Final Report of the Seventy-Fifth American Assembly,* Columbia University, New York, November 17–20, 1988, p. 6. Note that the Assembly called the federal deficit an urgent problem, not a looming disaster.

10. Albert Wohlstetler, "Morning of Prosperity in America," *Wall Street Journal,* November 3, 1988, p. A18.

11. Milton Friedman, "Why the Twin Deficits Are a Nation's Blessing," *Wall Street Journal,* November 3, 1988, p. A18. A similar position had been taken by Edward Yardeni, "Good Times Abound for America," *New York Times,* November 13, 1988, p. 2F.

12. Since commencement of America's trade deficit in the first quarter of 1983, the United States has created more than fifteen million jobs net. Its foreign deficit has not cost jobs but instead has provided the resources to facilitate the labor force's surge toward full employment.

13. W. Michael Blumenthal, "The World Economy and Technology Change," *Foreign Affairs* 66, no. 3 (1988): 529–50.

14. C. Paul Kennedy, *The Rise and Fall of Great Powers: Economic Change and Military Conflict from 1500 to 2000* (New York: Random House, 1987), p. 515. There has been considerable misreading of Kennedy's thesis. He spoke only of *relative* decline—nothing like the earlier experiences of Spain and

the Netherlands (p. 533). See also Aaron J. Frickberg, *The Weary Titan: Britain and the Experience of Relative Riches, 1895–1905* (Princeton, N.J.: Princeton University Press, 1989).

15. Mancur Olson has written that the ability of selfish interest groups to manipulate the government for their own ends is a phenomenon to be feared (*The Rise and Decline of Nations* [New Haven, Conn.: Yale University Press, 1982]). From a broad perspective, one is tempted to contrast today's pessimism with the brash optimism of Mike Fink, the nineteenth-century Mississippi keelboat operator who said he could outfight, outdrink, and outswear "any riverboat man from Pittsburgh to New Orleans." Quoted in David Nasawied, *The Course of United States History* (Chicago: Dorsey Press, 1987), p. 190.

16. Henry Steele Commager, *Theodore Parker* (Boston: Little, Brown, 1937).

17. Harry Newmann, "What Is Bigotry?" *Modern Age* 31 (Winter 1987): 45.

18. Alfred North Whitehead, *The Aims of Education* (New York: Macmillan, 1949), pp. 98–99. The conditional "if" was used because Whitehead himself was something of a riddle to his Harvard students: "If a poll was taken among Harvard undergraduates who heard him lecture, half would have said they did not understand him and a hefty minority would say that he did not understand himself." Lewis S. Fender, "Recollections of Alfred North Whitehead in the Harvard Setting, 1935–1937," *The Yale Review* 76 (September 1987): 541.

19. Peter Drucker, "Management and the World's Work," *Harvard Business Review* 66 (September–October 1988): 65.

20. Ibid., 67.

21. Frank J. Comes, Jonathan Kapstein, John Templeman, and Elizabeth Weiner, "Reshaping Europe: 1992 and Beyond," *Business Week,* December 12, 1988, pp. 48–51.

22. "The Harvard Business School Is Searching" (advertisement), *Harvard Business Review* 67 (January–February 1989): 162–63

23. David Granfield, *The Inner Experience of the Law* (Washington, D.C.: The Catholic University of America Press, 1987), p. 4.

24. Allan Bloom, *The Closing of the American Mind: How Higher Education Has Failed Democracy and Impoverished the Souls of Today's Students* (New York: Simon and Schuster, 1987).

25. Barry Schwartz, *The Battle for Human Nature: Science, Morality and Modern Life* (New York: Norton, 1988); Amitai Etzioni, *The Moral Dimension: Toward a New Economics* (New York: The Free Press, 1988).

26. Richard E. Mulcahy, *The Economics of Heinrich Pesch* (New York: Holt, 1952).

27. William Waters, "Social Economics—A Solidarist Perspective," *Review of Social Economy* 46 (1988): 116.

28. Edward O. Wilson, *Sociobiology: The New Synthesis* (Cambridge, Mass.: Belknap Press of Harvard University Press, 1975).

29. Richard Dawkins, *The Blind Watchmaker: Why the Evidence of Evolution Reveals a Universe Without Design* (New York: Norton, 1987). See also his earlier book, *The Selfish Gene* (New York: Oxford University Press, 1976).

30. Robert Brown, *The Nature of Social Law: From Machiavelli to Mill* (New York: Cambridge University Press, 1988), pp. 252–53.

31. Lionel Trilling, *The Uncertain Future of the Humanistic Educational Ideal,* quoted in Nathan A. Scott, Jr., "The New *Trahison des Clercs:* Reflections on the Present Crisis in Humanistic Education," *The Virginia Quarterly Review* 62 (Summer 1986): 403.

32. The writer served as rapporteur for the last two of the three meetings sponsored by these two groups.

33. Lyman Porter and Lawrence McKibbin, *Executive Summary of Management Education and Development: Drift or Thrust Into the 21st Century?* (New York: McGraw-Hill, 1988).

34. Jennifer Moore, "Autonomy and Legitimacy in the Liberal Arts," in R. Edward Freeman, ed., *Business Ethics: The State of the Art* (New York: Oxford University Press, 1991), pp. 60–66.

35. George Santayana, *The Life of Reason* (New York: Charles Scribner, 1905), pp. 214, 218–19.

36. Hannah Arendt, for example, whose intellectual interests would hardly classify her as an activist, willingly shared in attempts to annihilate ideas dear to Western civilization—including metaphysics, philosophy, and God. See her *Life of the Mind,* Vols. 1 *(Thinking)* and 2 *(Willing)* (New York: Harcourt Brace Jovanovich, 1978). Etienne Gilson had remarked caustically on a previous occasion, "Philosophy always buries its undertakers."

37. Renaissance humanists, though they preferred contemplation to action, recognized that the active life had legitimacy. As a matter of fact, some Renaissance thinkers said that straining the reasons to reach truth was not so productive a human effort as disciplining the will to serve others in action. They recalled Cicero's words: "Just as the horse learns to run, the ox to plow, the dog to scent a trail, so man, as Aristotle said, is born to two things: *to know and to act.*" Quoted in *The Columbia History of the World,* ed. John A. Gorroty and Peter Gay (New York: Harper and Row, 1981), p. 50. "What the Greeks called *paediea* (education or culture), we call *studia humanitas.* For learning and training in virtue are peculiar to man; therefore, our forefathers called them *humanitos,* the pursuit of activities proper to mankind." Ibid.

38. Anthony Grafton and Lisa Jardine, *From Humanism to Humanities: Education and the Liberal Arts in Fifteenth- and Sixteenth-Century Europe* (Cambridge, Mass.: Harvard University Press, 1986).

39. That it will not be easy is shown by Stanford's 1987 spirited debates on the appropriate content for its required courses in Western civilization, a debate that erupted at the University of Pennsylvania in 1988. Huntly Collins, "Penn Rejects New Culture Requirement," *Philadelphia Inquirer,* October 26, 1988, p. B1. The Penn debate reflects the contours of the Stanford debate, with advocates of change arguing that the emergence of women, minority groups, and developing nations dictates the need for emphasis on non-Western cultures; defenders of the status quo call "the reformers" ideallogues who are less interested in improving liberal education and more concerned with pushing their own political agenda. An editorial highly critical of "the Stanford mind" struck this theme: "The West is preserved not through the evolution of such ideas as faith and justice, but through the

prism of sexism, racism, and the faculties of its ruling class." "The Stanford Mind," *Wall Street Journal,* December 22, 1988, p. A14. For a rather comprehensive report on the Stanford project, see Carolyn J. Mooney, "Sweeping Curricular Change Is Under Way at Stanford as University Phases Out Its 'Western Culture' Program," *Chronicle of Higher Education* 35, December 14, 1988, pp. A1, A11–12.

40. "Text of 'Speaking for the Humanities,' a Report From the American Council of Learned Societies," *Chronicle of Higher Education* 35, January 11, 1989, p. A22.

41. Ibid.

42. Incidentally, Shakespeare's popularity began to wane when the plays were offered without entr'acte jugglers and acrobats. The removal of Shakespeare from the people occurred in the United States probably because the new immigrants, speaking English poorly, were easily excluded by rich and upper-class Americans. Yet all was not lost. The sacralization of art generally meant that museum crowds could no longer carry their dogs along, spit tobacco juice, or permit their children to urinate in corners. Lawrence W. Levine, *Highbrow/Lowbrow: The Emergence of Cultural Hierarchy in America* (Cambridge, Mass.: Harvard University Press, 1988).

43. Bruce Bawer, "High Priestess of Native American Lit," *Wall Street Journal,* November 9, 1988. What aroused Bawer's ire was the overly praised (in his view) work of the young poet-novelist Louise Edrich: "[W]hen Ms. Edrich came along she suited the current American publishing trends in at least three ways: She was young, she was a native American, and she was a she. So eager, one suspects, were many reviewers to help install a fictionist of this description on an upper tier of American letters that they were more than willing to overlook a few major aesthetic infelicities" (p. A21).

44. Arthur Schopenhauer, "On Books and Reading," in *The Works of Schopenhauer,* ed. Will Durant (New York: Frederick Ungar, 1928), pp. 533–35.

45. Perhaps the task is not so formidable as it seems after all. During the first thirty-two years of his life, Mark Twain's exposure to the humanities consisted of the Bible, church hymnbooks, and Sunday sermons—with curious results. The believer became a skeptic, the undefiled became the unwashed, the solemn books became the objects of satire and parody. See William Lyon Phelps, "Mark Twain," *The Yale Review* 25 (1935): 291.

46. Robert Maynard Hutchins, "University Education," *The Yale Review* 25 (1935–36): 668.

47. My indebtedness to Maurice Cranston will become evident by reading the book he crafted from essays (originally written for radio) entitled *Political Dialogues* (New York: Basic Books, 1968).

48. Richard Rorty, *Contingency, Irony, and Imagination* (Princeton, N.J.: Princeton University Press, 1989), p. xvi. See also Joanne B. Ciulla, "Business Ethics as Moral Imagination," in Freeman, ed., *State of the Art,* pp. 212–20.

49. L. T. Hobhouse, *The Metaphysical Theory of the State* (London: George Allen and Unwin, 1918), p. 7.

50. Karl Popper, *The Open Society and Its Enemies* (London: G. Routledge and Sons, 1945). See Bertrand Russell, *History of Western Philosophy* (New York: Simon and Schuster, 1946), esp. pp. 741ff.

51. Within this circle were such well-known theorists as Rudolf Carnap, Kurt Godel, Moritz Schlick, and Otto Neurath.

52. Karl Popper, *Conjectures and Refutations* (London: Routledge and Kegan Paul, 1963), pp. 350–51.

53. It should be noted, however, that Popper was himself skeptical of universal scientific laws and of what later came to be called social engineering. His was the pragmatic trial-and-error method that found favor with Franklin D. Roosevelt in the early days of the New Deal. So Popper wound up, curiously enough, in the company of Thomas Jefferson, who saw and dealt with abstraction yet favored the minimal state that Popper was later to justify on quite different grounds.

54. Two books that clearly reveal Yves Simon's thinking are his *Philosophy of Democratic Government* (Chicago: University of Chicago Press, 1951) and *A General Theory of Authority* (Notre Dame, Ind.: University of Notre Dame Press, 1962).

55. For his part, Bertrand de Jouvenel worked indefatigably to distinguish authority from authoritarianism, showing that without a clear sense of the first, the second was inevitable. Bertrand de Jouvenel, *Sovereignty,* trans. J. F. Hurlington (Chicago: University of Chicago Press, 1957).

56. Frederick A. Ogg and P. Orman Ray, *Essentials of American Government* (New York: The Century Co., 1932).

57. The *Historische Zeitschrift* was founded in 1859, the *Revue historique* in 1876, the *English Historical Review* in 1886, and the *American Historical Review* in 1870.

58. The loss is not total. To read Garrett Mattingly's brilliant history of the defeat of the Spanish Armada or Lacey Baldwin's tale of Henry VIII is to be reminded of what can be done.

59. The author critiqued business historians in a way that, in retrospect, seems rather harsh, even though the main point is still relevant.

60. This sketch is drawn from Gerald Graff's fascinating account in *Professing Literature: An Institutional History* (Chicago: University of Chicago Press, 1987), esp. chap. 3.

61. Ibid., p. 13.

62. Alvin Kernan, "Criticism as Theodicy: The Institutional Role of Literary Criticism," *The Yale Review* 77, no. 17 (Autumn 1987): 86–103.

63. Richard Kearny, "Ethics and the Postmodern Imagination," *Thought* 62 (March 1987): 39–78.

64. Sartre insisted that the very act of writing required the act of reading: "There is no art except for and by others." See his *What Is Literature?* (New York: The University Library, 1949), p. 38.

65. One may conjecture how many graduate students have exhausted themselves with writers who have critiqued Tolstoy without ever having read *War and Peace* or *Anna Karenina*. To say this is not to minimize the enrichments readers have been provided by Tolstoy scholars, which are endlessly fascinating to their successors, as noted by A. N. Wilson in his biography entitled *Tolstoy* (New York: Norton, 1985).

66. This is what the so-called German School of literary critics believed.

67. Frank H. Easterbrook, "The Influence of Judicial Review in Constitu-

tional History," in Burke Marshall, ed., *A Workable Government: The Constitution After 200 Years* (New York: Norton, 1987), chap. 7.

68. Ibid., p. 174.

69. See, for example, Ronald M. Dworkin's *Law's Empire* (Cambridge, Mass.: Belknap Press of Harvard University Press, 1986).

70. Jacques Derrida, *Margins of Philosophy* (Chicago: University of Chicago Press, 1982).

71. To this unsophisticate, Derrida seems to reflect positions stated by Herder (1744–1803), one of Germany's leading philosophers and literary critics. Herder taught that since language and poetry were spontaneous expression of human nature, language had to be created so that poetry could flower.

72. Rorty, *Contingency, Irony, and Imagination,* chap. 6.

73. Harold Bloom, *Ruin the Sacred Truths: Poetry and Belief from the Bible to the Present* (Cambridge, Mass.: Harvard University Press, 1989).

74. Scott, "The New *Trahison des Clercs*," 407.

75. Leon Kass, "What's Wrong with Babel?" *The American Scholar* 57 (1988): 54.

76. George Steiner, "The Lollipopping of the West," *New York Times,* December 9, 1977, p. A27.

77. Thomas J. DeLoughry, "Study of Transcripts Finds Little Structure in the Liberal Arts," *Chronicle of Higher Education* 35, January 18, 1989, pp. A1, A32.

78. Justification of this support was voiced in a rather widely shared comment by Leonard Sterling, the senior vice president and controller of American Can Company: "The dominant management technique of the 1970s is strategic planning, and how can you even contemplate without understanding the nature of forces of the world and how we bring our own beliefs and value systems to bear on our decisions?" "An Executive Crash Course in Liberal Arts," *Business Week,* August 14, 1978, p. 58. Yet the reality is that Dartmouth broke even only in the seventh year of the program.

79. Ted J. Smith III, *The Vanishing Economy: Television Coverage of Economic Affairs, 1982–1987* (Washington, D.C.: Media Institute, 1988), pp. 90, 94.

80. *Barron's,* October 31, 1988.

81. Charles J. Sykes, *Profscam: Professors and the Demise of Higher Education* (Chicago: Regnery Gateway, 1988). Sykes was a reporter for the *Milwaukee Journal* and the editor of the *Milwaukee Magazine.*

82. Hutchins, "University Education," 668.

83. As Professor Kim Lane Scheppele, who told the story, observed, "A good deal of scholarship probably starts from the intellectual equivalent of the countryside pub. We set out from unlikely places on major journeys, asking questions of those who haven't been where we are going and can't imagine why we want to go where we are heading." *Legal Secrets: Equity and Efficiency in the Common Law* (Chicago: University of Chicago Press, 1988), p. ix.

84. Mark Twain, *Adventures of Huckleberry Finn,* ed. Charles Neider (Garden City, N.Y.: Doubleday, 1985), p. 110.

85. Otto Bird, *The Idea of Justice* (New York: Praeger, 1967).

86. Thomas J. Donaldson, "Rights in the Global Market," in Freeman, ed., *State of the Art*, pp. 139–62.

87. *Swift* v. *Tyson*, 16 Pet. 1 (1842).

88. *Cooper* v. *Aaron*, 5 U.S. 137 (1803); *Marbury* v. *Madison*, 358 U.S. 1 (1958).

89. K. N. Llewellyn and E. Adamson Hoebel, *The Cheyenne Way: Conflict and Case Law in Primitive Jurisprudence* (Norman: University of Oklahoma Press, 1941).

90. H. Richard Hartzler and Radie Bunn, "The Mafia, *The Cheyenne Way*, and Undergraduate Law," *The Journal of Legal Studies Education* 6 (1987): 57–69.

91. James Tatum, "The Illiad and Memories of War," *The Yale Review* 76 (December 1986): 15–31.

92. Richard Posner, *Law and Literature: A Misunderstood Relation* (Cambridge, Mass.: Harvard University Press, 1988).

93. John M. Huelo, O.S.M., "Integrating Canon Law in Diverse Cultures," *The Jurist* 47 (1987): 249–53.

94. This is not intended to suggest that Langdell had only the method and Holmes the content of law. It is intended to mean that study of comparative legal traditions may require a new methodology and that law's content will come, as it did for Holmes, through awareness of its inconsistencies.

95. Plato, Cicero, Machiavelli, Locke, Fayol, Taylor, and Barnard are examples. Certainly the life of the mind need not stifle the life of the role.

96. In Great Britain the licensing body is the Council for National Academic Awards (CNAA), which was incorporated by Royal Charter in 1964. The CNAA was established in response to recommendations made by an advisory council, the National Council on Education for Industry and Commerce. Its document became known as the Crick Report. In the United States the AACSB might serve the same overall function as the CNAA. For a brief history of the British approach, see N. A. Basten, "Legal Education for Persons Embarking on Careers in Business: The British Experience," *Journal of Legal Studies Education* 6 (1987): 127–39.

97. The AACSB supports this goal. See the *Accreditation Policies and Students* (St. Louis, Mo.: AACSB, 1985–86).

98. Ibid., pp. 27–28.

99. Henrik Ibsen, *Peer Gynt* (New York: Charles Scribner, 1892), act 2, sc. 7.

Liberal Arts and Professional Education: A Response to Clarence C. Walton

W. Michael Hoffman and David A. Fedo

I

Clarence C. Walton's allusive, thoughtful, and often eloquent Ruffin lecture adds to the surprisingly public debate over the role of the humanities and other liberal arts in American higher education. This debate—much of it insightful, some of it rancorous—has played itself out in curious ways. On the one hand, it is heartening to see such "serious" books as Allan Bloom's *Closing of the American Mind* and E. D. Hirsch's *Cultural Literacy: What Every American Needs to Know* featured prominently in nearly every airport in Christendom alongside the mega–best-sellers by Danielle Steele and Judith Krantz.[1] On the other hand, with Bloom and former Secretary of Education William Bennett leading the charge, it is unfortunate that so much of the debate has been excessively fretful and negative and, in its characterization of what is actually happening in our colleges and universities, simply not accurate.

That the number of actual majors in the humanities declined during the 1980s is, or course, very real. A report summarized in the Winter 1988 *Newsletter* of the Modern Language Association outlines the extent of this decline: between 1974–75 and 1984–85 the number of bachelor's degrees awarded in the humanities dropped 13.3

142

percent. (In the social sciences, the fall was even worse: down 29.5 percent.) At the same time, the number of bachelor's degrees awarded in business rose 75.4 percent, and the number in engineering climbed an astonishing 105.1 percent.

Yet the rise and fall of numbers and percentages fails to convey the fact that students majoring in the professions and the technical fields—now the largest number of undergraduates, Professor Bloom notwithstanding—are taking more courses in the humanities and liberal arts than ever before. For example, at Bentley College, a medium-sized private institution that emphasizes business, students in 1980–81 selected business courses more than 66 percent of the time when they had unrestricted elective slots to fill—leaving the arts and sciences with a declining 33.6 percent share. By May 1988 that percentage had all but evened out, with students choosing far more of their courses—more than 49 percent—in the arts and sciences. Happily, the American Assembly of Collegiate Schools of Business (AACSB), the powerful accrediting body of which Walton speaks, encourages more—not less—integration of the humanities into the baccalaureate work of students seeking business degrees, and this sentiment is apparently having an impact.

Numbers of courses taken do not tell the whole story, of course, as the 1988 monograph *Structure and Coherence,* written by Robert Zemsky and published by the vigilant Association of American Colleges, reminds us.[2] But the true revolution in American undergraduate education—and here we are much more optimistic than Walton—is that the typical non–liberal arts major is graduating with a much broader education than did his or her predecessor ten or fifteen years ago. This young man or woman (or adult learner) is taking language and theatre courses, studying abroad, and enrolling in interdisciplinary seminars with instructors from the business, health sciences, engineering, and liberal arts faculties who are team-teaching in ways that seemed unthinkable a decade ago. The result these days is an accountant or pharmacist who in many cases (obviously not all) has learned to think clearly and communicate persuasively, who knows something about literature and world politics, who can deal comfortably with ambiguity, who understands that important decisions must be made with some appreciation of the organizational and human context, and who is cognizant of the ethical as well as the economic dimensions of management strategy and health policy. Thus, the decline in the number of English, history, and philosophy majors, while lamentable, is hardly catastrophic. Liberal learning is doing much better for those numerous students who have turned elsewhere for their baccalaureate concentrations than many are willing to acknowledge.

II

Walton's essay is so wise and so wide-ranging that any response to it must necessarily leave out much. Yet the key passage in his essay, which occurs at the end of the first section, hits on the central purpose of liberal learning and is well worth repeating:

> *Oneness* touches our common humanity before it touches our common economy; *oneness* impinges more on what we think in common than the language used to convey it; *oneness* requires each of the parts to identify the role that its own culture may play in the totality. Such a conception of *oneness* can then deal with the plurality of values. In all of these things humanistic studies play a part: they invite us to consider, in ways that economics and political science do not, the totality of the human journey as defined for each person by four sets of encounters: the *individual* (the I), the *bilateral* (the I-Thou), the *communal* (the We), and the *sacral* (the We-Thou). Classical economic theory (the self-interest maximizer) starts with the first, bargaining theory with the second, political science the third, and theology the fourth. But the humanities—philosophy, literature, and history—embrace all.[3]

Walton quoted earlier and at some length from the work of Alfred North Whitehead, and, indeed, there is much of Whitehead in our distinguished Ruffin lecturer from The American College. As Walton says, education must return to the goal of focusing on the *total* human being and abandon the pernicious drive toward overspecialization. Only by turning outward can academic departments avoid the tunnels which, by their very nature, provide no hope of interconnection.

Walton sees hope in the humanities because they invite us to consider the "totality of the human journey," thereby enabling us to deal more effectively with the plurality of values that forms our lives. As Shakespeare's Lear finally utters, "Ripeness is all"—the range and wealth of life's experiences, good and bad, are the exhilarating blessing and the cost of being human.

As Walton rightly points out, however, it will have to be a revitalized model of the humanities, rather than the barren one we have been offered over the past several decades. He points this out, for example, in his lucid analyses of the fields of history and literature. His review of recent trends in literary criticism is especially on target, and his healthy skepticism about movements such as structuralism and deconstruction is refreshing.

We would like to echo the insights of Walton by taking a brief look at the field of philosophy, which has suffered from a similar malaise. It is safe to say that we have found ourselves in a moral crisis, and the attention to and activities in applied ethics since the

1980s have been reactions to this crisis. In order to deal intelligently with this crisis we must uncover the reasons for its occurrence, which inescapably pushes us deeply into the history of ideas.

Our century has been weaned on *relativism*—the denial of ethical absolutes; on *pragmatism*—the belief that something is right if it works; on *positivism*—the equation of knowledge with observable experience; and on *behaviorism*—the interpretation of human actions as totally predictable. The unifying thread to these themes is the reduction of everything considered meaningful to the material or to sense experience, sometimes called *empirical materialism.* With such an ideological framework, science and scientific methodology have flourished and ethics and values have been relegated to matters of emotion, expressions of mere attitudes having no objective meaning. Walton speaks of the prevailing doctrine as preaching "whatever is not science is nonsense." With such an ideological heritage, there is no other level of meaning or being within which nonempirical, nonmeasurable dimensions of our lives such as freedom, morality, and divinity can be developed. Clearly, such an ideological picture is barren and valueless. And there is something about the human spirit that resists this dehumanization, a resistance that is today manifesting itself in many ways.

We are not saying that science and technology are the culprits causing this moral crisis. For far too long scholars in the humanities have managed to talk only to themselves and in a language and a context which for the most part were and still are unintelligible to the world of practical affairs. The closed world of scholarship in some disciplines—in certain modes of literary theory, for example—is scandalous. Departments and colleges of engineering, medicine, law, and business have therefore looked skeptically, if not disdainfully, at the so-called liberal arts. Furthermore, graduate students in philosophy often learned that good philosophy was synonymous with good linguistic analysis and that metaphysics and ethics were to be exorcised through continual and liberal doses of Wittgenstein and quantificational logic. Using the ideology of empirical materialism, philosophy declared an all-out war against nonobservable claims, or what were called ghosts in the machinery. Philosophical ethics focused on abstract methodology and metaethical problems, and when concrete moral problems were addressed, the emphasis was on individual personal ethics with no rational or objective grounding.

Little wonder, therefore, that many see ethics today as an empty discipline—either as a useless exercise in hair-splitting or as nonrational statements of personal taste and bias. On the other hand, applied ethics, including business ethics, is an attempt to bring moral issues into the concrete world of practical activity. This attempt will succeed or fail depending on what ideas the application is based on.

Only time will tell if we will shift from a barren empirical material-ism and broaden our metaphysical vision. We must reexamine our ideological presuppositions, and, if we find them wanting, then we must change them.

We used the word moral "crisis" earlier because it is an appro-priate one to denote what is today's critical turning point in the moral development of our race. More than twenty years ago Walton prophetically stated in his book *Corporate Social Responsibilities* that "the country stands poised on the edge of developing a style of life that probes more deeply than the material and physical realm."[4] And in 1974, in his "Overview" to his book *The Ethics of Corporate Conduct,* he concluded by saying: "A sense of expectancy permeates America—a feeling that new socio-philosophic fields remain to be explored . . . and a new human fulfillment made possible."[5]

Since Walton wrote these words, much has been achieved in and out of academe toward the realization of his insight into this poten-tially new and rich kind of human fulfillment. In his essay in this volume Walton cites a number of integrative programs that serve as encouraging signs. There are scores of others, of which we cite sev-eral at random.

The *University of Kansas* and the *University of Florida,* recipients of major grants from the National Endowment for the Humanities, have since the 1980s made important advances in establishing curric-ular and faculty links between the undergraduate professional pro-grams and the arts and sciences. At Kansas the bridges between the business school and the humanities are especially strong: manage-ment students are encouraged to take concentrations in the humani-ties and associated liberal arts; team-taught courses integrating lib-eral and professional learning are common. At Florida the effort to integrate learning has been even more comprehensive: all schools and colleges are urged to develop courses that allow their under-graduates to link their major courses with other fields, often in an interdisciplinary context. Cross-fertilization is the goal.

The *Claremont Graduate School* and *The Wharton School* encourage graduate students to integrate humanities learning into their M.B.A. programs. At Claremont courses designed to demonstrate humani-ties perspectives on business issues are well-established; MBA stu-dents on a special track at Wharton must acquire advanced language and cultural proficiency as they prepare for careers in international business.

The *Colorado School of Mines* and *Worcester Polytechnic Institute* are two engineering institutions that have fully embraced Walton's con-cept of "oneness." At Colorado a selective honors program in public affairs uses the humanities in an interdisciplinary setting to help fu-ture engineers understand the role of technology in society. At

W.P.I. interactive projects required of all undergraduates show how the humanities contribute uniquely to the solving of problems.

The Medical School at *Pennsylvania State University* and the Engineering School at the *University of Virginia* have humanities units *within* the professional schools, thus ensuring a broader perspective to the curriculum. Faculty teach literature, history, and religion to students about to embark on business careers.

These are but representative examples of hope-inspiring activity and reform; there are many others, at both the undergraduate and graduate levels, around the United States. We should also point out the contributions John Clemens and his Hartwick Humanities in Management Institute in Oneonta, New York (on the campus of Hartwick College), whose publications and conferences continue to explore the benefits and insights that come through the meaningful integration of liberal and professional learning. Business executives and practitioners play a strong supporting role at Hartwick. All of these initiatives provide a truly heartening antidote to the gloom of Professor Bloom and his followers.

We can also cite three books that give very useful accounts of both the new directions in liberal and professional learning and the resulting impact on society in general and business in specific. They are Michael Useem's *Liberal Education and the Corporation,* Joseph S. Johnston, Jr.'s *Educating Managers: Executive Effectiveness Through Liberal Learning,* and Peter T. Marsh's *Contesting the Boundaries of Liberal and Professional Education: The Syracuse Experiment.*[6] All are worth reading.

III

We would now like to turn once again to the subject of business ethics. Business ethics is surely one of the new fields Professor Walton foresaw fifteen years ago and, of course, helped build into what it has become today. We are optimistic that the establishment of business ethics, along with other efforts, will help in the realization of the goals of Professor Walton's vision of oneness and wholeness in the development of humankind. Yet it seems to us that business ethics is presently at a critical crossroads, which may be paradigmatic of other such efforts.

It was almost ten years ago that Peter Drucker in *Forbes* called business ethics "chic." He was not alone in thinking that the renewed interest in business ethics was nothing more than a fad, a flash in the pan. After all, even *The Wall Street Journal* referred to business ethics as being an oxymoron.

Although it is still too early to say if these skeptics were wrong, so far at least they have not been proven right. Business ethics is no longer an idea discussed and promoted by a few academic scholars around the country. It has developed into a full-fledged social movement. In fact, it is hard to pick up the morning newspaper without seeing some story on business and ethics.

More than 90 percent of business schools in the United States now offer their students business ethics studies in some fashion, and three-quarters of our major corporations indicate in surveys that they are in the process of building ethics into their organizations. Distinguished chairs in business ethics are springing up throughout academe, and corporate chairpeople are writing and speaking on ethics at conferences throughout the country.

In addition, business ethics consultants are in great demand by corporations and business schools seeking to beef up their programs in ethics. Consultants are constantly being called by members of the press for quotable news "bites" and are being asked to join the stables of large, established corporate consulting firms. They are even sought by litigation lawyers to serve as expert witnesses, by government departments researching issues for congressional action, and by corporate public relations firms to write in defense of their clients' positions.

Although the movement in business ethics began in the United States, it is growing internationally. Scholars from all over the world have been visiting business ethics leaders in this country to learn how to plant the seeds in their own turf. Perhaps the most significant development thus far is the establishment of the European Business Ethics Network, which held the first international business ethics conference in 1987 in Brussels.

With all of this growth and activity in business ethics, why are we still haunted by Drucker's accusation that the field is chic? Why do we feel that there is still a danger that the movement may not develop sturdy roots and grow into something that will provide a more ethical culture within which to do business? Will the potential be realized? From where we sit after more than a decade of work in the field, we see some disquieting signs.

On the academic front, American colleges and universities, despite the advances already alluded to, are not yet moving fast enough to build ethics into their graduate or undergraduate business curricula. Although everyone agrees that ethics is crucial, very few institutions, fewer than 10 percent, actually *require* that their business graduates take a *separate course* in business ethics. There are many reasons for this low figure. The difficulty of finding room in the curriculum is one common reason. Some programs have integrated ethics into existing courses, which is a start—but not the whole answer.

A few years ago the AACSB added to its requirements for accrediting business schools that bachelor's programs had to cover ethical and social issues. But what is lacking from the AACSB are any real guidelines about how this can be accomplished. We need stronger leadership within the academic community, from both the business and the liberal arts sides, to ensure that ethics is valued as much as accounting or marketing as a central part of the curriculum.

To take one specific example, two years ago the Harvard Business School, after receiving a gift of $30 million toward a business ethics program, began to rethink its commitment to business ethics. Just last year Harvard instituted a three-week minicourse in business ethics that was required for all its students. But it is not a graded course like other required courses, nor is it a full semester course like other required courses. What does this say to our students, our future business leaders, and to other business schools looking to Harvard's lead? It sends the wrong message, of course. We would hope that more colleges and universities will demonstrate their commitment to business ethics by requiring full-fledged courses.

On the corporate front, some executives can be seriously charged with only dressing up their windows with ethics instead of trying to remake their cultures and organizations into more ethical ones. This is true despite the fact that in the 1970s and early 1980s many corporations did jump on the business ethics bandwagon, and many have written or revised their codes of ethics. In addition, with the outbreak of the Wall Street scandals and defense contracting frauds, many corporations have hired business ethics consultants, but they are rarely asked to do much more than run a few sporadic training programs in ethics.

In a survey of Fortune 500 companies by Bentley's Center for Business Ethics, fewer than 15 percent of the respondents had ethics committees, only abut 5 percent had ethical ombudsmen, and only three responding companies had ethics judiciary boards. Generally, the large majority of corporations have no support structures to ensure that their codes of ethics provided for adequate communication, oversight, enforcement, adjudication, or review.

Although 80 percent of the companies in this survey said they were institutionalizing ethics, only 20 percent of those had made any structural or governance changes. And among that 20 percent, fewer than one-quarter had moved toward any worker participation in decision making, and only 7 percent had introduced an employee bill of rights.

In recent years many corporations have paid a lot of lip service to ethics, and some have even implemented worthwhile programs to foster ethical behaviors in employees. Both usually couch their rationale for their actions in the phrase "good ethics is good business." The Business Roundtable recently published a report entitled *Corpo-*

rate Ethics: A Prime Business Asset, in which it claimed that "corporate ethics is a strategic key to survival and profitability in this era of fierce competitiveness in a global economy."[7] Yet is the rationale that good ethics is good business a proper one for business ethics? We think not. We are not saying that good ethics is not good business. In most cases we think it is. We are claiming that it should not be advanced as the only or even the main reason for doing business ethically. We are saying that the ethical thing to do may not always be in the best interests of the firm. And when the crunch comes, when ethics conflicts with the firm's interests, any ethics program that has not already faced up to this possibility is doomed to fail because it will undercut the rationale of the program itself.

All of these decidedly mixed signs give ample testimony to the fact that business ethics is at a major crossroads. It has made great progress over difficult terrain to get to this point, and the contributions of educators and executives should be acknowledged. But without self-examination and courage, it is in danger of taking the wrong direction, which could lead to a dead end and the validation of Drucker's early skepticism.

Nonetheless, in business ethics and in the humanities in general, we remain more hopeful than not. A good deal is being accomplished, both in the classroom and in the world of practical affairs. That more remains to be accomplished is Walton's warning, and we agree. In his "President's Report" for 1987 President Derek Bok of Harvard called for higher education to demonstrate a deeper concern for the moral development of students in specific and the society at large. He concluded his report with a quote from Montaigne, which we think aptly serves to capture Walton's message to us in his Ruffin lecture as well as to symbolize his inspirational messages to all of us over the years:

To compose our *character* is our duty, not to compose books, and *to win,* not battles and provinces, but *order* and *tranquility* in our own conduct. Our great and glorious masterpiece is to live appropriately.[8]

NOTES

1. See Allan Bloom, *The Closing of the American Mind: How Higher Education Has Failed Democracy and Impoverished the Souls of Today's Students* (New York: Simon and Schuster, 1987), and E. D. Hirsch, *Cultural Literacy: What Every American Needs to Know* (Boston: Houghton Mifflin, 1987).

2. Robert Zemsky, *Structure and Coherence: Measuring the Undergraduate Curriculum* (Association of American Colleges, 1989).

3. Clarence C. Walton, "Management Education: Seeing the Round Earth

Squarely," in R. Edward Freeman, ed., *Business as a Humanity* (New York: Oxford University Press, 1994).

4. Clarence C. Walton, *Corporate Social Responsibilities* (Belmont, Calif.: Wadsworth, 1967), p. 141.

5. Clarence C. Walton, "Overview," in *The Ethics of Corporate Conduct*, ed. Clarence C. Walton (Englewood Cliffs, N.J.: Prentice-Hall, 1977), p. 27.

6. Michael Unseem, *Liberal Education and the Corporation: The Hiring and Advancement of College Graduates* (New York: A. de Gryter, 1989); Joseph S. Johnston, Jr., *Educating Managers: Executive Effectiveness Through Liberal Learning* (San Francisco: Jossey-Bass, 1986); and Peter T. Marsh, *Contesting the Boundaries of Liberal and Professional Education: They Syracuse Experiment* (Syracuse, N.Y.: Syracuse University Press, 1988).

7. James Keogh, ed., *Corporate Ethics: A Prime Business Asset* (New York: Business Roundtable, 1988). Emphasis added.

8. Derek Bok, "The President's Report, 1985–86." (The Report of President Bok to Members of the Board of Overseers at Harvard University, 1987.)

Liberal Education for Competence and Responsibility

Kenneth R. Andrews

Liberalizing management education by deliberately closing the gap between education or business practice and the humanities is no simple matter. Clarence C. Walton has made that clear in "Management Education: Seeing the Round Earth Squarely." I propose to build on his essay by examining further the decline in the influence of the humanities upon students throughout recent decades. The related shortfall of professional education in meeting the needs of the professions—amply evident in their practice—requires reduced expectations of advanced schooling or constructive redirection—one or both. The erosion of ethical standards is only one of the master problems confronting the professions. In this decline, as well as in other problems, the university implicates itself by inattention, if not by more direct participation.

My two-part excursion into these troubled waters will examine first the attitudes and then the actions required to strengthen the effectiveness of the university in preparing young people for morally responsible and technically competent performance. We will be led beyond the preprofessional training of vocation-oriented students to the conduct of professional education itself. We should all like the level of technical competence and moral or social responsibility to rise with the demands of an increasingly industrialized and interdependent world society. Discovering what is possible to do is much less difficult than finding the will to do it.

At an early point in their undergraduate years, today's students,

152

unlike the rebellious youth of the 1960s, feel pressed these days to decide what they want to be when they grow up and to shape their studies as narrowly possible toward that choice. A few years ago, when I was Master of a Harvard house and privy to decisions being made by five hundred undergraduates, a disproportionate number of very bright people were planning to go to law school—either to practice law or to keep related career options open. A substantial number of other students, admitted to Harvard in the first place to populate the science departments, had decided before they entered college to go to medical school. A very small number—since augmented by a notable change in sentiment—planned to attend business school, often after two or three years of work experience. A handful opted early for other professions and graduate work in fields such as divinity, education, and public health. And some happy-go-lucky blessed students paid no attention to how they were going to pay off student loans or repay their parents' anxious investment in their futures. They took courses that interested them and concentrated in exotic combinations of disciplines without regard for their utility. This minority was not so much clear (and never articulate) about the value of a liberal education as uncertain or adventurous enough to take their chances after graduation in finding something interesting to do. Student interests in the creative and performing arts, in journalism, in social work, and in politics were pursued in extracurricular activities. Except for those majoring in the sciences, students had considerable free time available for such interests.

In the situation I describe, prelaw students concentrated in government, premeds loaded themselves with heavy courses in chemistry and the biological sciences, prebusiness persons majored in economics. The few people then planning academic careers made a preprofessional curriculum out of their chosen discipline; even they spent little time (except for that required) in becoming acquainted with bodies of knowledge in other than their chosen field. All the rhetoric from the graduate schools about the desirability of a broad background (not really fervent in intent) fell on the deaf ears of a generation beelining to a professional school that would commit them to a set of predetermined careers they knew very little about. The core curriculum was reinvented to help determined careerists to achieve a nodding acquaintance with each of the main streams of knowledge. The return of requirements throughout our entire educational system poses the need, by the way, to be clear about the purposes they are supposed to serve.

Where undergraduate education and professional education have become clearly separated by the baccalaureate degree, it is especially difficult for prospective professionals to become informed about the nature of the profession they are considering, how professional practice differs from other forms of work, what the controlling standards and criteria are, and what the intellectual, material, and social satisfactions and rewards might be. One or more courses on the role of the professions in society might prepare students for more intelligent choice, might extend their sensitivities to the moral dilemmas of the profession they are entering, and might acquaint them with the nature of responsible competence and the ways in which it is extended or subverted. The intellectual and ethical challenges of the professions constitute a fascinating but neglected field of study. Rather than proposing a new discipline, however, I argue for now only that universities (and particularly the humanities faculty) should see themselves as preparing a large block of their students for professional careers. They should admit the fact and obligation. The limitations of uninformed and premature choice could be addressed by an interdisciplinary course, taught probably by a group made up of professional school faculty persons. Interchange between faculties overly oriented toward professional practice and theory-oriented academics caged by their disciplines is usually found to be stimulating and instructive.

Before choosing law (including legal practice and government service), medicine, or business as a career, candidates could inform themselves about the nature of professional work by giving disciplined attention to certain problems. Consequences of overabundant professionalism (such as a litigious society that keeps busy a surplus of lawyers), the materialism of a society in which the corporation is the dominant institution, the economics of medical care in which scientific advance outstrips the equitable distribution of benefits are as worthy of study as are more familiar subjects. Without inquiry into the nature of the professions, how are students to know that economics has actually very little to do with the management of business enterprises, that the practice of law might be informed as well by the study of history as by the study of political science, that the understanding by physicians of patients might be better informed by psychology, sociology, or literature than by biochemistry? If it is the excitement of professional practice that attracts students too soon away from their basic education, then a competing attraction must be established and maintained.

A much more fundamental remedy for rampant careerism would be a clarification of the purposes of a liberal education so that its claims on four years of an undergraduate's life could be seen as worth honoring for its ultimate contribution to professional practice and to living a rewarding life in an increasingly complicated society.

The relevance of the humanities has become less and less clear as opportunities for an academic career in its various forms have declined. This dismaying development must mean that the goals of liberal learning have not been clear. Personal benefits in terms of quality of intellect, taste, judgment, aspiration, self-knowledge, and confidence may be elusively intangible. They are nonetheless crucial to individual development of durable intelligence and to the achievement of deep-rooted happiness. Such benefits are seldom asserted, or even discussed—as if it were important that the humanities not be useful. But the skills of analysis and reasoning, of writing and speaking, and of human understanding are essential to the practice of the professions. Almost every aspect of leadership depends for its power on the spoken and written word; it should be possible for students to see the importance to their future lives of the study of their own and foreign languages. Professors in these subjects, accustomed to thinking that student devotion to their courses needs no justification, do not explore the implications for their students of liberal studies. Thus, they diminish further already languishing motivation.

Judgment in interpretation of contemporary society and knowledge of human capability are enhanced by the study of history, philosophy, and art. The capacity for mature emotional response to all aspects of life is developed by literature, music, and the graphic and performing arts. Respect for one's own personality and character and personal qualification for leadership are potentially the result of a liberal education. But all this seems to escape students drawn early to the simple obvious relevance of specialization. The decline in perceived relevance of the humanities is not to be laid, however, to the professional ambitions of the student. I am afraid we must charge it instead to the reluctance of professors to take interest in the fact that study in their discipline has rewards beyond pursuit of knowledge for its own sake. The purpose of education is the development of students, rather than of knowledge. Except for that pursued daily by devotees of research, knowledge quickly decays; it is the insight and skills associated with acquisition that remain with the student who has passed by. A shift of emphasis from knowledge for its own sake to knowledge for broadly defined uses requires a reorientation of the academic mind from research to teaching, from theory to application, from detachment to an intellectual interest in the life of action.

All dedicated teacher-scholars acknowledge the importance of balance in the relation of teaching to research and in theory to application. Striking that balance is the essence of fully professional conduct as a scholar. But the connection between the study of liberal arts and life as an adult, the usefulness of elementary research skills to real-world experience, and the role of college as preparation for lifelong learning are seldom addressed explicitly or passionately promoted.

Academic disdain for the application of ideas, for practical affairs, for life in business and government may motivate neglect of the ultimate purpose of liberal education. But if those offering education in the humanities to people bound for the world of work cannot find a way to know or discuss the real value of applying ideas to action, it will remain hard to persuade career-oriented students of the importance of the development of their own power of thought and capacity for moral decision.

Clarifying the purposes of a university education in terms of personal development and the acquisition of skills essential to being fully developed persons and leaders in professional achievement requires, then, a change in the perspective of teachers. It requires change as well in teaching methods to include more student interaction and participation in searching inquiry. The disadvantages of presenting in lecture form what can be read more quickly are so well known as to make curious the survival (except as a dramatic performance) of the lecture. At the very least, lectures could be written out and assigned in advance so that class time could be devoted to discussing and understanding them. Skills in problem-solving, analysis, comprehension of the relationship of variables, deciding the meaning of information, and drawing conclusions from analysis are developed in exercises, simulations, and analysis of case studies— in discussion and debate—and not only in solitary reflection. The excitement of liberal learning is felt in the interaction of persons and minds under intellectual leadership sensitive to the nature of human development—intellectual, moral, and social. It permits the assignment of more challenging work to which higher standards can be applied. The lack of rigor in judging student work, the erosion of grading standards, the indolence of students bored by what they consider irrelevant would all be leap-frogged by heavy schedules of exciting work. The slack that often characterizes the schedules of students and subjects other than in the sciences is extremely poor preparation for the pace and stamina all professional work requires.

It is not enough, then, simply to deplore the preprofessional zeal and course choices of students. I have said so far that the university can enable students to make a better informed choice of profession and to understand better the practical lifelong values of the skills, attitudes, and analytical methods that should be the products of the study of any substantial body of knowledge. If the role of the professions were to be critically examined rather than excluded from the undergraduate curriculum, then fascinating and difficult questions that still perplex the professions would challenge the minds of students and inform them of the nature of decision in the professions.

To exclude such matters from student attention is, from his or her point of view, to take everything interesting out of the curriculum.

The challenge somehow is to make such issues part and parcel of the liberal curriculum, if not in the way I have suggested, then in some better way.

The conduct of graduate professional education is similarly in need of clarification of purpose and elevation of quality. Because it is what I know most about, I will speak principally of business education. Despite the aversion of faculties of liberal arts, business education has become the elephant in the university tent. It began as undergraduate education at the University of Pennsylvania in 1881, spread to the universities of Chicago and California and to New York before 1900. Dartmouth invented the combination of three undergraduate and two graduate years at the Tuck School. Harvard became the first all-graduate school in 1908. At present more than two hundred thousand bachelor's degrees in business administration are granted each year. Such programs consist generally of two years of liberal arts or general education instruction and two years of a business major that introduces students to the functions of business. The bachelor of business administration is mostly the mark of an early decision about vocation. It is preprofessional in the sense of possibly leading to a career in management after graduate training or work experience, or both.

Because they are more directly professional than vocational and because their graduates are slated directly for management training in junior-management positions, the graduate program should be the focus of our attention. The number of M.B.A. degrees awarded annually has risen from 7,600 in 1965 to an estimated peak of 66,500 in 1985. Since the number of Ph.D.s granted each year has not exceeded six hundred, the problems of providing faculty to support this growth raise urgent doubts about the quality of graduate business education. In addition to degree programs, executive education in intensive short programs has become an influential instrument of business education.

The demographic depression projected to assault M.B.A. programs as student population declines may mean that many programs will and should fail. Those preparing for survival against severe competition will need to develop unique strategies to focus faculty recruitment and development and the selection of students. The shortage of both faculty and financial resources will require each professional school to develop its strengths, define the region or business communities it is to serve, balance its attention to teaching and research, and extend its reach into executive education—all to distinguish itself from the mediocre cohort.

The study of business organizations has developed the normative hypothesis that every organization should have a pattern of goals or objectives that is appropriate to the opportunity and risks in its environment, to its resources and special strengths, to the values and aspirations to which it is committed, and to the particular service it wishes to render to society. This discovery has seldom been applied to the university. Broad classes of institutions are recognized, grouped around either the public state-supported and service-oriented prototype or the private research-oriented university model. Generally, however, a university's purposes, as implied earlier, are taken for granted and, because of this inattention, have fallen behind the needs of their constituencies. Little attention is given to strategic planning. Some institutions, to be sure, have undertaken to define their mission and choose a course that will set them apart from the institutions that by default must drift with the rising and falling tide. Since the choice of purpose is so central to the development of persons and institutions, it is unfortunate that little time and conscious attention are devoted both to its determination and to the alternate courses of action that consciously articulated purpose soon makes clear.

The essential choice now confronting professional business schools is between two models—one we may call academic and theory-oriented, the other professional and practice-oriented. The academic model consists of disciplines relevant to the practice of management but leaves the problems of application largely to the student's subsequent experience. The development and explication of theory thus dominate the curriculum. Micro and macroeconomic theory, financial economics, computer science, all well developed bodies of knowledge, displace the other social sciences in students' attention. Management is conceived of as a science; whatever cannot be quantified is not scientific. Research is rigorous when measurement is possible; it is "anecdotal" when it reports on experience or moves into the realm of subjective judgment, where, alas, all management decision takes place. Needless to say, encounters with ethical quandaries are not encouraged. Professors in such a graduate school are almost indistinguishable from their counterparts in the social science and mathematical disciplines of the faculty of arts and sciences. They are primarily concerned with advances in knowledge within an established and separate discipline. Business becomes simply the environment in which they pursue their theoretical inquiry.

The faculty of the school following the professional model, on the other hand, is more concerned with relating theory to practice than with the development of mathematical models. It considers management an art. Its acceptance of the mission to prepare students for management responsibility requires knowledge of and experience with what management is and some value-laden conception of what it might become. It requires also direct study of the skills required to cope with its problems and realize its possibilities. Management is leadership in the continuous process of determining the appropriate objectives of an organization, of obtaining and allocating the resources for achieving those objectives, of overseeing the quality and effectiveness of work influenced by diverse individual goals, of reconciling personal aspirations and economic feasibility, and of developing a self-respecting organizational identity. In business, the process involves the identification of economic opportunity in a kaleidoscopic environment, the necessary invention or adaptation of product or service to meet perceived or revealed needs, and the mastery of the technology appropriate to product-market opportunities. In addition, an organization must be created or adapted to accomplish its chosen and changing purposes. This achievement must be encouraged by a variety of incentives, restrained and directed by a variety of controls, and evaluated by a variety of measures. The curriculum preparing for this universe of activity will certainly not be a departmentalized set of conventional academic disciplines.

The practice of any profession requires much more than knowledge, defined as information, concepts, and theory. The skills and attitudes appropriate to effective and responsible decision making become more important than knowledge. Because the breadth of knowledge required in industry is in technical detail impracticably vast, learning most of what needs to be known must be postponed until the choice of industry and company is made. The professional school purports to enable students, already broadly educated, to learn faster and better from subsequent experience than they otherwise would. Intellectual skills appropriate to the management of business can be learned through practice in the analysis of complex situations recorded from informed observation. Repeated exercises in such analysis leads to the identification of attitudes and points of view useful in meeting the needs for decision. The skills of leadership and the aspiration to maintain high ethical standards may not be as directly teachable, but sensitivity to the need for them can be extended and inculcated. The traditionally academic approach to research tends to avoid problems involving judgment, character, and moral discrimination. The management scholar must learn how to devise conceptual approaches that are capable of dealing with emotional and value-laden issues for various classes of problems.

The difficulties of conducting research in management are many. Skills of observation, interviewing, and interpretation, willingness to do patient clinical studies of unique organizations and situations, and judgment in identifying uniformities in diverse circumstances require recourse to the field more even than to the library. The education of faculty members of professional schools of management requires the conversion of the product of traditional doctoral programs to a new life of patient observation and construction of practitioner-oriented conceptual schemes. The product of a conventional Ph.D. program in economics, for example, is ill prepared to interpret the behavior of managers in real corporations. Management plays no role in microeconomic theory except as embodiment of the urge to monopolize; the corporation is a profit-maximizing black box.

The disparity between academic preparation and practice-oriented research exists also in other disciplines, where the end of scholarship (in more ways than one) may be further contribution to technical theory, rather than understanding the combination of intellect, energy, and morality that sustains responsible competence in executive positions. Rather than look for narrow problems that are tractable to precise quantitative techniques, researchers must be willing to apply imperfect approaches to important multidimensional problems. Although I cannot demonstrate this proposition in this confined space, let me assert flatly that it is possible to apply concepts originating in the study of business that reveal useful approaches to problems without making certain the outcome.

As is already clear, I think that the future development of professional preparation for the management of the business institution means abandoning the academic model of a graduate school that pursues advanced study of separate disciplines in favor of the model of the professional school that addresses the problems of practice. Since it is unrealistic to assume that a given school will go all one way or another, let me say that the dominant emphasis, conditioned by the capability of faculty, must be toward identification with the practitioner. If this is the case, then the coexistence of devotion to theory and to application becomes possible. If the graduate school model predominates, then as a matter of academic reality the practice-oriented faculty person never achieves tenure. The tentative emergence of practitioner-oriented theory cannot survive massive applications of artificial rigor made possible by unchallenged simplifying assumptions.

A more dangerous consequence of loyalty to academic theory is bad or incomplete theory that, rather than being rejected as unrealistic, is seized upon by businesspeople. It is in the area of financial economics that university-developed theory has been most influential in business. The economic and legal definition of the purpose of the corporation is the maximum enhancement of shareholder wealth, a definition central to corporation law and to the teachings of law schools. For the large, publicly held corporation that dominates our current business scene and will be an even more powerful force in the near future, the profit maximization model is obsolete. Because it leads, even though its proponents assume that legality and ethical custom will constrain it, to conclusions that behavior not blatantly illegal or immoral is acceptable in the pursuit of self-interest, it is at least an inherently moral proposition. Its obsolescence, however, lies in its ignoring the responsibility to customers, employees, suppliers and communities that leading corporations acknowledge. The elementary profit-maximizing theory also ignores noneconomic contributions to society that are worth making both on their own account and in the interest of furthering the reputation of the corporation for quality of product and service and for institutional integrity. Responsible behavior over and beyond that required by law is often rationalized as incurring short-run costs in order to contribute to long run-profit maximization. This ingenious logic is unsupportable as a substitute for doing what seems right after considering the conflicting needs of corporate constituencies. Commitment to a balance between self-interest and social concern is best made in the mind of a moral person. It is the product of will and judgment. To eliminate moral judgment in deference to theoretical profit maximization for shareholders is not a worthy goal of a professional school of business.

Much else in the theory taught by some of our business faculties is similarly incomplete and simplistic. The efficient market hypothesis (the principle that the share price of publicly traded stock is the accurate present value of the company's future earning stream) rests on the superficially plausible assumption that all available information about the company instantly pervades the investment community. What is unreasonable is the assumption that information *not* available is unimportant. The company's product development program, its long-term intentions, the quality of its decision making, its ability to convert high risk into high return in an atmosphere of great economic and geopolitical uncertainty, its capacity to outstrip competition via dedicated commitment to its purposes—all this and more does not immediately meet the eye.

Much mischief comes from the efficient market hypothesis, including executive concern for quarter-by-quarter earnings to sustain share price, conservatism in investing in international opportunity essential to growth but slow in return, and encouragement of hostile takeovers derived from depressed share prices. The truth is that nobody understands fully the process by which company shares are assigned value by the investment community. The market is in part efficient and in part inexplicable.

I do not mean to say that such theory is never useful or valid; it has limited usefulness as one view of a set of complex phenomena. When we consider whether professional education should be theory- or experience-based, we should be critical of both theory and experience. The development of theory adequate to the multidimensionality of executive decision is an important unfinished task. While it is being developed, all discipline-derived theories should be skeptically viewed and confined to the arenas where they are useful. In full recognition of the difficulties of identifying uniformities in practice, it is possible to develop organizing perspectives and conceptual schemes that permit a comprehensive overview of a company's situation and the variables that are part of it without unrealistically dictating the decision that should be made. Such concepts pave the way for, but do not supersede, informed judgment. Quantification informs and extends analysis but does not displace the intuition, aspirations, and judgment of the educated practitioner.

If the professional business school is to equip its students to think broadly about the relation of business and society, to analyze accurately economic opportunity, to be sensitive to the nature and quality of leadership exercised upon and by them, and to be technically competent in the analysis of quantitative data, it must be furnished by the university with students of innate leadership characteristics and diverse special abilities who are the product of a liberal education. If the purpose of a liberal education is to enable persons to live as fully developed human beings, the purpose of professional education must be to empower them to act effectively and responsibly and to equip them to lead.

My conclusion that liberal learning should encompass explicit attention to its uses in life and that professional education for business should meet the needs and challenge the performance of practicing managers will not be in itself influential. It flies in the face of the conventional static definition of the function of a university. Pursuit, maintenance, and communication of knowledge are not enough without responsibility for the development of attitudes, moral standards, and capacity for effective action that define a mature person as individual and citizen.

I have better reason to hope that business education will continue to inform and be informed by established practice. The most influential institutions are moving in this direction, with the support and encouragement of practitioners. Law and medical schools are moving closer to the problems of the practitioner. What is clear is that the evident need in years ahead for greater competence, higher levels of ethical concern and decision, and more creative adaptations to change is common to all the professions. The role of liberal education in developing intellectual power and moral values remains important as the professional schools continue the cultivation of capability to serve society. If, as we react to current wholesale questioning of our educational system, we conceive of a clearer definition of purpose embracing both the goals of liberal and professional education, we will make progress.

The collegial conventions of the university make glacial the rate of change and partially immunize it from the influence of leadership. But these days the shortcomings of our educational system are so widely documented and the practice of law, medicine, and business are so clearly flawed that at least we begin to realize our predicament. Liberal education can be linked to life, rather than to knowledge. Professional practice can become more responsible than self-centered in the pursuit of gain and increasingly more competent as society grows more complex. Professional education could recognize the need to apply the perspectives cultivated in liberal education to the special tasks of the professions and to shape the process through which responsible competence is learned from experience.

But progress in capitalizing these opportunities will be an act of individual and institutional will born of the recognition that the humanities are supremely useful in enabling us to learn how to live our lives. *Study* of the humanities would be more likely to galvanize than to bore young people if the *power* of the humanities for contributing quality and purpose to sheer achievement were rediscovered by each person somewhere in history, literature, philosophy, and art.

IV

Casuistry and the Case for Business Ethics

Joanne B. Ciulla

If you put your ear to the ground of history and listen closely, you will hear a variety of ongoing conversations about the moral problems of everyday life. Sometimes strange and sometimes familiar, these discussions take place at the crossroads of the humanities. Philosophers, theologians, historians, poets, and playwrights each, in their own way contribute to the dialogue. Today, real-life ethical problems sell newspapers and glue people to TV soap operas. As the stuff of gossip, moral problems titillate. As the foundation of comedy and tragedy, they move us to laughter and tears—reminding us that we are not simply spectators but participants in the human condition. Against the backdrop of this long-standing fascination with morality, it is odd to think that a subject such as business ethics is new.

History offers good news and bad news about business ethics. The good news is that we are not orphans but part of a family of scholars who systematically discussed cases about the moral problems of doing business. The bad news is that our ancestors, the Sophists and the casuists, were considered the quacks and horsethieves of moral philosophy. They were so disliked as a group that the words "casuistry" and "sophistry" became pejoratives that described a specious form of hair-splitting argumentation. In the court of history, the Sophists were charged with false advertising and dangerous practices. The casuists, known for their case approach to ethics, were indicted for recklessly disregarding moral principles and pandering to the interests of the rich and powerful.

The dubious reputation of our ancestors may in part explain why some people scoff and others giggle when they hear that we teach business ethics. Unfortunately, we can't choose our relatives. We can, however, try to understand where they went wrong. After a brief examination of the Sophists' problems, this essay will focus on casuistry, which is generally defined as the tradition of using of cases to discuss practical ethical dilemmas (sometimes called "cases of conscience").

The growth of interest in all areas of applied ethics has set the stage for an examination of casuistry, including two excellent books published on the subject: *The Abuse of Casuistry,* by Albert R. Jonsen and Stephen Toulmin, and *Conscience and Casuistry in Early Modern Europe,* edited by Edmund Leites.[1] Since this essay offers only some snapshots of the history of casuistry, I refer you to these books for greater detail. In my quick survey, I'm not interested in engaging in exegetic arguments about particular historical texts; instead, I offer a sampling of this rich history and of the provocative questions that it raises for those of us who teach business ethics today. Hence, I take as my guide the old casuist adage "Where the masters disagree, the disciples are free."

THE PROBLEM WITH SOPHISTS

You get a good sense of the Sophist's public image from the opening of Plato's dialogue the "Protagoras." Socrates and his friends knock on the door of the house where the Sophist Protagoras is staying. The porter opens the door, looks at them, and says, "Ha, Sophists!" and slams the door in their faces.[2] Protagoras later tells us: "Personally I hold that the Sophist's art is an ancient one, but that those who put their hand to it in former times, fearing the odium which it brings, adopted a disguise and worked under cover."[3] He says that some used poetry, religion, music, or physical training "as a screen to escape malice." There were several reasons why the Sophists were disliked. For starters, their name was presumptuous—it meant wise man. But the key reason was the fact that Sophists were usually foreigners whose ideas were seen as a threat to the traditional order. The most interesting criticism of the Sophists for our purpose, however, centers on the intent and methodology of their instruction.

The decline of polytheism in the fifth century led to a kind of superstition, found in the writings of Aristophanes, Sophocles, and Plato, that suggested that there is some higher authority or law. These factors, combined with the emergence of a democratic city-state, led to a new set of assumptions about morality. Prior to the fifth century, education was handed down through families of aristocrats, and moral virtue was considered an inherited quality.[4] The myth in the "Protagoras" tells us that the gods gave all men a sense of justice.[5] The notion that all people could have moral knowledge led to the belief that virtue could be taught.

The Sophists weren't just teaching ethics, they were teaching professional ethics. Their mission was to teach people how to be successful political leaders. This included the teaching of political virtue *(aretê)*, which encompassed both moral and technical excellence. For example, Protagoras says that in addition to teaching virtue, he teaches young men how to manage their personal affairs, household affairs, and state affairs "so as to become a real power in the city, both as a speaker and a man of action."[6] Unlike philosophic or religious ethics, political and business ethics rest on the assumption that people will have the technical competence to sustain themselves in their professions. Inherent in both these areas of knowledge is the potential for conflict between the demands of morality and the demands of winning an election or staying in business. In other words, you have to be a politician before you can be an ethical politician. For the Sophists the conflict between moral and practical excellence centered on rhetoric.

As intellectual descendants of Homer and Hesiod, the Sophists harnessed the force of the poetic tradition and used it as a tool for molding public opinion. They taught their students how to lay out both sides of a public issue so that each side appeared to be of equal value. Students were required to memorize cases and arguments. Lessons in rhetoric emphasized the timeliness of action, the mood of the audience, and the "opportune moment" for introducing a particular point. The Sophists also showed students how to use maxims and definitions to make their point. While the Sophists did not have a particular ideology, they did attempt to assign a coherent set of meanings to the evaluative vocabulary as a means of giving guidance for how to live well.

Socrates was accused of being a Sophist, even though he never formally had students. Plato's *Dialogues* show us how Socrates cross-examined and refuted interlocutors in hopes of encouraging and admonishing them into a better understanding of concepts such as courage and piety. In the early dialogues, Socrates demonstrates why the Sophists' definitions are inadequate. The difference between the Sophists' rhetorical method and the Socratic method rests more on the pedagogical goal; the techniques are similar. Rhetoric aimed at analyzing an argument and moving an audience; Socratic method aimed at exploring concepts and bringing forth self-knowledge. The problem with rhetoric was not that it was evil but that it could be misused to "make the weaker argument appear the stronger." Philosophy purged itself of rhetoric out of the fear that the form and aesthetics of language would overpower the substance of truth.

When Socrates raised the question "Can virtue be taught?" he was not casting doubt but instead asking "How can virtue be taught?" and "Who [meaning what sort of person] should teach it?" These questions are analogous to issues in the current debate over business ethics. Can the subject be adequately taught by any skilled case method teacher? Should the teacher have some broader understanding of moral concepts? Underlying these two questions is the question of intent in teaching business ethics. Is it to solve moral problems in business, or is it to gain a greater understanding of morality in order to solve moral problems in business?

Plato's intellectual disdain for the Sophists is based on their agnosticism and their disregard for universal principles.[7] They were interested in the good of particular actions, not the nature of "the good." For example, in *Double Arguments* the great rhetorician Gorgias uses rhetorical techniques to show that nothing general can be said about ethics—each case and each situation must be judged anew.[8] The Sophists were ethical relativists who had an anti-intellectual attitude towards theoretical or scientific knowledge. As Protagoras says, "Man is the measure of all things; which are, that they are, and of things which are not that they are not." Plato's dispute with the Sophists rests on the conflict between absolutism and relativism that reappears throughout the history of Western thought. He envisioned ethics as scientific or universal knowledge, while the Sophists saw ethics only in terms of experience or practical knowledge. For Plato morality needed to be pinned down to some larger order of things. In recent years, some critics have expressed a similar concern over business ethics. They worry that ethics in business is somehow disconnected with traditional values.

A question often raised today is, Don't people learn about traditional values when they are children? If they haven't learned them by college, why bother? Aren't business students too old to learn ethics? Aristotle says no. Unlike Plato, who thought ethics was a science *(episteme)*, Aristotle tells us that ethics is a form of practical knowledge *(phronesis)*, which can be learned only through experience. Hence, in *Nicomachean Ethics* Aristotle says that you shouldn't even bother trying to teach ethics and politics to young people; he asserts that this sort of education is useful *only* when one has had sufficient experience in life to appreciate it fully.[9]

For the Greeks the moral character of the teacher was as important as his skill. Teaching ethics for pay had a suspicious ring to it. In the "Protagoras" and the "Sophist" Plato uses commercial imagery to talk about the Sophist. He refers to the Sophist as a "hired hunter of young rich men," "a sort of merchant of learning as nourishment for the soul," and a "retail dealer" in knowledge.[10] Socrates warns us to be careful that the Sophist, "in commending his wares, does not deceive you like the wholesaler and retailer who deal in food for the body."[11] Well into modern times, people frowned upon the idea of paying teachers because they feared that education would then change to please the whims of the students. Since the Sophists usually taught men from wealthy families, there was a potential for conflict. This issue reemerged in the seventeenth-century debate over the Jesuit casuists, who were accused of being apologists for their rich patrons. Recently, the idea of paid ethics consultants and expert ethics witnesses has raised the eyebrows of skeptics. If anything, the issue of pay reminds us that throughout history people have demanded pure, disinterested intentions in those who aspire to teach virtue.[12]

WHY THE SOPHISTS WEREN'T CASUISTS

The word "sophistry" is sometimes used interchangeably with "casuistry." However, the debate over the Sophists had a somewhat different set of concerns than those behind the debate that emerges over casuistry. Casuistry has historically appeared in tandem with some ethicolegal or purely legal absolutism. In its most positive sense, casuistry corrected the excesses of overly rigid laws by bridging the gap between abstract principles and particular cases. This sort of legalism was not present in ancient Greek culture. There was no distinction between externally imposed moral principles and individual moral character. Thus, there was no real need for casuistry to fill the gap.

The second reason why the ancient world had no need for casuistry was that the notion of conscience was not developed until the time of the Stoics. While there were hints of conscience in the writings of Heraclitus, Hesiod, and Homer, there was generally no strong sense of self-condemnation. Prior to the fifth century B.C., the poets (notably Homer) provided moral instruction. The heroes of the *Illiad* and the *Odyssey* did not develop moral imperatives but instead showed people what they should be. The heroes embodied the virtues in spite of the fact that they were often manipulated by the gods, who were not regarded by the Greeks as the ultimate moral authorities.

Last, the Sophists emerged to meet the needs of a changing society with no system of moral principles. Polytheism was in decline, and the old ethical qualities were superseded by intellectual qualities. Democracy made achievement and success something that any male citizen could obtain. Traditional morality based on virtues gave the Greeks a clear sense of what they should be, but, in this new and chaotic environment, they needed guidance in what they should do.

Hence, unlike the casuists, the Sophists were trying to create standard procedures and definitions to bring order to the competitive world of politics. The common criticism of both, however, was that they were relativists and morally lax.

THE ROOTS OF CASUISTRY

Casuistry is the art of reasoning from from cases. The word itself is derived from the Latin *casus,* meaning "case." In grammar a "case" is the falling away or declension of a noun. By analogy, the term "casuistry" implies a kind of deflection or falling away from a law or principle. Casuistry serves the dual purpose of applying principles to cases and using cases to help us understand and sometimes alter principles. It is morality in detail. Parents are casuists when they explain to their children why certain acts are good and bad. Children learn the meaning of words such as "good" and "fair" not by definition but by observing a number of situations in which those terms are applied. If the ascetic moralist is like a mathematician, the casuist is like a medicine man,[13] the former is interested in knowledge and judgment, whereas the latter is concerned with understanding and diagnosis. Casuists have been accused of too much contact with the world, ascetics too little.

Jonsen and Toulmin trace the roots of casuistry to Aristotle's assertion that moral knowledge is *phronesis,* not *episteme.* We gain moral knowledge through experience, but, unlike science or geometry, moral knowledge is not certain, nor is it universal. Jonsen and Toulmin see the beginnings of case analysis in the third book of *Nicomachean Ethics,* where Aristotle outlines how to appraise the morality of an action. He asks (1) "Who did it?" (2) "What was done?" (3) "In what context was it done?" (4) "Using what instrument?" (5) "To what end?" and (6) "In what manner?"[14]

Classical rhetoric also played an important part in the development of casuistry, according to Jonsen and Toulmin. For example, in Cicero's *De Officiis,* written in 44 B.C., we see rhetorical methods being used to discuss cases related to business. Cicero tells the reader that his intention is not just to raise questions but to resolve the them completely. Some of Cicero's cases pop up in other texts over hundreds of years. The following is one such case:

> Suppose an honest man sells a house because of some defects that he is aware of but others do not suspect. Suppose the house is unsanitary but is considered healthy; suppose no one knows that vermin can be seen in all the bedrooms, that the house is built of poor timber and quite dilapidated. The question is, if the seller does not tell these facts to a buyer and

sells the house for much more than he thought he could get for it, did he act without justice and without honor?[15]

After raising the question, Cicero looks at both sides of the case. Using natural law, definitions, and recognized duties, Cicero points out that concealment is different from keeping silent. In a similar case that would be relevant in any business ethics class today, Cicero tells the story of a merchant who arrives with a grain shipment at the gates of the famine-stricken city of Rhodes. The merchant knows that other shipments are one day behind him, but the citizens of the city do not. The question is, "Should the merchant conceal this fact from the buyers and charge a higher price?"[16] In the discussion of this case Cicero pits self-interest against natural law and again discusses the buyer's right to know.

THE POTENTIAL IMMORALITY OF LAW

The most important characteristic of casuistry is the fact that it emerges as a means of discussing ethics in times when there is an overreliance on the law or when there exists a kind of legal or ethical absolutism. At its best, casuistry corrects the excesses of the law. This feature is one reason people are interested in business ethics today. For a long time we believed that laws and regulations were sufficient to effect ethical behavior in business. Any good corporate lawyer can ensure that a company adheres to the letter of the law. But we have seen many cases in which businesses act legally but unethically.

Extreme dependence on laws to regulate behavior is called nomism. Nomism is a tendency, found in some religions, to try to control personal and social life by making law the supreme norm. When a religion or a society degenerates into a mere formalism of conduct, it ceases to have moral conviction and ethical purpose. The founders of Judaism aimed at making all life conform to law and wanted obedience to the commandments to be both a necessity and a custom. They realized, however, the danger of overdependence on the law and softened their legalism by emphasizing sincerity of the soul. Following the letter of the law was not sufficient; the heart had to be inclined to the spirit of the law. In the covenant to be made with Israel, the Bible says that "the Law would be written in the hearts of the people."[17] We see this idea resurface in Kant, who also saw that what made an action moral was not just adherence to duty but a good will.

The rabbis who wrote the Talmud with the intention of immortalizing the law were skilled casuists. Some, like the fifteenth-century scholar Jacob Pollack, were notorious for taking the law literally. Pollack developed a method called "spicing" the law, which used ingenious disputations to circumvent the meaning of its language.[18] Under the reformed Judaism of the eighteenth century, this sort of procedure became irrelevant, because the law was regarded as an ideal that was subject to interpretation.

OCCUPATIONS AND SINS IN THE MIDDLE AGES

In Christianity, casuistry developed as a means for helping priests judge sinners. Texts of cases, called penitential manuals, started to circulate around the third century. These texts analyzed cases using the precepts of Roman law. The Pelagian controversy of the fifth century over free will and the all-knowing nature of God increased the need for casuistry to mediate between morality and religion. Since priests were like judges, their main function was *subsumptio* (i.e., placing a particular case under a general rule.). However, before a judge could do this there had to be *constructio,* which involved finding the identifying marks of a case.

Penitential manuals proliferated in the thirteenth century, after the Fourth Lateran Council of 1215 decreed that everyone had to go to confession once a year. The Scholastics turned the old legal casuistry of the Church into moral casuistry. Interest shifted from punishing souls to reforming them, and understanding the individual and his or her trade became an important part of the priest's task. The first confessors' manuals were also printed in local (or "vulgar") languages. The "best-sellers" were those texts that had the greatest number of questions about trade. These manuals were bought up by wealthy merchants who sought the Church's opinion on questions such as "Is it legitimate to work in the fields or sell at fairs on Sunday?" According to the historian Jacques Le Goff, three themes emerged from these manuals: (1) Every Christian is essentially defined in relation to his profession: vocation and salvation. (2) All labor deserves compensation: vocation and money. (3) Every profession based on labor is justified: vocation and labor.[19]

Until the 1600s ordinary Christians thought of sin in terms of the seven deadly sins—gluttony, lust, pride, envy, avarice, anger, and sloth—not the rules of the Ten Commandments. One reason for the sins' greater popularity is that seven things are easier to remember than ten. They also had the advantage of being easy to portray symbolically to an illiterate public.[20] You can draw a great picture of gluttony, but how do you draw "Thou shalt not kill?" (It is interesting to think about the relationship between a graphic view of morality based on types and an auricular or literary view of morality based on instructions.)

Confessors' manuals advised priests to watch out for gluttony in cooks, lust in innkeepers, and greed in lawyers. Sins were also related to the sinner's place in the hierarchy. There were academic sins, judges' sins, peasants' sins, and mechanics' sins. As the middle class grew, new categories had to be created. In his book *The Birth of Purgatory* Le Goff argues that the concept of purgatory became popular in the late thirteenth century because the Church needed a correlative place in the afterlife for the middle class. On earth they stood between the powerful and the poor, the clergy and the laity.[21]

By the end of the twelfth century the Church was changing its views on wage labor and the professions. Powerful guilds were established, and the Church was on a cathedral-building spree. In one famous incident, a group of prostitutes approached the Bishop of Paris and offered to donate a window to Notre Dame Cathedral. Unlike a guild donation, their window would not depict a scene from their trade but would honor the Virgin Mary. The embarrassed bishop refused. Nonetheless, a decision on the case was written in one of the first confessional manuals of the period by Thomas of Chobham. It reflects how casuistry can be used to move an activity into a different moral category. Chobham wrote:

> Prostitutes must be counted among the mercenaries. They hire out their bodies and supply labor. . . . Whence this principle of secular justice: she does evil in being a prostitute, but she does not do evil in receiving the price of her labor, it being admitted that she is a prostitute. Whence the fact that it is possible to repent of practicing prostitution while keeping the profits of prostitution for the purposes of giving alms.
>
> If, however, prostitution is engaged in for pleasure, and the body hired out to experience ecstasy, then one's labor is not being hired and the profit is a shameful as the act.[22]

Here you can see how casuistry might go wrong. In Chobham's rush to add prestige to paid labor, he almost forgets about the problem with prostitution. The result is an argument that would support "Robin Hoodism"—you can do anything as long as you give the money to the Church or the poor. Chobham, however, pushes on to consider other problems with the prostitute's trade. He says:

> If the prostitute perfumes and adorns herself so as to attract with false allures and gives the impression of a beauty and seductiveness which she does not possess, the client buying what he sees, which, in this case, is deceptive, the prostitute then commits a sin, and she should not keep the profit it brings her. If the client saw her as she really is he would give her only a pittance, but as she appears beautiful and brilliant to him, he gives a handsome sum. In this case, she should keep only the pittance and re-

turn the rest to the client she has deceived, or to the Church, or to the poor.[23]

In the emerging market economy of this time, the Church used cases to inch toward changes in its policies on trade and the professions. For an fascinating discussion of how a variety of cases helped the Church reconceptualized its view of usury, have a look at Benjamin Nelson's book *The Idea of Usury*.[24]

HARD TIMES FOR CASUISTS

Casuistry came under serious attack in the seventeenth century, most notably in Blaise Pascal's *Provincial Letters* (1656).[25] Pascal served as the hit man for the Jansenists, a group of rigorous Catholics who were violently opposed to the moral laxity of the Jesuit casuists. Jesuits of this period—including Escobar y Mendoza, Luis Molina, Thomas Sanchez, and John Azor—studied classical rhetoric and used it as a basis for refining their techniques of case analysis. Pascal's attack on them was so vicious and delightfully written that he turned the word "casuistry" into a derogatory term. His slurs on the casuist Escobar resulted in the word "Escobarderie," which became a synonym in French for duplicity.

Pascal's critique of the casuists was not always fair or loyal to the texts.[26] However, there was much to criticize in the Jesuit doctrine of probabilism. The Jesuits took their inspiration from the words of Jesus to the adulterous: "Neither will I condemn thee."[27] They sought a moral minimum, and their goal was to make objective and meaningful judgments by holding a person innocent of sin in cases where there was doubt. Probabilism was meant to address the fact that moral laws are not like scientific laws, so it is reasonable to doubt them in light of concrete examples. If the lawfulness of an action was in doubt, the Jesuits believed that it was reasonable to follow a probable opinion favoring liberty. Another way of deciding which opinion to follow was to choose the position held by the more famous scholar. Pascal interpreted probabilism to mean "When in doubt, do what you want." As Plato was displeased by the Sophists, so Pascal was offended by the casuists' relativism and by their failure to present some broader vision of morality.

Not all of the casuistry that came out of this tradition was bad, however, nor did Pascal's *Provincial Letters* kill off casuistry. By the nineteenth century, the methods developed by the Jesuits for clarifying the circumstances of a case were still being used in new texts. Consider, for example, Jean Gury's analysis of this case, called "Of the Indirect Will":

Richard, an inn-keeper, happy in having a large patronage, furnishes abundantly wine to the drinkers, incited by the love of lucre, and also by the desire to prevent blasphemous talk, though foreseeing that many of them will get drunk; in his conscience, he is not sinning. He harbors, even cheerfully, men who hold impious or obscene conversations, and he does not reproach them for it, because, says he, he is not responsible for their conduct.[28]

In question 1 Gury asks, "Does Richard sin gravely in furnishing wine to people who will get drunk, without any better reason than his love for gain?" The answer to this question is yes, if the innkeeper continues to serve wine to someone who is already drunk. Here he sustains a slight loss for the sake of preventing a certain sin. Question 2 asks whether the innkeeper sins by not preventing drinkers from committing blasphemy. Generally no, says the casuist, because charity does not require that we sustain a considerable business loss (by not serving wine) in order to oppose sins. It is morally sufficient that the innkeeper desires to prevent drunkenness and blasphemy.

ENGLISH CASUISTRY AND SCRUPLE SHOPS

The attack on Jesuits did not deter the English Protestants from writing their own massive books of casuistry in the late seventeenth century. The best-known English casuists were Bishop Sanderson, Jeremy Taylor, William Ames, William Perkins, and Richard Baxter. In contrast to Roman casuistry's reliance on canon law and the confessional, English casuistry was based on the Scriptures, tradition, and right reason, which made it more accessible to the general public. In the seventeenth century Oxford students would get together every week for "scruple shops," in which they would discuss interesting cases of conscience.[29]

English casuistry also made it into the American educational system. In the eighteenth century, Ames's work was standard reading at Yale, where casuistical instruction was part of the curriculum. Ames's writings were replaced in the nineteenth century by Francis Wayland's book *The Elements of Moral Science*, a best-seller that sold more than sixty thousand copies.[30] The second volume of this book, entitled *Practical Ethics*, was thoroughly casuistical.[31]

At Harvard the required text for young men in the eighteenth century was Richard Baxter's *Christian Directory*.[32] Like other English casuists, Baxter included a section that provided directions for the conscience on buying, selling, borrowing, lending, and usury and that included questions about bribes, contracts, and promises. In contrast to the Jesuits, the English casuists gave the benefit of doubt to the law only if more could be said against following it than could be said in favor of it. Notice how the principle works in the following case from Baxter's "Cases and Directions About Trusts and Secrets":

> What if a delinquent intrust me with his estate or person to secure it from penalty? Baxter answers, if the case has already been prosecuted and punishment required by the common good, then you shouldn't take it. However, if you think that your friend will repent and that his act will result in what a magistrate (if he knew) might agree is a greater good, then go ahead just don't lie or use other sinful means.[33]

CASUISTRY GOES PUBLIC

English casuistry soon found its way into literature and journalism. The best-known casuistical writer was Daniel Defoe. His novels *Roxana, Moll Flanders,* and *Robinson Crusoe* are chock-full of characters who are blameworthy but nonetheless evoke our sympathy. Defoe liked to write about how people rationalize immoral actions by making their situation the exception to the rule. In his essay "An Enquiry into the occasional Conformity of Dissenters" (1698), Defoe calls the tendency to misuse casuistry "playing Bopeep with the Almighty."[34] Many of Defoe's story ideas came from the magazine *The Athenian Mercury,* originally called *The Athenian Gazette: or Casuistical Mercury,* which printed readers' questions about moral problems. The magazine's subheading read "resolving all the most nice and curious questions proposed by the ingenious of either sex."

First published in 1690, *The Athenian Mercury* was the forerunner of magazines like *The Tatler* and *The Spectator.* John Dunton, its publisher and editor, wanted to "oblige the reader with a true discovery of the 'question project.' " By promising anonymity to his readers, Dunton hoped to elicit the "nice and curious questions" that people were too embarrassed to ask the divines.[35] We see in *The Athenian Mercury* the "Dear Abby" format that flourishes today, particularly in women's magazines.

Many of *The Athenian Mercury's* cases were about courtship and marriage. Some of the most interesting queries were actually retreads of famous cases discussed by casuists such as Jeremy Taylor. In one such case, an alleged reader asked: "Whether a man who has by mistake married his own daughter, coming afterwards to know it, is obliged to acquaint her with it, if he believe the knowledge of it will occasion her death; and how otherwise he ought to demean himself in that condition, having children by her, upon whom the reproach of being so born may bring a great affliction?"[36] Early on,

Dunton must have realized this sort of kinky moral problem sold magazines. Today we hear these types of issues discussed on TV talk shows sporting titles like "Cross-Dressers and the Women Who Love Them." Public discussion of private issues always seems to draw a crowd.

The cases from *The Athenian Mercury* were later categorized and republished in five volumes as *The Athenian Oracle*. Editors showed a mixture of respect for morality and pragmatism in their replies to readers' queries. One section of the reprint contains cases on business and employment. For example, a shop clerk wrote: "I needed money but didn't know anyone to borrow it from, so I cheated my master. After a time, I made up a greater sum and gave it to him for goods never sold, which will be a clear profit to him. In your opinion, is this a sin before God?"[37] Because you ought to "do unto others," it is a sin, the editors reasoned. They pointed out that the master might have needed the money before it was given back. Nonetheless, they went on to say, "We don't think that you are obliged to mention it to him [the master], for the world is reflective—beg for God's pardon and don't do it again."[38]

PHILOSOPHY ASCENDS

With the growth of literacy and the popular press, cases of conscience moved from the hallowed regions of religion and philosophy to the streets and coffeehouses. In his book *Lectures on the History of Moral Philosophy in England,* William Whewell traces the roots of modern moral philosophy to the English casuists of the seventeenth century, including Taylor and Sanderson.[39] Writing in 1852, Whewell maintained that Taylor's use of cases as illustrations of moral principles was the first step toward a systematic approach to morality.[40] During this time, however, philosophy was beginning its Platonic ascent into theory. As a sign of the times, Whewell changed the name of his chair at Cambridge from the Knightsbridge Chair of Casuistical Divinity to Professor of Moral Philosophy.[41]

By the twentieth century, G. E. Moore acknowledged in his *Principia Ethica* that "casuistry forms part of the ideal of ethical science: Ethics cannot be complete without it."[42] However, he washed the philosopher's hands of applied ethics when he asserted that it is not the business of a moral philosopher to give personal advice. Jonsen and Toulmin argue that modern philosophy's rejection of case ethics "is a lingering expression of the intellectual dream that, after all, ethics may yet be transformed into a universal theoretical science."[43] I don't think that we should take this to mean that philosophy should give up this quest. The infamous history of sophistry and casuistry tells us that case ethics without some larger picture of morality and tradition elicits outrage. Even if the search for scientific ethics is futile, we need to continue it so as to keep the dialogue between theory and practice alive.

In practical terms, business ethics must balance the demands of laws with the demands of particular circumstances. We also need, however, to convey some broader vision of the role that business plays in history and culture. I have been fascinated by the use of the word "greed" in recent discussions of business scandals. Public concern focuses more on an emerging disposition in our culture than on legal malfeasance. We live in a society filled with laws, codes, regulations, and "how to" books. Some are inclined to improve professional ethics by creating more rules and better codes. When President Bush entered office he appointed a lawyer to draft a new ethics code. The moral problem in government is not that public officials need instructions on how to act, however, but that they have lost sight of what it means to be a public official. They know that a conflict of interest is wrong, but they no longer possess a vision of what their interests should be. We could create more rules, but this approach is not sufficient because eventually it leads to an infinite regress of rules upon rules upon rules.

Modernity has been compared to a digital watch, which unlike an analog watch doesn't indicate where we've been or where we're going; it displays only the present. When we look at history, we see that few of our current moral problems are new. Most are just variations on themes—with new actors, props, and stage settings. Hence, it is not enough to teach business ethics by simply looking at cases or devising new rules to follow. We need to take our students to the crossroads of the humanities and engage them in the ongoing conversation about morality in everyday life.[44]

NOTES

My thanks to Kenneth E. Goodpaster, who saw the relevance of casuistry to business ethics and gave me valuable guidance in the early phases of my research.

1. Albert R. Jonsen and Stephen Toulmin, *The Abuse of Casuistry: A History of Moral Reasoning* (Berkeley: University of California Press, 1988). Edmund Leites, ed., *Conscience and Casuistry in Early Modern Europe* (Cambridge: Cambridge University Press, 1988).

2. Plato, *Protagoras,* in *The Collected Dialogues of Plato,* ed. Edith Hamilton and Huntington Cairns (Princeton, N.J.: Princeton University Press, 1971), 314d–e. All references to Plato are from this edition.

3. Ibid., 316d–317b.

4. Werner Jaeger, *Paideia*, vol. 2 (New York: Oxford University Press, 1943), p. 287. See also George Grote, *A History of Greece*, vol. 3 (London: John Murray, 1869).

5. Plato, *Protagoras*, 349e.

6. Ibid., 318e–319.

7. There were also cultural and personal reasons why Plato disliked the Sophists, but here I focus only on what he tells us in the text of his dialogues.

8. See Mario Untersteiner, *The Sophists*, trans. Kathleen Freeman (Oxford: Basil Blackwell, 1954).

9. Aristotle, *Ethica Nicomachea*, ed. David Ross (Oxford: Oxford University Press, 1980), bk. 2, 1103a11–a37.

10. Plato, *Sophist*, 331c–e.

11. Plato, *Protagoras*, 313c–d.

12. Jacques Le Goff points out that in the Middle Ages the argument against paying teachers was similar to the argument against usury: one should not pay teachers because that would be like selling knowledge, and knowledge belongs to God. In the case of usury, the same prohibition was made against selling time. See Jacques Le Goff, *Time, Work, and Culture in the Middle Ages*, trans. Arthur Goldhammer (Chicago: University of Chicago Press, 1980), p. 29.

13. This analogy is suggested in Jonsen and Toulmin, *Abuse of Casuistry*, pp. 42–6.

14. Ibid., p. 71.

15. Marcus Tullius Cicero, *De Officiis*, trans. Harry G. Edinger (Indianapolis, Ind.: The Library of Living Arts, 1974), bk. 3, 54.

16. Ibid., bk. 3, 50.

17. Jer. 31.33.

18. Robert Mark Wenley, "Casuistry," in *Encyclopedia of Religion and Ethics*, vol. 3, ed. James Hastings (New York: Charles Scribner, 1929), p. 243. See also his *Modern Thought and the Crisis in Belief* (New York: Macmillan, 1909).

19. Le Goff, *Time, Work, and Culture in the Middle Ages*, p. 118.

20. John Bossy, "Moral Arithmetic: Seven Sins in to Ten Commandments," in Leites, ed., *Conscience and Casuistry in Early Modern Europe*, p. 220.

21. See Le Goff, *The Birth of Purgatory* (Chicago: University of Chicago Press, 1984).

22. Le Goff, *Time, Work and Culture in the Middle Ages*, p. 66.

23. Ibid., pp. 66–67.

24. Benjamin Nelson, *The Idea of Usury* (Chicago: University of Chicago Press, 1969).

25. Blaise Pascal, *The Provincial Letters*, trans. A. J. Krailsheimer (New York: Penguin Books, 1982).

26. For an excellent discussion of this debate, see Jonsen and Toulmin, *Abuse of Casuistry*, chap. 8.

27. John 8.11.

28. Paul Bert, trans., *The Doctrine of the Jesuits* (Boston: B. F. Bradbury, 1940), p. 55.

29. Robert Barclay, *The Inner Life of Religious Societies of the Commonwealth* (London: Hodder and Stoughton, 1876).

30. Francis Wayland, *The Elements of Moral Science* (Cambridge, Mass.: Belknap Press of Harvard University Press, 1963).

31. Wenley, "Casuistry," p. 245.

32. Richard Baxter, *A Christian Directory* (London: Robert White, 1673).

33. Richard Baxter, *Baxter's Works*, vol. 1 (London: Henry G. Bohn, 1854), p. 866.

34. G. A. Starr, *Defoe and Casuistry* (Princeton, N.J.: Princeton University Press, 1971), p. 4.

35. Gilbert D. McEwen, *The Oracle of the Coffee House* (San Marino, Calif.: The Huntington Library, 1972), p. 3.

36. *The Athenian Oracle*, vol. 2., p. 183.

37. Ibid., p. 155.

38. Ibid.

39. William Whewell, *Lectures on the History of Moral Philosophy in England* (London: J. W. Parker, 1852).

40. William Whewell, *The Elements of Morality*, vol. 1 (London: J. W. Parker, 1845).

41. Jonsen and Toulmin, *Abuse of Casuistry*, p. 163.

42. G. E. Moore, *Principia Ethica* (New York: Cambridge University Press, 1968), p. 5.

43. Jonsen and Toulmin, *Abuse of Casuistry*, p. 20.

44. In addition to the works already cited, the following sources have also been consulted: William E. Addis and Thomas Arnold, eds., *A Catholic Dictionary* (London: Kegan Paul & Trench, 1885); Morton W. Bloomfield, *The Seven Deadly Sins* (Mich.: State College Press, 1952); James Broderick, *The Economic Morals of the Jesuits* (London: Oxford University Press, 1934); Jack H. Broome, *Pascal* (New York: Barnes & Noble, 1965); Jospeh Butler, *The Analogy of Religion* (London: Oxford University Press, 1934); Enrico Castelli, ed., *Tecnica e Casistica* (Rome: Instituto di Studi Filosofici, 1964); Dwight Cathcart, *Doubting Conscience: Donne and the Poetry of Moral Argument* (Ann Arbor: University of Michigan Press, 1975); Thomas De Quincey, *Uncollected Writings*, vol. 2, ed. James Hogg (New York: Books for Libraries Press, 1972); Peter Drucker, "What Is 'Business Ethics'?" *The Public Interest* 63 (Spring 1981); George A. Grote, *A History of Greece*, vol. 8 (London: John Murray, 1869); Richard M. Hare, "Medical Ethics: Can the Moral Philosopher Help?" in Stuart F. Spicker and H. Tristram Engelhardt, eds., *Philosophical Medical Ethics: Its Nature and Significance* (Boston: D. Reidel, 1977); Frank L. Huntley, *Jeremy Taylor and the Great Rebellion* (Ann Arbor: University of Michigan Press, 1970); Kenneth E. Kirk, *Conscience and Its Problems: An Introduction to Casuistry* (London: Longmans, Green, 1927); Roger L'Estrange, *The Casuist Uncased* (London: Sign of the Gun, 1680); George Lewis, *Robert Sanderson* (New York: Macmillan, 1924); Edward Leroy Long, Jr., *Conscience and Compromise: An Approach to Protestant Casuistry* (Philadelphia, Pa.: Westminister Press, 1950); Martin Luther, *Luther's Works*, ed. Walther I. Brandt, vol 45 (Philadelphia, Pa.: Muhlenberg Press, 1962); Alasdair MacIntyre, *A Short History of Ethics* (New York: Macmillan, 1973); W. I. Matson, "Kant as Casuist," *The Journal of Philosophy*, vol. 51 (December 1954); Freder-

ick Denison Maurice, *The Conscience: Lectures on Casuistry* (London: Macmillan, 1868); Robert James Merrett, *Daniel Defoe's Moral and Rhetorical Ideas* (Victoria, B.C.: University of Victoria, 1980); Edward Caldwell Moore, *Christian Thought Since Kant* (New York: Charles Scribner, 1915); Raymond Mortimer, ed., *The Seven Deadly Sins* (London: Sunday Times Publications, 1962); J. Clark Murray, *A Handbook of Christian Ethics* (Edinburgh: T&T Clark, 1980); Benjamin Nelson, "Conscience, Casuistry, and the Cure of the Souls," unpublished ms., 1950); G. B. Nicolini, *History of the Jesuits: Their Origins, Progress, Doctrines, and Designs* (London: Henry G. Bohn, 1854); George R. Noyes, ed., *Collection of Theological Essays from Various Authors* (New York: Walker Fuller, 1866); Chaim Perelman and Lucie Olbrechts-Tyteca, *The New Rhetoric: A Treatise on Argumentation* (Notre Dame, Ind.: University of Notre Dame Press, 1971); Nicolas Perrault, *The Jesuits Morals*, trans. Exerel Tonge (London: John Starkey, 1679); Robert Sanderson, *Lectures on Conscience and Human Law*, ed. Charles Wordsworth (London: James Williamson, 1877); Jerome B. Schneewind, *Sidgwick's Ethics and Victorian Moral Philosophy* (Oxford: Oxford University Press, 1977); Henry Sidgwick, *Outlines of the History of Ethics* (Boston: Beacon Press, 1968); Thomas Slatter, S.J., *Cases of Conscience for English-Speaking Countries*, vol. 1 (New York: Benziger Bros., 1911); Camille Wells Slights, *The Casuistical Tradition in Shakespeare, Donnne, Herbert, and Milton* (Princeton, N.J.: Princeton University Press, 1981); Jeremy Taylor, *Whole Works*, vol. 12 (London: Thomas Davison, 1828); Stephen Toulmin, *The Place of Reason in Ethics* (Chicago: University of Chicago Press, 1986); Eduard Zeller, *Outlines of the History of Greek Philosophy*, trans. Sarah Frances Alleyne and Evelyn Abbott (London: Longmans, Green, 1886); *Zeller's Pre-Socratic Philosophy*, trans. Sarah Frances Alleyne (London: Longmans, Green, 1881).

Some Lessons and Nonlessons of Casuist History

Manuel G. Velasquez

In her interesting essay Joanne B. Ciulla suggests that history can make an important contribution to business ethics. In particular, she suggests, a study of the history of casuistry can yield a wealth of material on business ethics, from the discussions of the Greek Sophists and of Socrates, Plato, and Aristotle, through the writings of the Roman Cicero, who discussed a variety of cases relating to trade in Book III of *De Officiis,* through the penitential manuals of the thirteenth century, and on to the writings of the classical casuists in the sixteenth and seventeenth centuries and of the English casuists in the seventeenth, eighteenth, and nineteenth centuries. Ciulla holds that examining what these writings have to say about morality in business situations might provide us with some interesting and helpful insights that might be put to use in resolving similar quandaries in contemporary business ethics.

Although, as we will see, I agree with Ciulla's suggestion that a study of the history of casuistry will shed some light on contemporary business ethics, I do not think that the illumination is of the kind that she assumes will shine forth. I will argue that there is a significant problem raised by attempts to apply the moral concepts of earlier periods of history to the business problems encountered in our own age. The problem is that the social context of the casuists radically affected their moral pronouncements about business. Since our own social context is so radically different from theirs in several significant respects, it is inappropriate to apply their moral judgments to our own business institutions. I will then try to show that there is nevertheless an important lesson to be drawn from the discussions of the casuists. This lesson is not concerned with the substantive moral judgments of the casuists but is, rather, an important lesson about how moral reasoning itself should be conceived.

SOME NONLESSONS OF HISTORY

Let me begin with Ciulla's suggestion that we might learn something about business ethics by looking at the moral discussions of the early Greeks. These discussions, I would argue, are inextricably tied to the social and economic contexts in which they took place in a way that calls into question our ability to simply transfer them to a contemporary context.

The economy of the early Greeks was predominantly agrarian, and Greek city-states were almost uniformly organized into rigidly stratified hierarchical social systems. At the top of the social order sat the aristocratic citizenry, which alone could own land and hold political office. Crowded at the bottom were the serfs and slaves who provided the labor required to work the farms and mines. Somewhere in the middle were the Metics, resident foreigners who settled in the Greek cities but who were barred from citizenship and from owning land, although they (unlike slaves) had access to Athenian courts, where they could initiate legal actions against citizens as well as other Metics.[1]

Although the bulk of the early Greek economy remained agrarian for centuries, toward the end of the sixth century B.C. the economy of the Greek cities, especially Athens, developed a brisk market in international trade. The landed aristocracy of Greece, however, for the most part did not take part in these new commercial and industrial opportunities. Its members were content to farm their land holdings and exploit the mines on their lands. It was the Metics, the resident foreigners who could not own land, who quickly plunged into the business of acquiring wealth through commerce and industry.[2]

The Metics in Athens dominated the ceramic and textile industries and controlled most retail trading and the bulk of the shipping and trade industries. Through their business ventures, they managed to amass considerable capital, enough that some were able to rent the lands away from the aristocracy, buy slaves whom they would then hire out to the aristocracy, and provide loans to the aristocracy at interest rates of from 10 to 60 percent. Not surprisingly, considerable enmity arose between the Metic foreigners and the native Greeks.

Moreover, the trade and shipping activities of the Metics brought them into contact with the intellectual perspectives of the non-Greek world and introduced them to non-Greek ideas. The Metic travelers imported these ideas from abroad and became the nucleus of a new class of thinkers, the so-called Sophists to whom Ciulla refers.[3] The Sophists, who traveled to foreign markets as part of their trading activities, naturally concluded that all social norms were arbitrary, thereby challenging the settled morality of the native Greeks who stayed at home on their farms. And, since the Sophists were legally prohibited from owning land, they had to find other ways of making money: naturally, they sold their services like modern teachers.

When Socrates, Plato, and Aristotle came along in the fifth and fourth centuries B.C., they, of course, sided with the native landed aristocracy against the Metics. Socrates was himself a citizen, as was Plato, who was also a member of the aristocracy, and Aristotle was Plato's student. That they all should have argued against the Sophists is not surprising since the Sophists belonged to the Metic class. The attacks of Socrates, Plato, and Aristotle against the Sophists, then, have to be understood in terms of the social class to which they and the Sophists belonged and the extent to which one class was seen as a threat to the other.[4] Their attacks, for example, on the fact that the Sophists hired themselves out as teachers was an attack on one of the economic activities of the Metics.

Moreover, when Plato and Aristotle discussed the ethics of business activities, their positions were strongly biased by this class enmity.[5] In the *Republic* Plato argued that all commercial activities—that is, the economic activities of the Metics—should be subordinated to the control of an educated elite; that the ruling elites should be prohibited from entering the corrupting activities of the commercial world—that is, the world of the Metics; that business profits—that is, the profits of the Metics—should be strictly limited to compensation for services rendered; that foreign trade—that is, the trade of the Metics—should be rigorously regulated; that prices—that is, the prices charged by the Metics—should be fixed; and that lending at interest—that is, the lending of the Metics—should be outlawed. In short, Plato condemned the economic activities of the social class that had become a threat to his own by characterizing these activities as immoral.

Not surprisingly, the writings of Plato's student Aristotle reflect the class biases of his teacher. In his *Politics* Aristotle wrote that "citizens must not lead the life of . . . merchants, for such a life is ignoble and inimical to virtue."[6] Earlier, he told us: "There are two sorts of wealth-getting; one is estate management, the other is retail trade; the former is necessary and honorable, but [retail trade] which consists in exchange, is justly condemned, for it is unnatural, and a way by which men try to gain from one another."[7] In short, the profit motive—the economic motive of the Metics—is wrong and unnatural.

But the most unnatural means of making money, Aristotle argued, was wealth generated by charging interest. He wrote that "the most hated kind [of money making], and with the greatest reason, is usury, which makes a gain out of money itself, and not from its natural purpose. For money is intended to be used in exchange, but not to increase at interest. . . . Which is why of all ways of getting wealth, this is the most unnatural."[8] So much for the moneylending of the Metics.

In short, both Plato and Aristotle united to heap moral condemnation on business activities, including exchanging for profit and lending at interest. But these moral pronouncements were condemnations of the activities of the wealthy foreigners living in their midst, the Metics, against whom they had a strong class bias. These moral judgments of Plato and Aristotle, then were deeply influenced by the economic and social circumstances in which they found themselves. Their attacks against the Sophists and their moral evaluations of business, of the profit motive, and of interest have to be understood in terms of the social class structure within which they lived.

Our class structure, of course, is utterly different—so different that today the banker, whose core activity is the lending of money at interest that the aristocratic Greeks despised, is among the most respected members of our communities and trading for profit is no longer scorned but is seen as the foundation of our economic life. Given the radically different social and economic contexts of the Greeks and ourselves, then, and given that the moral judgments of the Greeks were tightly linked to those contexts, it is difficult to see exactly how much light their moral judgments can shed on our own questions about the morality of various business practices.

A similar point can be made about the second set of historical writings to which Ciulla calls our attention: the writings of the Roman Cicero. The educated Roman aristocracy, of which Cicero was a part, also had its economic base in land holdings.[9] Farming was its most characteristic source of income. The Roman aristocracy, therefore, inherited the Greek aristocracy's distaste for business. There was an exception, however. The business enterprises of very wealthy merchants were grudgingly approved, but only if the merchant had washed off the stink of business and retired to the purer life of a gentleman farmer.

In fact, Cicero, who was a member of the Roman upper class, began his discussion of ethics in commerce with these words:

> I will now discuss trading and money-making: some methods we have been taught to consider gentlemanly, others sordid. The first to be condemned are those which make for unpopularity, such as . . . lending at interest. . . . Retail dealers are little better, for they have little to gain un-

less they are very dishonest, and then deserve no credit. . . . The career of a merchant is to be despised if pursued on a small scale, but if it includes large and valuable transactions and imports from all over the world resulting in a large clientele from honest dealing, it is not so much to be condemned; in fact, if those who indulge in it become satisfied or at any rate are prepared to be content with their profits, and retire from the harbor to their country estates . . . this seems to be entirely commendable. But of all the sources of income, the life of the farmer is the best, pleasantest, most profitable and most befitting a gentleman.[10]

Thus, the moral judgments of Cicero to which Ciulla calls our attention, like those of Plato and Aristotle before him, are biased by Cicero's social class standing. They heap moral approval on those economic activities of their own social class and characterize as immoral the economic activities of opposing classes.

My conclusion, again, is that it is not altogether clear that one can so easily draw upon the moral concepts and arguments of one period of history and use them to elucidate the moral quandaries of another age. The social context of the ancient Roman moralists deeply influenced their moral views, and their context was radically unlike ours.

It is equally dangerous, I believe, to take the moral judgments of the medieval casuists at face value and to think that we can easily transfer their insights to a modern setting. Let me take but one example that illustrates the difficulty: the casuist discussions of lending at interest, that is, of usury.[11] As is well known, usury was unanimously condemned throughout the whole of the Middle Ages, and medieval casuists frequently cited the arguments of Aristotle to support their condemnations. But it is important to realize that the agrarian and localized economies of the Middle Ages had little use for moneylending. So long as moneylending was economically unnecessary, the casuists condemned it.

However, as European economies developed, as trade routes opened up, as transportation improved, as business enterprises grew, the opportunities for investment proliferated, and moneylending became a necessity. Once moneylending became an economic necessity, casuists changed their views on its morality. Whereas moneylending was unanimously condemned by the casuists who lived in the agrarian societies of the early Middle Ages, the casuists of a later, more economically developed Europe advanced some rather novel moral justifications for this heretofore condemned activity.

This change in the treatment of the morality of moneylending by the casuists was driven almost wholly by profound changes in their economic institutions. The lesson to be drawn, again, is that moral concepts and moral judgments are deeply influenced by their social context and that they cannot simply be plucked from one historical context and applied to the problems of another age.

SOME LESSONS OF HISTORY

That having been said, there is nevertheless an important lesson to be learned from the casuists. It is a lesson which Ciulla hints at but does not develop. The most important lessons that the casuists can teach us, I believe, do not concern their substantive moral judgments about the morality of business practices, which, as I have suggested, are socially conditioned. The most important lessons of the casuists concern the *method* they used and the *assumptions* behind this method. Let me develop this idea, and let me begin by painting a picture, using very broad strokes, of our current conception of the method that is appropriate for ethics.

Contemporary ethics is dominated by a certain conception of moral reasoning. In spite of some stinging attacks by Alasdair McIntyre[12] and others, this conception of moral reasoning continues to be the governing assumption in most contemporary writings on ethics and in virtually all writing in what is called "applied ethics," including, I am embarrassed to admit, much of my own writings on business ethics.

The conception I have in mind patterns moral reasoning on the model of a deductive syllogism. The syllogism contains two main premises and results in a conclusion about what ought to be done in a particular situation or type of situation. The first premise of the syllogism is supposed to consist of a highly general moral principle. The second premise is supposed to consist of a factual description of the situation. By putting together the moral principle and the facts about the particular situation, one may draw a conclusion about what ought to be done in that particular situation.

The utilitarian, for example, assumes that the utilitarian principle is supposed to function as the fundamental premise in moral arguments, the Kantian assumes that this is the function of the categorical imperative, and the Rawlsian assumes that this is the function of the difference principle. Each of these will then further assume that in order to apply the respective principles, we need to supply some factual information—that is, the second premise—concerning the situation to which the principles are to be applied. The utilitarian will want to know which courses of action are available and what utilities attach to each of these actions; the Kantian will want to know what forms of deception, manipulation, coercion, or other forms of treating people as mere means are present in a situation; the Rawlsian will want to know what kinds of social arrangements would have the highest probability of leaving the least advantaged group best off. Once we supply these kinds of factual information, it is a fairly straightforward task to apply the general principle to the facts of the situation and derive a conclusion about what ought to be done in the particular situation.

The task of applied ethics in this view is simple: to provide the second or factual premise and to derive the conclusion. Not surprisingly, applied ethics in this view is perceived as being a derivative and intellectually uninteresting discipline. It is not theoretically interesting because it is not fundamental and because its core activity is empirical information gathering, rather than analytical inquiry. It is, therefore, somewhat disreputable in an academic context. Business ethics, as a form of applied ethics, becomes a poor cousin of the fundamental research being conducted in ethics. The truly interesting and important ethical problems are believed to lie in the discussion and establishment of the fundamental premises of moral arguments—the highly abstract moral principles—which is where the real work of ethics, it is assumed, is being done.

Moreover, in this view of moral reasoning, cases serve merely an illustrative and pedagogical function. They serve to explain, through example, the meaning of moral principles, and they provide the student with practice in using these principles. The moral principles on the basis of which cases are resolved are determined prior to the case, and case applications have little to say about the shape of these rules. The normative burden in moral reasoning is carried by the general moral principles, to which the cases are supposed to add nothing more than an illustration. This view of the role of particular examples is most clearly stated by Kant, one of the prime architects of this view of moral reasoning. He writes in the *Groundwork:* "We cannot do morality a worse service than by seeking to derive it from examples. Every example of it presented to me must first itself be judged by moral principles in order to decide if it is fit to serve as an original example—that is, as a model: it can in no way supply the prime source for the concept of morality." [13]

Now I want to describe another, very different conception of moral reasoning, one that is quite alien to the approach that currently dominates contemporary philosophy. It is the conception that lies behind the casuistry of the late medieval casuists. [14]

Reading the works of the medieval casuists is a strange experience. For there is little of the discussion of principles that we have become accustomed to expect in treatises on ethics. Instead, we find a listing of situation after situation, case after case, preceded by the question "Is it legal to"?

Let me take as an example Alphonsus Ligouri, a late casuist, who in 1763 authored a fifth edition of his *Theologia Moralis.* [15] In the tract on the seventh commandment, "Do not steal," he discusses contracts.[16] After giving some examples of clear cases of legitimate contractual exchanges and reviewing the obligations created by such contracts and several other related issues, he goes on to discuss buying and selling through contracts.[17] After a general discussion, he gives a series of "doubts" under these headings:[18]

- Does a hidden defect in a commodity render the sales contract void?
- What if the defect concerns the substance of the commodity?
- What if the seller sells an adulterated substance as a pure one?
- What if it is wine that is mixed with water?
- What if the defect concerns the quantity of what is sold?
- What if the defect concerns the quality of what is sold?
- Is it licit to sell a promissory note at its ordinary value when the debtor is insolvent?
- Is it licit to sell an annuity that will soon decrease in value?
- If a thing is entrusted to you to sell at a fixed price and you manage to sell it for more, is it licit for you to keep the surplus?
- If a thing happens to be sold twice, who owns it?
- If a thing perishes before it is handed over to the purchaser, who suffers the loss?
- What if it perishes after it is handed over?

As he discusses these matters, Ligouri tends to follow a more or less set pattern. He begins his discussion by setting out particular situations about whose morality or immorality he is particularly confident and that he classifies under a simple moral rule such as "Do not steal" or "Honor your promises." Then he sets out a series of situations, similar to those I just listed, that resemble the paradigm situation but that involve some complicating circumstance that renders him less sure about the application of the simple rule. He describes the new situation and attempts to assimilate it to the earlier clear paradigm situations, or else he notes the features that set off the present situation from the earlier paradigm he has discussed. He then renders his opinion on the new situation and notes the other casuists who concur with his opinion and those who dissent. Where there is dissent, he again notes the features of the situation around which the dissent turns. He ends by stating what he takes to be the most probable judgment on the situation and goes on to the next complicating circumstance.

To our modern eyes, it is astonishing to see that Ligouri the casuist does not attempt to construct a deductive argument that somehow applies a high moral principle to a particular case. Instead, he proceeds by building up a large repertoire of particular cases that serve as paradigms of a simple and ordinary moral rule ("Do not steal") and whose morality is therefore obvious and uncontroversial. Questions about new cases are then solved by analogy to the cases in this repertoire of settled cases or by identifying the features that differentiate the new case from these cases, rendering it an exception to these paradigmatic cases. The normative burden of this form of moral reasoning is thus carried by particular cases, not by abstract moral principles, and moral reasoning proceeds by analogy and differentiation, not by deductive syllogism.[19]

For the classical casuist, then, moral reasoning is not seen as proceeding from highly abstract moral principles through facts to particular conclusions. Moral reasoning consists instead of moving from paradigmatic cases of ordinary moral rules through a process of analogy and generalization to conclusions about new cases. As experience adds more settled cases to the repertoire of the casuist, he is able to extend the scope of his analysis; as new cases that embody new features are brought forth, the casuist is able to branch off into a new way of judging these cases by differentiating them from the old. (This form of moral reasoning is therefore much more flexible and attuned to the changing nature of the moral life than is our contemporary method of proceeding from fixed general principles; and that explains why, of course, the casuists were able to change their treatment of usury when new circumstances called for a change.)

There are several lessons to be drawn from this consideration of the methods of the classical casuists. First, the view of moral reasoning that today continues to dominate the philosophical world and that still holds us in thrall in applied ethics in general and in business ethics in particular is not the only or necessarily the most important form of moral reasoning. There is a form of moral reasoning, exemplified by the casuists, that begins with concrete cases and that returns to those concrete cases to evaluate the moral quality of new cases.

Second, if the method of the casuist mirrors a correct form of moral reasoning, then applied ethics is not a poor cousin to general theory building, as we presently tend to think it is. If the casuist method of moral reasoning is more fundamental, then the real action in ethics ought not to be in abstract theory building but in the minute analysis and dissection of concrete situations, in short, of cases. Contemporary ethics should not look with disdain upon applied ethics, because that is where the real foundational work of ethics should be done.

Third, the casuist method of moral reasoning suggests the possibility of reconceiving practical reasoning in general. We tend today to conceive of all reasoning, including practical reasoning, as essentially deductive. It is assumed that in order to decide what one is to do in a given situation, one must have at hand a set of rules about the types of behaviors that are appropriate for given types of situations. Decisions are made by scanning one's environment to gather information about the type of situation one is in. Then this information is put together with the rules, and a decision is made about the appropriate type of behavior.

The problem faced by this model of practical reasoning is that if practical reasoning proceeded in the fashion the model proposes, the number of rules required by everyday living would have to be impossibly large. For concrete situations are so very different, changing, and detailed that the number of rules that would have to be written to cover even a small class of different types of situations and circumstances quickly multiplies beyond the ability of any intellect to handle.[20]

Examination of the casuist method of the medievals suggests that it is possible to abandon the assumption that practical reasoning proceeds by applying general rules to particular situations. Suppose, for example, that as a person moves from childhood through adulthood, he or she acquires a larger and larger repertoire of stored memories of particular situations. When a person encounters a new situation, she determines what to do by a process of analogy: by asking which of the concrete situations that she has encountered in the past is most analogous to this new situation? Then, by doing what worked in the earlier situation, she solves the problems facing her in the new situation. Practical reasoning, then, may move not from general rules through deductive processes to particular concrete situations but from particular concrete situations through analogy to concrete situations.[21]

Fourth, the example of the casuist points to four elements that are desperately needed in contemporary applied ethics, particularly in business ethics. First, we need what is central to a casuist method: a rich collection of paradigm cases of exemplary and wrongful behaviors. Second, we need a delineation of the categories of circumstances that can alter a judgment about new cases and a rich collection of cases that serve as paradigms of such exceptions. Third, we need the development of a logic of analogy and differentiation that can allow us to move systematically from a repertoire of settled cases to new cases involving new features and circumstances. And, fourth, we must introduce a change in the pedagogical role of cases. In the casuist method, cases are not intended to show the student how to apply abstract principles. Rather, the point is to give the student a large repertoire of paradigm cases so that, when confronted with a new situation, the student can resolve it by selecting from the repertoire those cases to which the new situation bears some resemblance and then, by analogical reasoning, reaching a decision about the new situation.

CONCLUSION

Let me summarize. I have argued that it is improper to use history to search the past for substantive moral concepts and moral judgments that we can then use to shed light on contemporary business ethics. Substantive moral concepts and moral judgments are too conditioned by their social and economic contexts.

Nevertheless, I have suggested that history can show us a method of moral reasoning that is quite different from the methods assumed by contemporary ethics. And this method, I have argued, is one that can play a major role in the development of applied ethics in general and of business ethics in particular.

NOTES

1. I am here relying on the standard account of the Greek social structure as given, for example, by Sarah C. Humphreys, *Anthropology of the Greeks* (London: Routledge & Kegan Paul, 1978), who writes: "Citizens were farmers, slaves supplied domestic services and unskilled labour, while traders were foreigners or [M]etics" (p. 144). This account has recently been somewhat amended by G. E. M. de Ste. Croix, who has pointed out that not all traders were Metics; see his book *The Class Struggle in the Ancient Greek World* (Ithaca, N.Y.: Cornell University Press, 1981), pp. 95–96. De Ste. Croix nevertheless continues to maintain the fundamental points that the ruling class "was the landed class, from which merchants and traders were largely excluded, and that the condemnations of trading of Aristotle and Cicero were based on class bias (pp. 114–33).

2. This, again, is the standard view. See, for example, J. W. Roberts, *City of Sokrates* (London: Routledge & Kegan Paul, 1984), who writes: "Metics were, it seems, dominant in large-scale manufacture, foreign trade and banking" (p. 29).

3. This, again, is a commonplace. See, for example, Joint association of Classical Teachers (hereafter JACT), *The World of Athens* (London: Cambridge University Press, 1984): "Almost all the sophists who taught in Athens were foreigners, men like Protagoras of Abdera and Hippias of Elis (a sophist of prodigious memory and learning)" (p. 176).

4. For example, Roberts, *City of Sokrates* states: "To conventional Athenians, not necessarily of the upper class, the notion that clever, skeptical foreigners should be telling some of the most gifted of their young men how to live was abhorrent: that task had always, and properly, fallen to fathers and uncles and others accounted 'brave and fair.' . . . It was intolerable that

the formal instruction of foreigners should supersede the informal instruction of responsible and respected citizens" (p. 224).

5. According to JACT, *The World of Athens:* "Trade and manual craftsmanship are despised [in the fifth and fourth centuries B.C.], being deemed suitable only for slaves, foreigners or the urban proletariat. Here more than anywhere else the leisure-class bias of our sources can seriously mislead. These are long-standing upper-class attitudes, traceable as far back as Homer and Hesiod. But they were intensified as political power swung away from the landed elite to the *demos* (in the sense of the mass of poor Athenians) and as slavery became ever more prevalent in agriculture and manufacture" (p. 177).

6. Aristotle, "Politics," in *The Basic Works of Aristotle,* ed. Richard McKeon (New York: Random House, 1941), pp. 1288–89.

7. Ibid., p. 1141.

8. Ibid.

9. See E. Badian, *Publicans and Sinners: Private Enterprise in the Service of the Roman Republic* (Ithaca, N.Y.: Cornell University Press, 1972): "Landed property was the basis of membership of the upper class—on the whole, the basis of 'equestrian' wealth as of senatorial; and below the august ranks of the officer class as a whole, the basis of municipal eminence" (p. 50). De Ste. Croix makes the same point in *The Class Struggle in the Ancient Greek World,* pp. 120–33.

10. Cicero, *Cicero on Moral Obligation: A New Translation of Cicero's "De Officiis,"* trans. John Higginbotham (Berkeley: University of California Press, 1967), p. 92.

11. The best history of the development of medieval views on usury is provided by John Noonan, *The Scholastic Analysis of Usury* (Cambridge, Mass.: Harvard University Press, 1957).

12. Alasdair MacIntyre, *After Virtue: A Study in Moral Theory* (Notre Dame: Ind.: University of Notre Dame Press, 1981).

13. Immanuel Kant, *Groundwork of the Metaphysic of Morals,* trans. Herbert J. Paton (New York: Harper & Row, 1964), p. 76.

14. This conception is wonderfully described in Albert R. Jonsen and Stephen Toulmin, *The Abuse of Casuistry: A History of Moral Reasoning* (Berkeley: University of California Press, 1988). I am obviously heavily indebted to their work in what follows.

15. Alphonsi de Ligorio, *Theologia Moralis,* 5th ed. (1763). This work is not discussed in any detail by Jonsen and Toulmin. My reason for focusing on it is simple: it was very easily available to me locally.

16. Ibid., pp. 216ff.

17. Ibid., pp. 230ff.

18. Ibid., pp. 234–36.

19. Jonsen and Toulmin, *Abuse of Casuistry,* pp. 250–59.

20. This criticism is made by Herbert L. Dreyfus and Stuart E. Dreyfus in their essay "Copying with Change: Why People Can and Computers Can't," *Logos: Philosophic Issues in Christian Perspectives* 7 (1986): 17–33.

21. Ibid.

Business Ethics and Modes of Ethical Reasoning

George Brenkert

A central problem in the development and understanding of business ethics is the relation between moral principles or laws and particular cases. Does business ethics, for example, simply apply the principles of theoretical ethics to concrete cases?[1] Is it "merely" a concern that what theoretical ethicists do gets applied to the real world and not simply left to gather dust in the halls of academia? Or, on the contrary, does business ethics focus on particular cases because the principles and abstract issues of theoretical ethicists are largely, if not wholly, irrelevant? In short, is business ethics a practical extension of modern ethics, or does it represent a revolution in the relation between moral principles and particular cases?[2] It is crucial that we sort out these relations if we are to understand the nature of business ethics.

The modern view that principles are basic to ethics has been challenged by those who advocate casuistry, an ethical method (developed in medieval times) of reasoning from particular cases to resolve moral problems. For casuists, cases rather than principles are basic. In her essay "Casuistry and the Case for Business Ethics," Joanne B. Ciulla aligns herself with contemporary casuists such as Jonsen and Toulmin, who defend not only this different view of ethics but also (as a consequence) a distinctive view of business ethics.

In reflecting on the claims and arguments made by Ciulla and other contemporary casuists, I am not concerned with the historical connections they draw between business ethics and traditional casuistry (or sophistry).[3] Rather, I wish to focus on the philosophical view of ethics and business ethics they defend. Of specific interest is the

196

light that is shed on business ethics by their argument that it is (or should be) a form of casuistry.

Although contemporary casuistry provides a provocative context within which to explore the nature of business ethics, I shall argue that it leaves the central issues unresolved and little clarified. Like the conservatives they unwittingly ape, modern casuists seek to take us into the future by returning us to the past. Too simply do they contend that we are faced with a dichotomy between two ways of discussing ethical issues.[4] The situation is much more complex. At most, I can indicate some of the directions in which we must go.

ALTERNATIVE MODES OF ETHICAL REASONING

Members of the contemporary casuist movement would have us believe that we face two different ways in which ethics can be done. On the one hand, there is Principle Ethics, which holds that principles are basic to ethics, that such principles are absolute, universal, and exceptionless, and that all moral conclusions are deductively derived from these principles. Like stern, gray, Prussian fathers, our principles lay down what we are to do with no chance of appeal.

On the other hand, there is Case Ethics, which derives from the developments of traditional casuists. Case Ethics pays primary attention to particular cases and their details. It looks to paradigms, analogies, and taxonomies of moral problems. Exceptions may be made for individual cases. This ethics is a rich tropical forest of interesting paths and motherly concern for persons who have moral problems.

In reality, contemporary casuists are able neither to stick to this starkly drawn picture nor to agree on what course we should take. Ciulla argues that business ethics must seek to resolve moral problems by balancing both principles and cases. Jonsen and Toulmin seem, variously, to think that we must simply adopt some form of Case Ethics or some view that combines principles and cases, as Ciulla argues.

To sort these matters out, I suggest that the issues concerning principles and cases that contemporary casuists discuss divide into (at least) four different possibilities. One might opt for the *Rigorist* view that ethics (including business ethics) is concerned primarily with absolute and exceptionless principles. The *Particularist* view holds that cases or particular experiences alone are the stuff of ethics. The *Compatibilist* view contends that a combination of principles and cases is both possible and necessary for an ethics. Fourth, one might adopt the *Practicalist* view in which we focus on particular cases but within an understanding informed by paradigms, moral taxonomies, consensus, and common moral institutions.

THE RIGORIST VIEW

The Rigorist view is the starkly painted interpretation of Principle Ethics noted earlier. According to contemporary casuists, the Rigorist holds that ethics is simply a set of law-like principles.[5] Moral knowledge consists in knowing these principles, and ethics is a kind of moral geometry. Second, these principles are eternal, invariable, universal, and not subject to exception.[6] Thus, ethics (like math) can be a matter of knowledge and, indeed, a rigorous science. As such, moral problems are essentially theoretical; a Rigorist ethics is a matter of episteme. This view of ethics, then, is analogous to a realist view of physics. There are certain eternal laws to be discovered by the ethicist. It is the study of these that occupies the ethicist.

Third, the Rigorist deduces practical ways of acting from these principles or laws. These deductions require little concern for circumstances themselves. After all, what is right is right.[7] Furthermore, since our moral answers are logically deduced from Rigorist moral principles, our answers constitute certain knowledge. Finally, the application of such laws to real cases is no more the business of the ethicist than the application of the laws of physics to real cases by an engineer is the business of the physicist. No wonder real ethicists disdain those who lower themselves to business ethics. Just as Plato's forms do not encompass hair, mud, or dirt, so pure ethicists remain above the arena of business and medicine. Indeed, in this view there really is no place for applied ethics within ethics, any more than engineering is simply a province of theoretical physics. The two endeavors are quite distinct. For this reason, ethicists are not out to give personal advice or practical answers. The role of the ethicist is primarily to study principles from which practical imperatives can be deduced.

Although some past philosophers might be identified as Rigorists, it is noteworthy that contemporary casuists seem hesitant, and with good reason, to pin this view on anyone today. Surely any number of criticisms can correctly be brought against such a view. Indeed, one suspects contemporary casuists of setting up stalking horses only to mask problems they have in using their own philosophical lariats.

It is interesting, then, that the crux of Ciulla's objection to the Rigorist view is not that its understanding of principles is mistaken or that moral conclusions cannot be derived deductively from universal laws. Rather, she objects that this view overly emphasizes or relies on principles. Thus, she claims that this view is a matter of excess. It is a form of nomism, the extreme dependence on laws to regulate behavior. It is a "purely legal absolutism."

Accordingly, Ciulla maintains that we are to reject the Rigorist view because it is excessive, not because it is fundamentally mistaken.

By analogy, racists would be condemned because they insist too forcefully, not because they insist at all.

This is, however, a strange criticism. It is much weaker than those brought by other contemporary casuists, and much less forceful than we need. How, one wonders, can Rigorists be charged with being overly concerned with principles, given their view of principles? This would be like objecting to deductive geometry because geometers relied too much on their basic principles. How could they do otherwise within such a system? Ciulla's criticism of Rigorism as excessively relying on principles makes sense only if she has a different understanding of principles in mind and she unwittingly is claiming that Rigorists use these kinds of principles excessively. But, of course, a Rigorist could not or would not adopt those kinds of principles. Hence, her criticism is misdirected.

Nevertheless, surely we must reject Rigorism. Jonsen and Toulmin offer more convincing criticisms. To begin with, they argue that the Rigorist view of ethics is incomplete. Principles and rules can take us only part of the way in resolving our moral problems. Beyond them we need human perceptiveness and judgment; wisdom, discretion, and discernment are required to apply present rules.[8]

Second, they note that today we hold a different view of the supposed absolute claims of geometry. The claim that the rules of geometry and science are absolute and unchanging is no longer widely accepted. Similarly, they contend that we need not believe that ethics must be based on such principles.

Finally, they claim that "we understand general maxims and principles . . . because, and to the extent that, we are familiar with the central unambiguous kinds of cases (the 'paradigmatic' cases) that they are commonly understood to cover."[9] Once we go beyond the simple paradigmatic cases to which the chosen generalizations were tailored, it becomes clear that no rule can be entirely self-interpreting; we must go behind the simple rules and principles themselves.

These criticisms are forceful and persuasive. We might also add, that the Rigorist view is simply that of the hidebound dogmatist, rather than that of the reflective moralist. If moral principles are to direct or guide our actions and the nature of those actions is altered by the circumstances in which they occur, then moral principles must take circumstances and particular cases into account. Contemporary casuists may present Rigorism as an ethics that is based upon principles, but, in fact, it is a caricature of such an ethics. Thus, the rejection of this view is not only correct but also not surprising. Although we can identify philosophers who have held this position (or something similar to it in the past), we would be hard pressed to find such philosophers today.[10]

THE PARTICULARIST VIEW

The Particularist view insists on the sufficient nature of Case Ethics. Thus, it might appear to be the view that contemporary casuists advocate, in contrast to the Rigorist form of Principle Ethics. The Particularist proceeds by examining each case in all its details. He or she does not recognize principles or rules but judges each case on its own merits. Thus, the Particularist also does not look at moral problems within a context of customs or traditions.

Since Particularism has so little to draw upon, it is not surprising that it quite generally ends up appealing simply to individual choice, conscience, or intuition. From these sources there can be little appeal. On this view, we could, perhaps, speak of a theoretical ethics, if we could draw a sharp distinction between analyzing morality (metaethics) and engaging in morality (normative or substantive ethics). On the other hand, we could hardly speak, in any ordinary sense, of an applied ethics, since without principles, rules, customs, or traditions, there would be little to apply. All normative or substantive ethics would be a matter of spontaneity or the moment.

This is surely an extreme view. It amounts to what some have called "antinomianism."[11] Ciulla links Particularism to Gorgias when she attributes to him the view that "nothing general can be said about ethics—each case and each situation must be judged anew."[12] To the extent that Joseph Butler simply relied on conscience, he has been said to have been a Particularist.[13] Toulmin claims that Tolstoy held this view.[14] Finally, some claim that existentialists hold this kind of ethics.

If Particularists hold that one can appeal only to circumstances, not principles, analogies, or moral taxonomies, then this view is the mirror image of the Rigorist view. Indeed, it seems to arise as an extreme response to the dogmatism of the Rigorist. But both views are clearly inadequate. Ironically, then, Particularism shares the implausibility of the Rigorist view, albeit from the other side. Quite correctly, contemporary casuists reject Particularism.

First, even if Particularism is a Case Ethics, it could not be a traditional casuist view, since traditionally casuistry has appealed to some principles or laws, even though they lie on the most outer reaches of the moral firmament and may be circumvented by any of a number of tactical procedures (e.g., Probabilism). As such, the traditional casuist may play loose and free of such principles in all but the most clear-cut cases. What the casuist offers, however, is a distinctive way of approaching such objective rules in the light of fallible human knowledge, different interests, and divergent impressions. That is, traditional casuistry, even as Ciulla presents it, requires that there be principles.[15]

Second, Ciulla's opposition to Particularism is evident throughout her article. Thus, she argues that if we do not appeal to principles, almost any kind of activity can be justified. Her example of the prostitutes is said to show that the argument involved might be used to justify any kind of activity so long as one gives the proceeds to the Church or to the poor. It is a view that has been indicated, Ciulla notes, for "disregarding moral principles."

Third, Jonsen and Toulmin also distinguish between contemporary casuistry and Particularism. Although they mistakenly attempt to pin Particularism on situation ethics, their argument that we should reject Particularism is correct. They note, for example, the development of Particularism in the 1960s and register its differences with casuistry:

> Where the casuists had worked with a multitude of moral paradigms, principles, and maxims, particularists acknowledged no general principles, or only a single principle. . . . Where the casuist had been attentive to "circumstances" as one feature of moral life among many others, particularists reduced the moral life to a bare succession of circumstances. The casuists analyzed novel cases by analogy with prior or paradigm cases: situationists focused on moral choices that were concrete but unique and isolated.[16]

Two further comments are relevant here. First, situation ethics is not, in fact, Particularism. Jonsen and Toulmin's comments on Joseph Fletcher and other situation ethicists are prejudiced and misleading. Specifically, it is false that situationists focus on moral choices that are unique and isolated.[17] On the contrary, they admit the important place of principles, even though all but their central principle of love merely sum the result of past experience.[18] Still, for situation ethicists, individual cases are seen within the context of other situations. Their view merely emphasizes the extremity of Particularism.

Finally, Particularism should be rejected not merely as an exercise in spontaneity but as a headlong rush into subjectivity. It encounters difficulties on both scores. It is impossible in ethics, as in other areas, to proceed without some generalizations or at least some rules of thumb. Although the Particularist denies this, the weight of evidence is opposed. Further, if it is to be admitted that some choices are correct and others incorrect, or some better than others, we need some standards, paradigms, or principles by which to make such claims. As Ciulla complains, without some standards or paradigms, any activity can be justified. In fact, the real upshot would be that the very idea of justification in ethics would be drained of any meaning. Ethics and our moral life would be impoverished. Accordingly, contemporary casuists such as Jonsen and Toulmin do not accept this view. Ciulla does not accept it. Neither should we.

ferent strengths. Some demand that principles and experiences be quite closely related. Others allow that principles provide a looser and more distant correction of particular experiences and cases. In either case, however, a Compatibilist must hold that principles are basic. It is only by recourse to them that we can justify our particular actions, as well as the characters and virtues we ought to foster.[19]

Compatibilists need not hold that moral principles are exceptionless or eternal; they may hold a more moderate view. Nor need a Compatibilist claim absolute certainty for the answer that he or she derives from applying a principle. Compatibilism may allow for forms of moral knowledge other than deductive knowledge.

Compatibilists hold that moral principles are applied appropriately only if they are applied sensitively in light of the complexities of the situation. Pedagogically, they may allow that cases, rather than basic principles, should be presented first to individuals. Thus, a Compatibilist might *use* cases to illustrate underlying principles or *use* cases to arrive at important conclusions on the basis of those principles. Still, the cases theoretically play a secondary, although important, role. Ultimately, we must appeal to a principle that transcends each case; we must appeal to something that is universal and objective, on the basis of which we arrive at our conclusion.

In this view, business ethics is truly an *applied* ethics. It applies various principles and concepts to situations involving business. In addition, it analyses those concepts in light of the work of (pure) ethicists. In doing so, it takes circumstances into account.

What is clear, then, is that cases play a role primarily *after* principles are derived. It is a pedagogical question whether in the classroom or a text one wishes to begin with cases or principles. Most current texts reveal their logical biases by discussing the basic principles involved that are to be applied during the course. Once cases are presented, we are to move back up through them to the level of principles. Although those in applied ethics are doing important work, they are not necessarily doing important *philosophical* work insofar as they are concerned about particular cases. They may be doing philosophical work to the extent that they continue the explication, analysis, and clarification of intermediate concepts such as friendship, loyalty, and trust. Still, looming beside these activities are the pillars of Hercules, the moral principles, that hold up the moral roof.

Now it appears that some such view is close to what traditional casuists have held. Traditional casuists thought that moral principles were already given by God; man had to discover and interpret them. Leites describes casuistry as relying on first principles (that everyone knows) and practical judgment whereby they are applied.[20] This is also the view of casuistry held by G. E. Moore and Immanuel Kant.

Moore did not pursue casuistry, not because it is unworthy, but because we do not know enough, he claimed, to pursue it.

It follows that if casuistry requires principles that are basic, it is a form of Compatibilism. If, however, this were the view that contemporary casuists really defend, we would have to wonder why they claim that such a view is notably a descendent of traditional casuistry, when most moral philosophers would agree with Compatibilism but reject casuists (and sophists) as their ancestors. I suggest that traditional casuistry signals a dispute not over whether moral principles should be abandoned but over the strength and relation of principles to experiences. Compatibilists reject traditional casuistry, not because the latter denies a role to principles, but because the role of principles it affirms is very limited and subject to arbitrary exception.

What are we to say, then, about Compatibilism? First, it seems terribly familiar. It has been held by a wide variety of moral philosophers, such as Brandt, Rawls, and Hare. In short, this seems to be the way that most of those who believe that principles are important for ethics proceed when seeking to solve practical problems. Kant, Moore, and others also seem to agree.

If philosophers of such different stripes can agree that both principles and cases are important for ethics, we must ask whether this view secures any special importance for the study of circumstances, let alone cases. Both may be important, but one had also better be well versed in the principles themselves.

In addition, this is the approach that is followed by virtually every current text in business ethics. Initial chapters are on Kantianism, utilitarianism, and so on, after which the text gets into particular cases (or topics) within business ethics. Hence, if contemporary casuists are advocating this view, they are on well-trod ground.

Second, it is some such view that Ciulla, in spite of her excursus into sophistry and her toying with contemporary casuistry, seems ultimately to adopt. Ciulla says that casuistry is the "using of cases to *discuss* practical ethical problems (or cases of conscience)." But this is something that the Compatibilist might allow, for using practical cases to discuss practical ethical problems is something that a Compatibilist can do, if only as a pedagogical device. Ciulla says that "casuistry corrects the excesses of the law" by attempting "to balance laws with the demands of particular circumstances."[21] But this means that laws or universal principles are still part and parcel of morality and ethics. In applying them, however, we must pay particular attention to the details of the situations. Again, a Compatibilist may grant this.

By itself, Ciulla claims, casuistry risks dangers such as extreme relativism and "specious hair-splitting argumentation." A Principle Ethics, on the other hand, runs the dangers of absolutism and irrele-

vance. We need some kind of mixture of the two. But this is what a
Compatibilist might hold. In this Ciulla proves herself to be not a
contemporary casuist but at most a traditional casuist. In fact, the
view that Ciulla defends seems much more conventional or common
than she makes it seem. We might say that Ciulla's dogged good
sense abandons either of the two more radical views. She is, I believe, a contemporary casuist manqué.

If Ciulla is, then, advocating a doctrine seemingly as familiar as
Compatibilism, she might seek to advance our understanding of
Compatibilism's views of the relation between principles and cases.
But it is just at this point that a crucial unclarity exists in Ciulla's
essay. To begin with, although she would have us balance principles
by cases, part of the way in which she would have us do so is by
continuing the search for scientific ethic of principles. One is then
perplexed to read that "the search for scientific ethics is futile." If
this is the case, one can only wonder what the relation of principles
and cases is in her view. Would she have business ethicists knowingly
engage in a self-frustrating activity? How, we must ask, would engaging in such an impossible task help "to keep the dialogue between
theory and practice alive"?

Further, Ciulla does not tell us what it means to balance principles
and cases. On what balance are we going to make this attempt? What
are we going to do when they conflict? To "balance" makes it seem
as if principles and cases are to be given equal weight. But what does
this mean, and how is it to be interpreted? Unfortunately, Ciulla
answers none of these questions.

Finally, what is being said to be compatible? "Business ethics," she
says, "must balance the demands of laws with the demands of particular circumstances."[22] But if the principles or laws are those of the
Rigorist, this could not be done. Laws of an absolute, universal, and
exceptionless nature can hardly be balanced with the demands of
particular circumstances. What, then, are the principles we are to
adopt? Ciulla does suggest that "moral laws are not like scientific
laws," but we hear little more about what moral laws are like. It
seems that Ciulla mistakenly thinks that the question is simply one
of balance, not of difference in kind. It is not only the relation of
principles to cases about which we must worry but also the nature of
the principles.

Whether contemporary casuists such as Jonsen and Toulmin
adopt Compatibilism is less clear. At least in some essays Jonsen
seems to be a Compatibilist.[23] In *The Abuse of Casuistry*, Jonsen and
Toulmin sound like Compatibilists when they say that "the pursuit
of Justice has always demanded both law and equity."[24] They claim
that "we need to respect not only the general principles that require
us to treat similar cases alike but also those crucial distinctions that

justify treating dissimilar cases differently." [25] We need not question, they tell us, the truth of our principles as they apply to ideal type cases; only historical novelties compel us to rethink the scope of moral concepts and rules. A morality built on principles alone becomes too easily tyrannical; we must learn to make equitable allowances. Such comments sound like Compatibilism.

As I suggested earlier, if this is what Ciulla and they accept, then they have not really broken new ground. In this interpretation, the contemporary casuists are not saying something new. However, even if they are not saying something new, they might be saying something important. As I noted earlier, it might be that the issue is not one of principles at all. Rather it might be the complaint that current theoretical ethicists never get down to cases. They are concerned with the nature of ethical relativism, the foundations of morality, the meaning of moral words, the nature of morality, and so on. But they do not, as a result, get to the point that they take up the problems of friendship, individualism, creation, work, love, courage, or the virtues. Or, when they do so, they do not look to these as they come embodied in particular instances. Furthermore, if they take up these issues, they treat them conceptually and abstractly. Their discussion is terribly theoretical; it is about concepts, rather than about particular cases. They do not seek to solve particular problems; their focus centers not on the practical, concrete level but on the level of speculation, theorizing about the nature of our concepts, their conceptual and logical structure. The objection then would be not so much that this logical and conceptual approach is mistaken as that its defenders do not carry it far enough. They should be willing to get their hands dirty. The objection is not one of justification or logic; it is their conception of the role of the ethicist that is lacking. There is nothing in the views they hold of the logic of justification that prevents them from considering particular cases or giving advice. If this is, indeed, the criticism of contemporary casuists, then it is manifestly a good criticism.

Second, it might be objected that contemporary casuistry points out the limits of principles. Equity is needed to fill the interstices of, and the areas of conflict between, our laws, rules, principles, and other general formulas.[26] This objection, however, would also not undercut Compatibilism. Compatibilism is not (or need not be) a legalism: it can allow for equity. Its laws are not overly rigid: it is not a legal or ethical absolutism. It can allow for the virtues. It is not simply deontic laws and rules. Compatibilist ethics is more than right or wrong. It also includes the good and the bad. However, it might well be that the basic thrust of Compatibilist ethics has been mistakenly abstract. An appropriate objection, then, would be not to the logical structure of Compatibilism but to its emphasis. Compatibilists may say that once we are clear about these concepts and principles, we can seek to apply them to particular cases. The contemporary casuist objection would be that this does not happen. There is much to this criticism, although more in the past than at present.

THE PRACTICALIST VIEW

There is a fourth view, which may be what contemporary casuists are actually advocating. It strikes me as potentially the most interesting and significant for business ethics. On this Practicalist view, ethics (casuistry) is the art of reasoning from cases.

The orientation of this view is wholly practical. Its concern is to solve particular moral problems. Such problems are questions of *phronesis*, not of abstract knowledge or theory. What is needed for their resolution is moral experience. However, this is not simply the particular moral experience of individual agents who seek solutions that they can personally live with. Rather, the relevant moral experience extends back into customs, traditions, and knowledge gained from other similar experiences. Thus, practical moral experience is as much collective as personal.[27] It is for this reason that the Practicalist view depends heavily on moral consensus and common moral institutions through which moral problems can be resolved.

The focus of Particularist moral inquiries, accordingly, falls on classifying actions and circumstances into different species and on developing "moral taxonomies" rich and subtle enough to cover all the serious problems that typically arise in different sectors of human experience. Moral taxonomies provide "a detailed and methodical map of morally significant likenesses and differences."[28] In addition, the ethicist must identify paradigms and analogies by which problems can be solved.

Moral knowledge, then, is knowledge of particular analogies, metaphors, paradigms, etcetera. The attempt to apply abstract moral principles is not helpful—and may be harmful—in solving practical problems. When Jonsen and Toulmin speak about moral taxonomies that allow people with different basic moral beliefs to reach agreements in moral disputes, they suggest that moral principles are neither crucial nor even necessary.[29] Moral knowledge lies not in accepting universal principles but in our ability to note subtle distinctions and the like. Accordingly, Toulmin claims that the point of "appealing to principles [is] . . . not to give particular ethical judgments a more solid foundation, but rather to square . . . ethical conclusions [with] other *non*ethical commitments. . . . The principles of Catholic ethics tell us more about Catholicism than they do about ethics, the principles of Jewish or humanist ethics more about Judaism or humanism than about ethics."[30] To the extent that we can draw on paradigms, taxonomies, and analogies, moral principles can be jettisoned in the resolution of moral problems.

Jonsen and Toulmin defend this view by asserting that "ethics deals with a multitude of particular concrete situations, which are themselves so variable that they resist all attempts to generalize about them in universal terms."[31] Accordingly, they contend that "the primary locus of moral understanding lies in the recognition of paradigmatic examples of good and evil, right and wrong; the typical cases of, for example, fairness or unfairness, cruelty or kindness, truth-telling or lying, whose merits and shortcomings even a small child knows at a glance."[32] In the clearest cases, one need simply appeal to the paradigm cases to justify one's views.

Consequently, the Practicalist holds that we must overthrow Principle Ethics and turn to a Case Ethics as described. In contrast to Principle Ethics, which is a top-down ethics, Practicalism purports to be a bottom-up ethics.

Finally, the Practicalist claims that "in the realm of Practice, certitude . . . depends on accumulated experience of particular situations; and this practical experience gives one a kind of wisdom— *phronesis*—different from the abstract grasp of any theoretical science—*episteme*."[33] Instead of demonstrable or certain conclusions such as the Rigorist seeks, moral argument leads to presumable conclusions. Practical moral reasoning is topical or rhetorical, not geometrical or formal. Thus, ethics is not and cannot be a science. It is "a field of experience that calls for a recognition of significant particulars and for informed prudence: for what [Aristotle] called phronesis, or "practical wisdom."[34]

Now this is an interesting view. It involves a very different way of looking at morality, one that is incompatible with a Principle Ethics. Thus, it differs from Rigorism. However, the Practicalistic view is not a mixture of Principle and Case Ethics. As such, it differs from Compatibilism and is similar to Particularism. On the other hand, unlike Particularism, Practicalism appeals to features of our moral experience that transcend the individual experience and problem. It does not simply focus on the particular instance. The appeal to consensus, tradition, and a common morality are crucial.[35]

If the Practicalist view can be defended, it would have direct implications for business ethics, as well as other applied and nonapplied ethics. For example, talk about theories of utilitarianism or Kantianism would be much less appropriate. Business ethics texts would begin in very different ways than they currently do. They might begin by discussing various paradigm cases, analogies, methods of analysis of these cases, and the like. Furthermore, the work of philosophers on the logic of principles would be of doubtful help. At best it would be an activity in which they should indulge on vacations, rather than when attempting to advance our understanding of morality and to aid in the resolution of moral problems.

For the Particularist, business ethics would not be an applied ethics—"at least not in the sense that cases are resolved by application, through operations of formal logic, of an ethical theory, be it utilitarian, contractarian, or whatever."[36] Practical ethics would be the basis or foundation of ethics. We would have to look to practical ethics, rather than to theoretical ethics, for advances in ethics. "Business ethics" would refer simply to that form of practical ethics which deals with business. "Business" would not indicate a field of application but rather a particular set of phenomena or an area within which moral issues arise and are resolved.

Finally, this view of business ethics would seem to tie in very nicely with the case method used in business schools. Indeed, to learn more about morality, it might well be that moral philosophers should beat a path to the classroom of those in business schools who teach case methods, rather than the other way around.

There are, however, a number of significant problems that contemporary casuists must address if they are to win our allegiance to a Practicalist ethics. To begin with, how are we to avoid any purely conventionalist interpretation of this view? Since traditions and conventions may conflict, which are we to follow? Casuistry flourished when common moral institutions and views of ethics were more widespread than they are today. How, then, can Particularism be defended when consensus and the common institutions required for this view are breaking up? To the extent that casuistry worked as contemporary casuists portray it, it may have worked only because it occurred within institutions that no longer exist in contemporary society.

Jonsen and Toulmin are sensitive to this point. They argue that common institutions and consensus are developing among those in medical ethics.[37] But since problems of medical ethics do not occur simply for those within the medical community but as it interfaces with the public and government, surely we need something broader for Practicalists to resolve moral problems. The breakup of shared cultural conditions and world views raises problems for the Practicalist view that are both practical and theoretical.

Second, contemporary casuists do not seem to realize that what they defend comes much closer to the view that traditional conservatives have espoused, rather than to the view of traditional casuists. Conservatives such as Edmund Burke have strongly objected against the use by liberals and radicals of universal, abstract principles.[38]

The extent to which Particularists (or contemporary casuists) are traditional conservatives is unclear, since they do not openly appeal simply to tradition. Still, they appeal to consensus within, for example, the medical profession. If this is placed within an historical and social setting, we have the makings of an appeal to tradition. This appeal was important for traditional casuists. Thus, Leites argues that the casuists held that "Christians were living within a tradition and that it was the possession of a common tradition which enabled Christians to talk, to explain, and to justify themselves to one another."[39] But then we find ourselves back in the problems noted in my first objection. Which tradition should we appeal to? How can we determine which traditions are corrupt? To the extent that traditional casuists could appeal to basic moral principles, they had an answer. Contemporary casuists cannot make the same appeal.

Third, Jonsen and Toulmin note that "casuistry" refers to an "art": the art of "the practical resolution of particular moral perplexities, or 'cases of conscience.' "[40] It is "the art of analyzing moral issues in terms of cases and circumstances."[41] Like other arts, it can be put to good use or misused. And surely there is a great amount of art to resolving difficult moral problems. But this does not in itself imply that principles are not relevant and are not needed to determine when that art is misused. In particular, to be able to speak of the misuse of Practicalism we must have some standards or principles. We cannot simply abandon them.

Fourth, argument by analogy or paradigm is only as strong as the analogy or extension of the paradigm. Obviously, it is quite possible to push analogies and paradigms in ways that open up the ethical door to immorality. What constraints exist on such "inventive" moral reasoning are unclear. It is at this point that traditional casuistry foundered. How can contemporary casuists avoid a similar fate? As argued earlier, the Practicalist cannot simply appeal to historically or socially accepted paradigms or analogies. The appeal to an historical or general consensus is also fraught with dangers. Surely this would have justified any number of immoralities in the past. What safeguards the Practicalist can offer here are unclear.

Fifth, even the appeal to analogies and similarities is an appeal to the general features of each case. We cannot live, it seems, let alone solve moral problems, without looking to what is general, if not universal, within the situations we face. To try to do so is a misguided route for escaping Rigorism. But then we need to consider the relation of these general or universal features to principles and rules. Does our appeal to such features count as an appeal merely to second-order principles rather than to first-order, or primary, principles? If so, is the dispute between Practicalists and Compatibilists really over the order of principles to which we must appeal, rather than whether we must appeal to principles at all? If it is, as seems likely, it appears that the Practicalist approach to ethics either assumes (even if only implicitly) various principles and rules of which its proponents are unaware or risks collapsing into a form of Particularism.

Finally, if the Practicalist advocates appealing to experts, those with a depth of moral experience, in order to avoid any appeal to principles, we face the problem of identifying these moral experts. Jonsen and Toulmin acknowledge that "the authority of wise men" gradually became, for traditional casuists, the "preponderance of experts." And "the weight of scholarly opinion, in the modern sense of 'heads counted,' replaced the weight of reason and argument."[42] But then how does the contemporary casuist suggest that we avoid these problems?

These problems point in the direction of principles and Compatibilism. Perhaps these problems lie behind the uncertainty noted above that contemporary casuists seem to have concerning the exact role of principles in their views. The Practicalist view rejects principles. But as we have seen in this and the preceding section, various statements of their views call for the use of principles. Further, it has been the argument of this section that, at least as far as the position has been developed, it cannot really do without principles.

CONCLUSION

In conclusion, the tendency of contemporary casuists to paint the moral world into two groups, Principle Ethics and Case Ethics, should be rejected. The situation is more complicated. Indeed, it is clearly more complicated than the fourfold picture sketched in this essay. The Rigorist view should be rejected. But such a view is less a real alternative today than a foil by which contemporary casuists highlight their own views. The Particularist view is an extreme response to the Rigorist view. It too should be rejected. The jettison of all principles is a false alternative to the Rigorist view of principles.

Compatibilism not only allows a place for both principles and the particular details of individual cases, it also allows for various relations between the two. Most contemporary ethicists are Compatibilists. However, traditional casuists also hold to a form of Compatibilism. Although Ciulla links business ethics to forms of sophism and casuistry that reject principles, her own position seems most straightforwardly (although not entirely unambiguously) to be that of a Compatibilist. This has the merit of defending a position which seems least problematic in itself, although as a consequence her position does not seem to stake out any new philosophical ground.

The Practicalist view is the most interesting and potentially significant for business ethics. It offers a radically different view of business ethics and theoretical ethics. In Copernican fashion, the Practicalist would reverse the relation between the two: practical ethics, rather than abstract principles, would be the center of the ethical universe. Indeed, for contemporary casuists such principles are more epicycles than any real feature of the moral heavens. We can do without them. Nevertheless, Practicalists (or contemporary casuists) have yet to work out a host of serious problems that stands in the way of acceptance of their view.

NOTES

1. It should be obvious that this question also arises for other areas within applied ethics (e.g., medical ethics). Albert Jonsen is quite explicit that this is one of the questions with which he is concerned in his discussion of casuistry. See his "Casuistry and Clinical Ethics," *Theoretical Medicine* 7 (1986): 71.

2. By "modern ethics" I refer to ethics as it has been pursued by such diverse philosophers as Immanuel Kant, John Stuart Mill, G. E. Moore, and John Rawls.

3. With Ciulla, I include Albert R. Jonsen and Stephen Toulmin, *The Abuse of Casuistry: A History of Moral Reasoning* (Berkeley: University of California Press, 1988).

4. Ciulla suggests such a simple dichotomy in her essay, as do Jonsen and Toulmin. See the latter's *Abuse of Casuistry*, pp. 2–23.

5. Ibid., p. 6.

6. Ibid., p. 2.

7. Locke seems to hold a Rigorist view. He claims that "the law of right and wrong is in itself eternal and unalterable"; see John Locke, *An Essay Concerning Human Understanding*, vol. 1, ed. Alexander Campbell Fraser (New York: Dover, 1959), p. 477, n. 478. He also holds that morality can be demonstrated, as can mathematics; we can have certain knowledge of them (p. 65).

He does not think that the application of moral laws to actions is really any problem: "[T]he mind is easily able to observe the relation any action hath to it, and to judge whether the action agrees or disagrees with the rule; and so hath a notion of moral goodness or evil, which is either conformity or not conformity of any action to that rule: and therefore is often called moral rectitude." The explanation for this is: "[T]his rule being nothing but a collection of several simple ideas, the conformity thereto is but so ordering the action, that the simple ideas belonging to it may correspond to those which the law requires" (p. 480).

8. Jonsen and Toulmin, *Abuse of Casuistry*, p. 9.

9. Ibid., p. 8.

10. Jonsen and Toulmin, as well as Ciulla, mention Plato as one who held this view. They also briefly refer to Grotius, Pufendorf, and Christian Wolff as Rigorists (*Abuse of Casuistry*, pp. 276–78). I cannot think of anyone today who holds this view. Even Jonsen and Toulmin do not argue that Kant holds this view.

11. Harvey Cox, ed., *The Situation Ethics Debate* (Philadelphia, Pa.: Westminister Press, 1968), pp. 246, 251.

12. Edmund Leites, "Conscience, Casuistry, and Moral Decision," *Journal of Chinese Philosophy* 2 (1974): 54.

13. Stephen Toulmin, "The Tyranny of Principles," *The Hastings Center Report XI* (1981), pp. 34–35.

14. For general principles that casuists used, see Jonsen and Toulmin, *Abuse of Casuistry*, pp. 170, 174.

15. Ibid., p. 272. Obviously, the comment that Particularists can appeal to a single principle is at odds with the present characterization of Particularism. Given the remainder of the quotation, however, I take the general thrust of this comment by Jonsen and Toulmin to be relevant against the present form of Particularism discussed in this section.

16. Cf. Cox, *Situation Ethics Debate.*

17. Cf. Joseph Fletcher, *Situation Ethics* (Philadelphia, Pa.: Westminister Press, 1966). Fletcher maintains that situation ethicists adhere to one norm or principle, namely, that of love, which is "binding and unexceptionable, always good and right regardless of the circumstances" (p. 30).

18. Cf. William K. Frankena, *Ethics,* 2nd ed. (Englewood Cliffs, N.J.: Prentice-Hall, 1973).

19. Edmund Leites, "Casuistry and Character," in *Conscience and Casuistry in Early Modern Europe,* ed. Edmund Leites (Cambridge: Cambridge University Press, 1988), p. 124. Saint Thomas Aquinas claims that "the human act of reasoning ... proceeds from the understanding of certain things—namely, those which are naturally known without any investigation on the part of reason, as from an immovable principle—and ends also at understanding, inasmuch as, by means of those principles naturally known of themselves, we judge of those things we have discovered by reasoning," adding "wherefore the first practical principles are bestowed on us by nature." Quoted in *On Law, Morality and Politics,* ed. William P. Baumgarth and Richard J. Regan (Indianapolis, Ind.: Hackett, 1988), p. 2. Further, "conscience ... implies the relation of knowledge to something: for conscience may be resolved into *cum alio scientia,* i.e., knowledge applied to an individual case" (p. 3). These comments fit closely with Leites's view of casuistry.

20. Jonsen, "Casuistry and Clinical Ethics."

21. Jonsen and Toulmin, *Abuse of Casuistry,* p. 10.

22. Ibid., p. 14.

23. Toulmin, "Tyranny of Principles," p. 34.

24. Jonsen and Toulmin, *Abuse of Casuistry,* p. 314.

25. Ibid., pp. 14, 17, 251.

26. Ibid., pp. 17, 18, 40, 43, 44, 251.

27. Toulmin, "Tyranny of Principles," p. 32.

28. Jonsen and Toulmin, *Abuse of Casuistry,* p. 19.

29. Ibid., p. 330.

30. Ibid., p. 26.

31. Ibid., p. 19.

32. Given the view of casuistry defended in the preceding section, contemporary casuists are offering a new reading of traditional casuistry. How-

ever, even if it is historically questionable, this may be an interesting way to think about business ethics or medical ethics. It would make them primary and theoretical ethics secondary.

33. Jonsen, "Casuistry and Clinical Ethics."

34. Jonsen and Toulmin, *Abuse of Casuistry*, pp. 337–41.

35. Cf. Edmund Burke, *Reflections on the Revolution in France* (Garden City, N.Y.: Anchor Books, 1973).

36. Leites, "Conscience and Character," p. 125.

37. Jonsen and Toulmin, *Abuse of Casuistry*, p. 13.

38. Ibid., p. 15.

39. Ibid., 168.

40. Ibid.

41. Ibid.

42. Ibid.

Epilogue

R. Edward Freeman

I

What does it mean to see business as a humanity? What are the contributors to this book recommending for the institutions that make up Business? What are the politics and the ethics of these recommendations? In this brief epilogue I want to suggest a program for change—for one institution in particular, namely, the professional school of business—that can enable us to come to see business as a humanity.

Business is not now understood as a humanity, and the very title of this book of essays seems at best contradictory, at worst fuzzy-headed. In fact, business theorists for the most part want the study of business to become even more scientific, and business decision makers would like nothing more than to be able to rely on some quick-fix rules that rest on some authority other than the consultancies of the authors.[1] So, to issue a call to see business as a humanity, to juxtapose the tropes of business with those of literary studies, theology, philosophy, and history, to recommend change in the very background disciplines of business is first of all nonsense. After reading these essays, however, it is easy to see that they imply a very different idea of business, one in which "the human condition," "the moral point of view," "the joys and sufferings of humankind," "the human person," and the like can become the centerpiece of thinking about business. In a sense these essays call for no less than a reversal of margin and center. The role of economics and its subordinate disciplines, such as finance and marketing, must move into the shadows, while ethics and the humanities begin to occupy the center stage.[2]

215

While I believe that such a call is ultimately futile given the current state of the professional school of business, I want to argue that such a reversal offers a way to revitalize business schools and business theory. To make such an argument I shall examine in the first section of this epilogue the history of business schools and suggest that we can see three important phases in the development of business schools that have ended in a contradiction of sorts. In the second section I suggest a reorientation of professional schools of business along more pragmatic lines. Finally, in the last section I offer some concrete suggestions for how business schools can change to open up the possibility of seeing business as a humanity.

II

The Formative Period

According to L. C. Marshall, one of the earliest proposals for a collegiate business school was made by Robert E. Lee, the first president of what is today Washington and Lee University. Although the proposal was not put into action, Lee's idea was not confined to the business details of bookkeeping and the like "but [aimed] to teach the principles of commerce, economy, trade and mercantile law."[3] At its very beginning the American collegiate business school sought to articulate and teach the basic principles of commerce and economics, as well as their partners in the law. It is ironic that almost 125 later American business thinkers and government policy makers are still searching for these principles.[4]

The Wharton School of the University of Pennsylvania was founded in 1881 with funds from the steel magnate Joseph Wharton, and a rapid increase in the number of business schools continued for the next forty years in both the United States and Europe. Assessing this trend in 1928, L. C. Marshall wrote: "In view of our general acceptance of the idea that the higher levels of practical education are quite properly a function of a university, it is only to be expected that business—overwhelmingly our largest practical activity—should have its training schools at the university level."[5]

Frances Ruml argued that the existence of business courses in secondary schools and so-called commercial colleges

made it easy and natural for the university and collegiate schools of business to focus its attention more on professional and social ends; to place an emphasis upon dealing with the complicated social organization in which the business man does his work; to accept as its objective the training of persons with a social point of view for executives and professional positions in business.[6]

While there is a great deal of debate about the original purpose of business schools, it is reasonable to believe that multiple outcomes occurred, such as (1) replacing the apprenticeship system, largely dismantled by the industrial revolution; (2) training businesspeople in the fundamentals of scientific management; and (3) training an elite capable of managing more complex social organizations.[7]

Ruml summarized Joseph Wharton's initial stated purpose as being "to establish means for imparting a liberal education in all matters concerning Finance and Economy."[8] In his address to the trustees of the newly formed Wharton School, Wharton remarked: "It is reasonable to expect that adequate education in the principles underlying successful business management would greatly aid in producing a class of men likely to become pillars of the state, whether in private or in public life."[9] And on this original theme of imparting "moral education" to managers, Ruml approvingly quotes E. P. Cubberly's *History of Education:*

> As the industrial life of the nation has become more diversified, its parts narrower, and its processes more concealed, new and more extended training has been called for to prepare young people to meet the intricacies and interdependencies of political and industrial and social groups and to point out to them the importance of each one's part in the national and industrial organization.[10]

The American Assembly of Collegiate Schools of Business (AACSB), founded in 1916, reinforced this idea of a liberal education for businesspeople by requiring accredited schools to require students to take at least 40 percent of their credit hours in subjects other than economics and commerce.

To reinforce the argument that the original purpose of business schools was grounded in the idea of moral education, consider Joseph Wharton's original plan, most ironic for the contributors to this volume. Wharton proposed and implemented a program to take humanities faculty, trained in the liberal arts, and put them in the classroom to teach business subjects. This experiment, tried in 1882, failed miserably, according to Ruml, because the liberal arts professors were resentful and did not necessarily believe that knowledge should be practical. By 1883 the Wharton School had hired instructors versed in business, leaving the ensuing one hundred years or so barren of meaningful interchange between business and the humanities.

The early history of business schools is rife with arguments about the same controversies that dominate discourse today. Should faculty be trained in economics? Were graduate economics departments sources of ignorance about business? Could businesspeople be used as adjunct professors, and if so, how many? What was the proper balance between research and consulting? Should the study of business be scientific or largely storytelling? Was business to be a profession with ethical norms, or were schools of business merely to socialize students into the practices of business and prepare them for the world of work? While these questions are relevant for us today, a second phase in the history of the American business school makes answering them all the more difficult.

The Scientific/Modern Period

Two well-known reports published in the 1950s gave voice to a crisis of legitimacy in the business school. The Carnegie Report and the Ford Foundation study by R. A. Gordon and J. E. Howell both recommended that business schools were in need of academic legitimacy and essentially proposed the adoption of a social sciences approach to the subject matter of business.

According to Thomas Mulligan, writing in an important retrospective in no less than *The Academy of Management Review:*

> The landmark studies of business education by Pierson (1959) and Gordon and Howell (1959) have had great influence. The often unsubstantiated descriptive content of earlier business school curricula and research has been replaced by quantitative description based on rigorous data collection, computer-assisted mathematical modeling, and the foundational concepts of science—testable hypotheses (or, at least, testable networks of hypotheses), correlated observations, and causal explanation.[11]

Mulligan concludes that the culture of science that emerged in the business schools was successful in getting established, and it has only recently begun to be challenged by the introduction of humanities-based ethics courses. Mulligan argues that the current state of business schools suggests a desperate need for something like the humanities.

While Mulligan's conclusion is certainly shared by the scholars represented in this volume, and while certainly he is correct that the culture of science is dominant in journal reviews, tenure decisions, and business school politics, I want to suggest that there is an alternative to his view of the two cultures of arts and sciences as incompatible. Mulligan rightly points out the emergence of "practitioner" books critical of the scientific approach, but there is more at issue here than practical criticism of academic abstractions.

The Porter/Peters Era

Two seemingly unrelated events catapulted business thinkers out of their obsession with description and explanation and gave rise to scholarship that was normative in nature. In the 1970s economist Michael Porter published a series of articles on the economic basis of business strategy. These articles formed the basis for his groundbreaking book, *Competitive Strategy*. From this book it was easy to reestablish the dialogue between social scientists and businesspeople. Porter had a theory with particular implications for how to manage.[12]

During roughly the same time period, Tom Peters and his colleagues at the consulting firm McKinsey and Company embarked on a study of why some organizations seemed to be successful year after year. The report they produced formed the basis for Peters's and Robert Waterman's best-selling *In Search of Excellence*,[13] which has sold more than twenty-five million copies worldwide. The power of *Search* was its systematic, albeit unscientific, story about what real companies did and did not do to achieve success. *Search* was grounded in the real world and coherent as a narrative, enhancing its believability.

My argument is not that the scientific period is over in business schools. The existence of so-called scholarly journals ensures an appetite for trivia in excess of either its production or its value. It is not that Peters and Porter provide examples of how to do research that is rigorous and relevant. Rather, I want to suggest that Porter and Peters show us the power of narrative, of telling a good story about how we can create and manage our organizations. In short, they give us, in this pragmatist reading, a basis for reintroducing the humanities in business education. For if the humanities are anything, they are powerful narratives and metanarratives about human societies and cultures. These narratives are more or less coherent and more or less normative.

III

The Functions of a Professional School

To understand how narrative can serve as a powerful force for change in business schools, we need first to set forth a conception of the professional school. I want to suggest, in a simple and straightforward way, that we think of professional schools as having two main aims: socialization and practical criticism.[14]

The first aim of any professional school will always be the socialization of students into the habits and practices of the profession. Students go to medical school to learn how to be and act like doctors and to understand the subjects and sciences necessary to the practice of medicine. Similarly, business schools train students in the practices of businesses. Students study the techniques and frameworks and disciplines that business managers use. They learn the language of business. They come to understand the norms of business, from the differences in use of "net present value" versus "payback" calculations to the dress and speech codes of companies and industries. Students become facile with the methods of recognizing and solving ordinary business problem and issues.

But they also do more. Any business school worth its salt teaches students to be skeptical and critical, that is, teaches the methods of practical criticism. A profession is a critical practice, one that contains the seeds of its own improvement. Medicine, by committing to the alleviation of human suffering, must allow the analysis of questions that are critical of current practice, for current practice is instrumental, although importantly instrumental, to the alleviation of human suffering. The following questions—(1) What's the best practice? (2) How can we improve the practice in area X? (3) Is this case a kind of human suffering that we can and should try to alleviate? (4) Is this case, such as a factory, a case of human life?—are all appropriate for students of medicine; their training and their teachers' research is incomplete if these critical questions are not a part of the curriculum. If they are absent from a school's curriculum, we would not call that school "professional."

Similarly, business is about the creation of value. How such value is created is instrumental to its creation. Value creation admits a whole host of critical questions: (1) How can we create value more efficiently? (2) How can we create *this kind* of value? (3) How should value be distributed? (4) Who owns/controls the value production process? and (5) Should business create value regardless of its effects? As with medical schools, we have to see the business school that does not produce a large dose of "practical criticism" or train its students in the methods of "critical practice" as incomplete and unprofessional.

It is a mistake, however, to see the socialization function of business as based on science and the critical function as based on the humanities. Both the sciences and the humanities have much to say to both functions. If we think of the current practice of business as "the narrative(s) of business" or "the story(s) of business," then the functions of business school are to teach the old/current stories and to invent new ones. If we think about the work of Peters and Porter, they claim to be basing new narratives on old ones. Theories, understood this way, evolve and change over time, sometimes piecemeal, sometimes wholesale. Science and art both produce narratives, and both are important for business.

For example, let us suppose that one of the standard stories of business is that managers can, do, and should act in a fiduciary manner for stockholders. That they can and do is shown by elaborate scientific studies, and that they should is argued for normatively, usually from the moral standpoint of utilitarianism, (as in the work of Adam Smith or Ronald Coase, but sometimes on libertarian grounds, as in the work of Michael Jensen. Any *standard story* has descriptive (scientific) and normative (moral) bases.

Now the pragmatist should argue that if the goal of the professional school is to teach and improve or replace the standard story by a better one, then it doesn't much matter whether that story is improved or replaced by science or morality. In fact, the savvy pragmatist points out, ultimately both will be entwined in a story of human practice whose test will be the way it allows us to live.

For example, suppose we tell a story about the practice of business that has more characters than the standard one. In this new narrative there are stakeholders,[15] and businesses create value for stakeholder groups such as employees, suppliers, customers, and communities, as well as for stockholders. Now we want descriptions of "stakeholder practice," and we want to know what the texture and meaning of stakeholder practice can be.

Any business school worthy of the description "professional school" must teach its students to evaluate multiple narratives and to create or at least improve the messy story of business as it is practiced in the world. If this argument is valid and sound, then business schools can be more professional by embracing the humanities as a partner in the socialization and critical processes of education. How can such a partnership be accomplished?

IV

I want to make some concrete suggestions in four areas of business education: (1) curriculum, (2) faculty, (3) students, and (4) institutions. Each of these suggestions is meant more to provoke conversation than to end it. Take them as half-baked suggestions that merit further thought.

The Curriculum of Business Schools

Far too little time is spent on the critical function of professional schools. With the exception of accounting courses, which induce deep skepticism about the "truth" of accounting statements, and ethics courses, which explicitly question the stockholder ideology, the pickings are slim indeed.

I want to make four related points about how to deepen the critical function of business education. First, ethics has to be a part of the curriculum whose purpose is to challenge the implicit values and assumptions in the rest of the curriculum. Ethics should be the course that explicitly leads the critical function.

Second, we need courses on culture studies and language. The globalization of business itself challenges the status quo, yet the response of some schools is to deny course credit for the language skills their graduates need. Courses in these areas must be supplemented with projects, events, and other pedagogical devices that give students experiences in dealing with other cultures and thus coming to see their own from a critical perspective.

Third, in areas where the application of theories, models, and frameworks from the humanities are most easily applicable—organization studies, strategy, leadership—courses must be revised to take account of the humanities. It is difficult to imagine that it is a rare exception when Freud is mentioned in a business classroom, yet the first chapter of Karen Horney's *Neurotic Personality of Our Time* is a stunning self-description for many executives.[16] Of course, these areas must continue to draw on the social sciences, but they must not fall prey to an instrumentalism that buys the dominant ideology wholesale. Thus, a course in organizational behavior that professes to teach the students "how to get more out of people to maximize shareholder value" would fail the criteria I have in mind here, as would a course that fails to mention the necessity of efficiency as a business value.

Finally, where critical attention points up conflict between the received narrative and a new one, we should "teach the conflicts."[17] After all, we are building the critical judgment abilities of our students, abilities that we hope will outlast a two-year M.B.A. program. If they cannot deal with conflicting ideology or challenges to their very assumptions about business, they will not make very effective business leaders in today's world.

There are more curriculum changes that need to take place. I am suggesting these four as necessary to any meaningful attempt to teach the critical function. I have left open the question of pedagogy because it seems to me that there are many ways to learn. Even while I remain a devoted follower of the Socratic method, I recognize that it too may be bound by culture.

The Faculty

The question of designing a business school faculty is at once simple and intractable. It is simple because we need some new faces with new backgrounds. Historians, literary theorists, legal scholars, linguists, and others could easily find their way around a business school, if invited to do so. It is intractable because at the margin their presence would make little difference, as has been the case with the few philosophers who now slink about the b-school hallways.

Rather, we must find ways to reinvigorate the intellectual processes of the disciplines of business. In addition to adding humanities people, we must add "humanities questions" to the intellectual life of marketing, accounting, finance, decision science, operations, and organizational studies. Donald McClosky and his colleagues have begun this process in economics.[18] A group of scholars, writing in the journal *Accounting, Organizations and Society,* has adopted a critical approach to accounting, and scholars in business ethics and business and society have given a critical turn to issues of strategy, governance, and organizational studies. However, there is much work to be done.

We need to undertake an explicit program of lectures, conferences, institutes, joint research projects, and joint courses among business scholars and humanities scholars. Such a program of faculty development would try to build the intellectual capital of business faculty and could offer a rich and varied setting in which members of the humanities faculty could test their ideas.

The Students

In addition to the standard package of M.B.A. students, ranging in age from twenty-five to thirty-five, with experience in business, I believe that we can make business schools relevant to another group.

Imagine a program designed for one hundred of the very best liberal arts graduates from the best liberal arts programs. These students should have highly developed critical faculties, but they would have little knowledge of business. With the right curriculum design, one combining socialization and the continued development of critical faculties, these students could easily emerge as candidates for business leadership. What I have in mind is a joint program, with humanities and business faculty playing roughly equal roles.

There are many ways to design such a program, and it would have to include a heavy dose of experiential learning about business, but programs such as these never get designed because we do not question critically the ideology that says one has to know business to learn about it in depth.

Institutions

Finally, we need some new institutions, such as a Center for Business and the Humanities. The goal of such a center would be threefold:

1. to produce new knowledge and insights into the human experiences in organizations
2. to provide intense executive development experiences that rely on innovative methods of learning from multiple disciplines
3. to provide a rich atmosphere of interaction and mutual learning among scholars in business and in the humanities, business executives and humanities practitioners such as artists, writers, and musicians

A broad range of activities, including research projects on race, gender, culture, the environment, the role of institutional reinvention, and leadership, could be undertaken, and conferences could be staged to share and build learning from theory to practice and practice to theory.

While the Aspen Institute has attempted the executive development part of this mission, and while various ethics centers have attempted other parts, so far no one has tried to confront the issue on the main ground—integrating business with the humanities, or, as we have put it here, coming to see business as a humanity.

V

I conclude with the challenge that if professional schools of business are to be relevant in today's multicultural, technologically wired, rapidly changing world, something like a reinvention of the business school must occur. The forces of stability must not be underestimated, however. From issues of tenure to the reluctance of recruiters to hire culturally divergent people, change will not come easily. It is incumbent on the intellectuals who see themselves as telling better stories about business to try to lead this change, enlisting our colleagues, our students, and our "practitioners."

NOTES

1. The genealogy of the business self-help book is another story, one worth telling on another occasion.

2. Daniel R. Gilbert, Jr., has recently moved the concept of corporate strategy fully into the shadows and hence begun this task for the business disciplines allied with economics. See his *Twilight of Corporate Strategy* (New York: Oxford University Press, 1992).

3. L. C. Marshall, "The American Collegiate School of Business" in L. C. Marshall, ed., *The Collegiate School of Business: Its Status at the Close of the First Quarter of the Twentieth Century* (Chicago: University of Chicago Press, 1928), p. 3.

4. See, for example, books by Robert Reich, Lester Thurow, Peter Drucker, and others for different views of what the principles are that connect these disciplines.

5. Marshall, "American Collegiate School," p. 9.

6. Frances Ruml, "The Formative Period of Higher Commercial Education in American Universities," in Marshall, ed., *Collegiate School of Business*, p. 47.

7. Drew E. VandeCreek, "Power and Order: The Ideology of Professional Business Training at Wharton and Harvard, 1881–1933, draft of masters thesis in history, University of Virginia.

8. Ruml, "Formative Period," pp. 54–55.

9. VandeCreek, "Power and Order."

10. Ruml, "Formative Period," p. 53.

11. Thomas M. Mulligan, "The Two Cultures in Business Education," *Academy of Management Review* 12, no. 4 (October 1987): 593–99.

12. I am not claiming that Porter was the first to do this; of course he was not. I am claiming that without a landmark of the magnitude of his book, normative scholarship would not have achieved the power that it has today. The same applies to the argument about Peters.

13. The work of Peters and Waterman and others is noted by Mulligan, "Two Cultures," pp. 594–95. Porter's work is not, probably because it is clearly couched in the scientific idiom.

14. There is a large literature here with a number of complicated questions that I am going to ignore. I take the dual purposes outlined here as necessary, but not sufficient, conditions for a school to have the label "professional."

15. Notice the ironic twist on stockholders, for new narratives are often ironic retellings of old ones.

16. Karen Horney, *The Neurotic Personality of Our Time* (New York: Norton, 1937).

17. Gerald Graff, *Professing Literature: An Institutional History* (Chicago: University of Chicago Press, 1987).

18. See, e.g., Donald N. McCloskey, *Second Thoughts: Myths and Morals of U.S. Economic History* (New York: Oxford University Press, 1993); Donald N. McCloskey, *If You're So Smart: The Narrative of Economic Expertise* (Chicago: University of Chicago Press, 1992); Donald N. McCloskey, John Nelson, and Allen Megill, *The Rhetoric of the Human Sciences: Language and Argument in Scholarship and Public Affairs* (Madison: University of Wisconsin Press, 1987).

INDEX

Rand, Ayn, 67
Ransom, John Crow, 124
Rawls, John, 6, 71, 74n22, 83, 85,
    94, 97n11, 99
Ray, Orman, 121
Relativism, 145
Renaissance, 15
Ricardo, David, 114
Richards, I. A., 109
Rights, 53–54, 94
Roosevelt, Franklin D., 139n53
Rorty, Richard, 84
Rousseau, Jean-Jacques, 73, 93–94,
    97n13
Royce, Josiah, 69
Ruml, Francis, 216–17
Russell, Bertrand, 120

Sanchez, Thomas, 176
Sanderson, Bishop, 177, 179
Santayana, George, 117
Sartre, Jean-Paul, 139n64
Saussure, Ferdinand de, 124
Say, Jean Baptiste, 114
Schiller, Friedrich, 58
Scholastics, 174
Schumpeter, Josef, 110, 121
Schwartz, Barry, 114
Scott, Nathan, 126
Scruton, Roger, 93, 95
Shakespeare, William, 118, 124–25,
    138n42
    Hamlet, 131
    King Lear, 73, 144
    Macbeth, 73
    Measure for Measure, 131
    Merchant of Venice, 50, 131
Shame, 69, 71
Shils, Edward, 121
Shopenhauer, Arthur, 119, 138n44
Situation ethics, 59, 201
Smith, Adam, 51, 63, 68, 99, 102,
    104, 106n3, 114, 219
    "invisible hand," 47
Smith, Ted, III, 127
Snell, Bruno, 49–50, 73n3
Social choice theory, 63
Social responsibility, 8
Social sciences, 16

Sociology, 14
Socrates, 7, 65, 184, 186
"Soft" skills, 12, 30
Solomon, Robert C., 5–6, 76–85,
    88, 93–96, 98–105
Sophists, 168–70, 172, 176–77, 179,
    186
Sophocles, 49
    Oedipus Rex, 49
Spectator, The, 178
Stakeholders, 66, 105
Stalin, Joseph, 112
Steinbeck, John, 65
    East of Eden, 65
Steiner, George, 126
Stoics, 171
Stoppard, Tom, 73
Story, Chief Justice Joseph, 130
Swift v. Tyson, 130

Tatler, The, 178
Taylor, Charles, 55, 74n14
Taylor, Jeremy, 177
Thomas of Chobham, 175
Tolstoy, Leo, 124, 200
Toulmin, Stephen, 168, 172, 179,
    196, 200–201, 204, 206–7,
    209
Townsend, Robert, 58, 74n18
Trilling, Lionel, 115, 137n31
Trivium, 15
Turgot, Anne-Robert-Jacques, 114
Twain, Mark, 6
    Huckleberry Finn, 79, 129

Union Carbide. *See* Bhopal, India
    (Union Carbide spill)
University, 19
University of California, 157
University of Chicago, 157
University of Florida, 146
University of Kansas, 146
University of Pennsylvania, 37, 127,
    146, 157, 216–17
University of Texas, 48
University of Virginia, 147
Unseem, Michael, 147
Utilitarianism, 7, 189